THE GOLDEN

HOME AND

THE GOLDEN HOME AND HIGH SCHOOL ENCYCLOPEDIA, while sufficiently comprehensive and detailed for family use, has been created principally for students at the high school level.

The aim of this reference work is twofold: first, to serve the student's immediate need for authoritative information on a wide range of subjects, and, second, to set forth and explain the many areas of knowledge, so that a student may explore them and thus more competently plan his educational future.

Arranged alphabetically in twenty volumes, here are thousands of full, accurate entries, written and reviewed by experts. The text is abundantly illustrated with full-color photographs and paintings.

Designed to complement the high school curriculum, this encyclopedia offers help with assignments and valuable guidance in the use of other reference tools —dictionaries, atlases, and various library materials. Extensive cross-references and a complete index direct the reader quickly to the information he seeks. A special feature of this work is the sound career information it offers in scores of job and professional fields.

Among the many subjects encompassed in these volumes are the newest developments in science, from microbiology to radioastronomy; fine arts and literature; history and government; religion and philosophy; the physical world, its plants and animals; the social sciences; invention and industry. Four-color maps and latest census figures contribute to an up-to-date view of the world, its continents, nations, and peoples.

Every care has been taken to make *The Golden Home and High School Encyclopedia* lively and stimulating, without sacrifice of accuracy. It is the hope of the editors that these volumes will be used with both advantage and pleasure.

VOLUME VIII

HIGH SCHOOL ENCYCLOPEDIA

in 20 Volumes

✳

Geometry · Hippocrates

GOLDEN PRESS · NEW YORK

FIRST PRINTING, 1961

Library of Congress Catalog Card Number: 61-13292

© Copyright 1961 by Golden Press, Inc. Designed and produced by Artists and Writers Press, Inc. Printed in the U.S.A. by Western Printing and Lithographing Company. Published by Golden Press, Inc., New York.

Illustrations from GOLDEN BOOKS, © 1949, 1950, 1952, 1953, 1954, 1955, 1956, 1957, 1958, 1959, 1960, 1961 by Golden Press, Inc.; and from the Basic Science Education Series (Unitext), published by Row, Peterson and Company, Evanston, Illinois © 1941, 1949 by Row, Peterson and Company.

GEOMETRY is a part of mathematics that treats of space and figures in space. It grew out of early attempts to measure shape and size, as its name—which means "earth measurement"—partly indicates. The ancient Greeks built geometry into a system of logic that remained unsurpassed until recent centuries. Subsequent developments in the field include analytic geometry, which relates geometry to algebra, and projective geometry, which treats properties of figures that do not change under projection. Differential geometry, which relates calculus and geometry, is important in the theory of relativity.

A major change of thought in geometry followed the comparatively recent discovery that more than one geometric system of describing space is possible. Geometric systems are now understood as abstract mathematical systems having no necessary reference to the space of our physical world. Such systems refer to the physical world only as models that fit our present understanding of the universe. New information could change that understanding and make a different geometry more suitable.

Early investigations of geometry centered in practical problems of surveying and building. The ancient Egyptians, for instance, used knowledge of geometry to resurvey property lines after annual floods of the Nile River washed away landmarks.

The Greeks were first to take the step from known properties of geometric figures to a system of logic that could be used to derive unknown properties. The famous Greek geometer Euclid founded his geometry on a small group of definitions, postulates, and axioms, which he accepted as self-evident. Step by step from these he deduced the whole set of theorems of classical geometry. His achievement still stands, and much of it is included in the elementary geometry taught today. It involves plane geometry, which treats figures on a flat surface, and solid geometry, which treats figures in three dimensions.

After Euclid the next great development in geometry did not come until the 17th century, when René Descartes discovered a way to study geometric problems by methods of algebra called analytic geometry. This involved a coordinate system centered at a point called the origin. Among several different kinds of coordinate systems the most familiar is rectangular like the grid pattern of city streets. In this type two lines,

The Egyptians knew some of the simple geometric relations embodied in present-day tools.

called the axes, run through the origin at right angles to each other. The location of any point can then be described by its perpendicular distance from each of the axes, and the two distances can be represented algebraically as two variables. A third axis through the original perpendicular to the plane of the other two axes extends the coordinate system to three dimensions.

Other mathematicians investigated the effect of projecting a geometric figure from one plane to another, which is somewhat like comparing the shape of an object with the shape of its shadow. In projection a different line is passed through each point of a figure from a single point outside the figure. Sometimes the point is considered to be at infinity, in which case the lines are parallel. In any case the set of lines is then cut by a plane, and the intersection of the lines and the plane forms what is called a projection of the original figure. Projective geometry studies the properties of a figure that remain unchanged under projection. An application of projective geometry important to engineers and artists is called descriptive

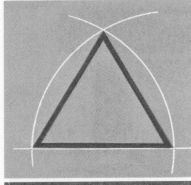

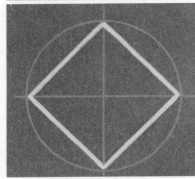

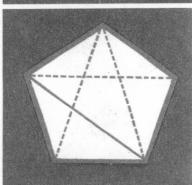

In Euclidean plane geometry, special attention has been given to regular polygons, or polygons with equal sides and equal angles. The four simplest regular polygons—equilateral triangle, square, regular pentagon, and regular hexagon—are shown above.

geometry. It treats methods of drawing two-dimensional and three-dimensional objects on a flat surface from different angles of view.

Until the 19th century Euclid's geometry was understood as a description of the geometric properties of the physical world. His famous axioms and postulates were accepted as self-evident truths about the real world, and it seemed obvious that to change them would lead to absurdities and contradictions. However, one of the postulates had bothered mathematicians—the postulate that for any straight line there is one and only one other line parallel to it through a point outside the line. Because the postulate seemed less self-evident than the others, many persons tried to deduce it from the other axioms, but all attempts failed.

In the 1820's two men working independently—János Bolyai and Nikolai Lobachevski—decided upon a different approach. They would prove the parallel postulate indirectly by showing that to define parallelism differently would produce theo-

rems contradicting each other. They substituted a different postulate stating that for any straight line there are at least two other lines parallel to it that pass through a point outside the line. When they deduced theorems from this changed set of postulates, they found no contradictory result. Instead of confirming the Euclidean geometry they had discovered a new system of geometry. Georg Riemann tried a similar approach but substituted for Euclid's parallel postulate the statement that for a straight line there is no other line parallel to it passing through a point outside the line. He also deduced no contradictory theorems. These two new non-Euclidean systems of geometry are now called hyperbolic geometry and elliptical geometry.

Once it was known that systems of geometry other than the Euclidean could exist, it was no longer so enormous a leap of thought to the idea that Euclid's geometry might not accurately represent the real world. Euclid's system had been the

Analytic geometry, conceived by Descartes, treats geometric figures algebraically by using a grid system. Thus the equations $y = x + 2$ and $x + y = 10$ may represent the lines graphed below, and their common solution is the coordinates of the point where the lines intersect.

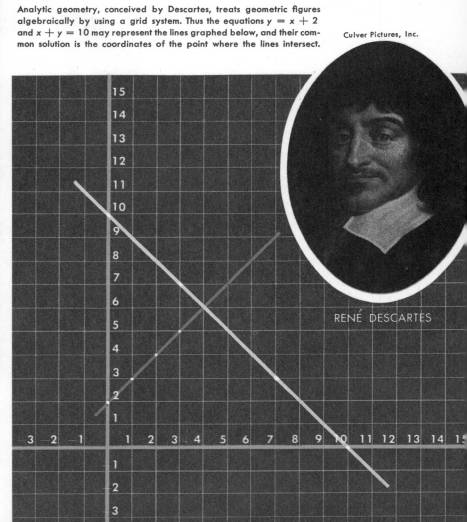

RENÉ DESCARTES

first step toward mathematical abstraction by setting up a system based on logic instead of measurement. The non-Euclidean geometries showed that even the system of logic need not be tied to the physical world. Many new systems of geometry were constructed, including systems with more than three dimensions. It was found that the very ideas of point, line, and angle can be replaced by completely arbitrary terms and that a geometry can be erected totally without reference to physical space.

As a result geometries are now regarded as theoretical models interesting in themselves quite apart from any reference to physical

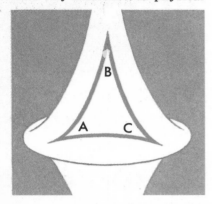

Non-Euclidean geometry deals with surfaces and spaces in which Euclidean geometry does not hold. One kind of non-Euclidean geometry can be represented in the three-dimensional space of our experience on the pseudosphere, of which a limited section is represented here. On its surface the sum of the three angles, A, B, and C, of a triangle is equal to less than 180 degrees. There is only one shortest line between any two points on the surface, but more than one parallel to a line can be drawn through a point outside it.

space. Some of them are given a physical reference, but this reference is no longer confused with the logical system. Fitting geometries to physical space is more like finding a map that will approximately depict a terrain. Einstein found, for instance, that Riemann's elliptical geometry fit his theory of space in a strong gravitational field better than Euclidean geometry, but that Euclidean geometry was a better fit where gravitational strength is low. It is interesting to note that as geometry was freed from reference to physical space and became a wholly abstract study of mathematical structures, it also became a better instrument for describing the physical space revealed by empirical science.

GEORGE III (1738-1820) was king of Great Britain and Ireland. A member of the Hanoverian Dynasty, he succeeded his grandfather George II in 1760.

George III ascended the throne amidst great popularity, for unlike the two preceding Hanoverian monarchs he had been born, reared, and educated in England to be a patriotic Englishman. So strong was George's education in British patriotism, royal prerogative, and Christian morality that he determined not only to govern his realm himself but also to break the influence of the Whigs, whose control of Parliament and country since 1688 rested upon vast property, enormous patronage, and a not insignificant amount of corruption. During his first years as king he was not powerful enough to solve what he considered his life task, but he tried. He succeeded in building up in Parliament, largely through bribery and patronage, a substantial group of loyal supporters who were willing to vote for the king's measures regardless of party ties. By means of this group, known as the king's friends, George created the first real threat to Whig political supremacy since its establishment. The resulting conflict between crown and Parliament produced a rapid succession of governments.

This internal contention did not, however, reduce the effectiveness of British power abroad. The French and Indian War, known in Europe as the Seven Years' War, was successfully concluded. No longer was France to be a serious rival for empire in North America or in India.

If the war had given Britain an unrivaled position of power, it had also given it a large debt. Like a majority of Englishmen, George believed that the North American colonists, for whose protection so much of the debt had been incurred, should share in its payment. But what was more, he saw that by publicly advocating the taxation of the colonists he could add to his own popularity and power at home. Neither he nor the average Englishman concerned himself with the constitutional question of the right to tax a subject unrepresented in Parliament. By 1770 George achieved the object of his ambition: He chose his own first minister, Lord Frederick North. Six years later the tactlessness of George's North American policy resulted in open rebellion. Still, the majority of Englishmen supported him, for he was their representative against an unrepresent-

Colonial Williamsburg

George III

ative Parliament. The war, which arrayed France and Spain on the side of the colonists, dragged on until the defeat of Cornwallis at Yorktown in 1781. The treaty of peace that was signed two years later recognized American independence.

During these years there occurred agitation for economic reform, the need for which was in no little way tied to George's war policies. But the king himself retained his popularity. When the French Revolution began to sweep across France in 1789 and to scatter its sentiments abroad, his Whig opponents quickly ceased struggling against him. For them the preferred basis of government was no longer merely aristocratic but became aristocratic and monarchic. George became the symbol of struggle against France, which was at last defeated in 1815.

But George was unable to enjoy the victory, for the fits of insanity that had troubled him throughout his life became permanent in 1811. From then until his death nine years later he was king in name only. The duties of the crown were exercised by his eldest son, known as the Prince Regent, later George IV. After George III lost control of the royal office, his popularity increased greatly. This was due in part to the people's growing sympathy with George's condition and their indignation toward the behavior of the Prince Regent, who made little effort to conceal his contempt for his father. Early in his reign George's sturdy conservatism and homely personal ways had won him the nickname "Farmer George." At first applied out of derision, in his later years it became an expression of his subjects' affection for him.

GEORGIA, the Cracker State, is the largest state in area east of the Mississippi. It is located in the southeastern United States. Atlanta, the capital, is the largest city. Savannah, Columbus, Macon, and Augusta are other important cities.

Georgia has an area of almost 59,000 square miles. It is nearly the size of New York, New Jersey, and Connecticut combined. Twenty-first among the states in size, it measures 254 miles in width and 320 miles in length. Georgia's population in 1960 was 3,943,116.

The elevation of Georgia ranges from sea level along the Atlantic coast to almost 5,000 feet at its highest point in the northeast. The state has three topographic sections. Northern Georgia is mountainous. The central upland, known as the Piedmont Plateau, is chiefly rolling terrain cut by numerous rivers. The south is a coastal plain that comprises approximately three-fifths of the state. One of the most interesting attractions in Georgia is the Okefenokee Swamp in the southeast. A wealth of unusual plants and animals may be found here. Many fine beaches and islands along the coast make popular vacation spots. Georgia has a subtropical climate. Most of the state has warm humid summers and short, mild winters.

Georgia is historically an agricultural state. It has a climate favorable for the growth of many different crops. The leading cash crops of the state are cotton, peanuts, and tobacco. However, Georgia also ranks high as a producer of peaches, watermelons, pecans, sweet potatoes, and other truck crops. Livestock and poultry raising are gaining importance.

Textile manufacturing, cotton milling, and wood processing are the state's leading industries. Other important industries include food processing and the manufacturing of apparel, transportation equipment, and chemicals.

Georgia was visited by Hernando de Soto, the Spanish explorer, in 1540. In 1733 James Oglethorpe established Savannah, the territory's first permanent settlement. During the Revolutionary War many of the important towns were seized by the British. The destructive, triumphal march of General William T. Sherman, during the Civil War, was from Atlanta through Georgia to the sea.

Since the Reconstruction era, Georgia has made rapid progress in the establishment of industries and the development of the state's many resources. After World War I, diversification of crops was introduced.

Georgia's Capitol in Atlanta, modeled after the national Capitol, contains the Georgia State Museum and the State Library. Another notable attraction is the Cyclorama Building, a structure that houses the Cyclorama, a mammoth painting measuring 400 feet in circumference and 50 feet in height. The painting depicts the Battle of Atlanta.

Courtesy of Georgia Department of Commerce

Herbert Lanks—Black Star

Granite is quarried (above) in Georgia, one of the nation's leading suppliers. Naval stores (below), such as rosin and turpentine, are tapped from Georgia's pine trees.

Robert Thomas—Camera Clix

GEORGIA

Nickname: Cracker State

Seal: An arch with *Constitution* written above it—three columns carrying the inscriptions *wisdom, justice,* and *moderation*

Flag: Blue vertical band next to staff with seal—remainder (the confederate flag) two blue stripes on a red background

Motto: Wisdom, justice, and moderation

Flower: Cherokee Rose

Bird: Brown thrasher

Capital: Atlanta

Largest cities: Atlanta, Savannah, Columbus

Area: 58,876 sq. mi. (including 393 sq. mi. inland waters)

Rank in area: 21st

Population: 3,943,116

Chief universities: University of Georgia, Georgia Institute of Technology, Emory University

Chief rivers: Savannah, Altamaha (with tributaries Ocmulgee and Oconee), Ogeechee, Flint, Chattahoochee

Average temperature: Atlanta, 45° F. (Jan.), 79° F. (July)

Average annual rainfall: 50 inches

Chief economic activities: Agriculture, manufacturing

Chief crops: Cotton, peanuts, tobacco, corn, pecans, peaches

Chief mineral: Kaolin

Chief manufactures: Textiles, food and wood products, transportation equipment

Notable attractions: Warm Springs, Okefenokee National Wildlife Refuge, Andersonville National Cemetery

Important historical dates:

1569 Spanish missions established on Sea Islands and mainland

1733 Arrival of first colonists from England under James Oglethorpe

1778 Savannah seized by British during Revolutionary War

1788 First southern state to ratify the Constitution

1864 General Sherman's destructive march from Atlanta to Savannah

Ga. Agric. & Ind. Development Bd.

Savannah, Georgia's oldest city, is an important commercial and shipping center on the Savannah River. The port's naval-stores market is one of the largest in the world.

Stone Mountain, which is a huge dome of granite located near the city of Atlanta, is 1,686 feet high and measures 7 miles around the base.

State of Georgia Dept. of Commerce

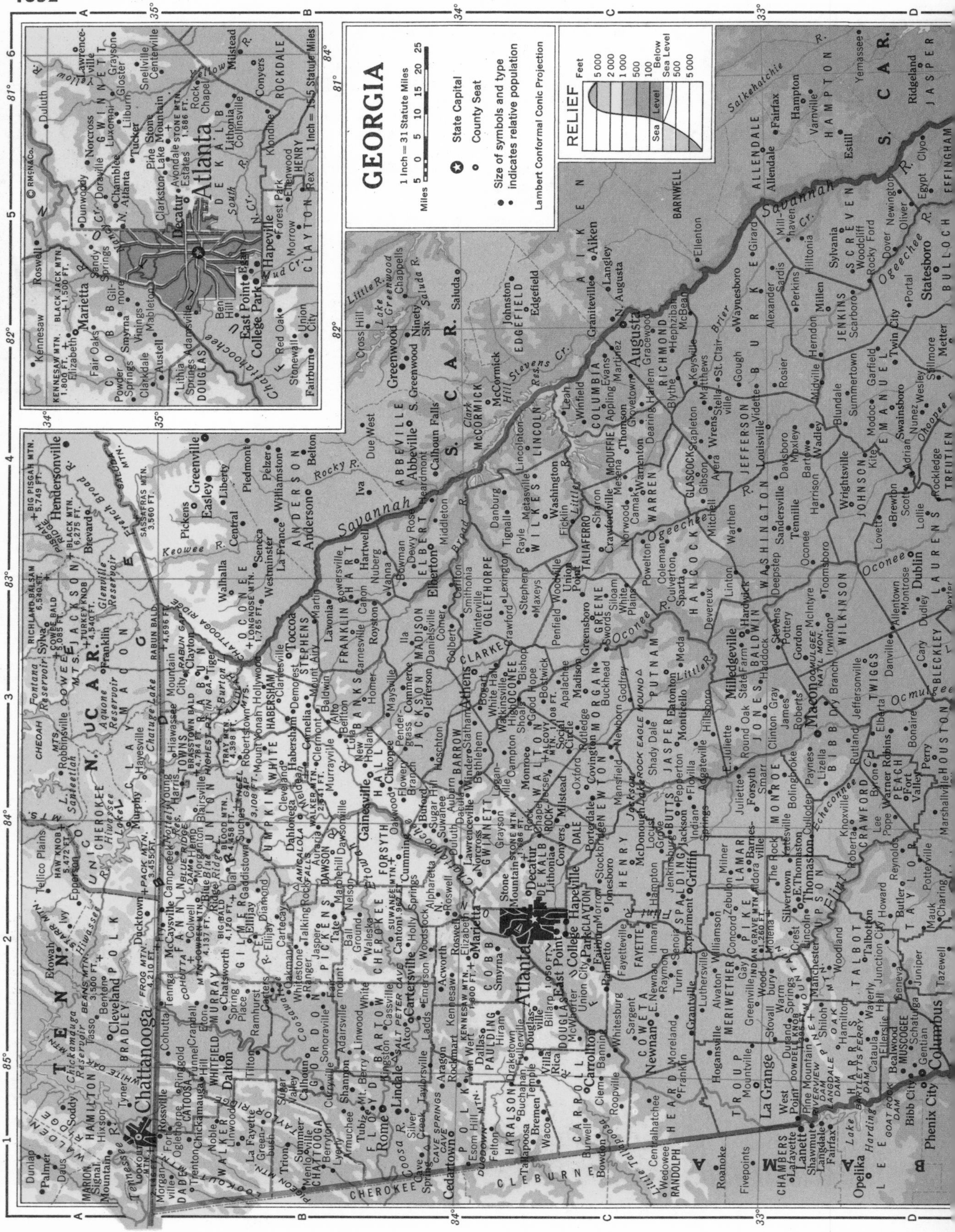

GEORGIA

1 Inch = 31 Statute Miles

Miles 5 0 5 10 15 20 25

★ State Capital
◎ County Seat

Size of symbols and type indicates relative population

Lambert Conformal Conic Projection

RELIEF

Feet
5 000
2 000
1 000
500
100
Sea Level
Below Sea Level
5 000

Rex 1 Inch = 15.5 Statute Miles

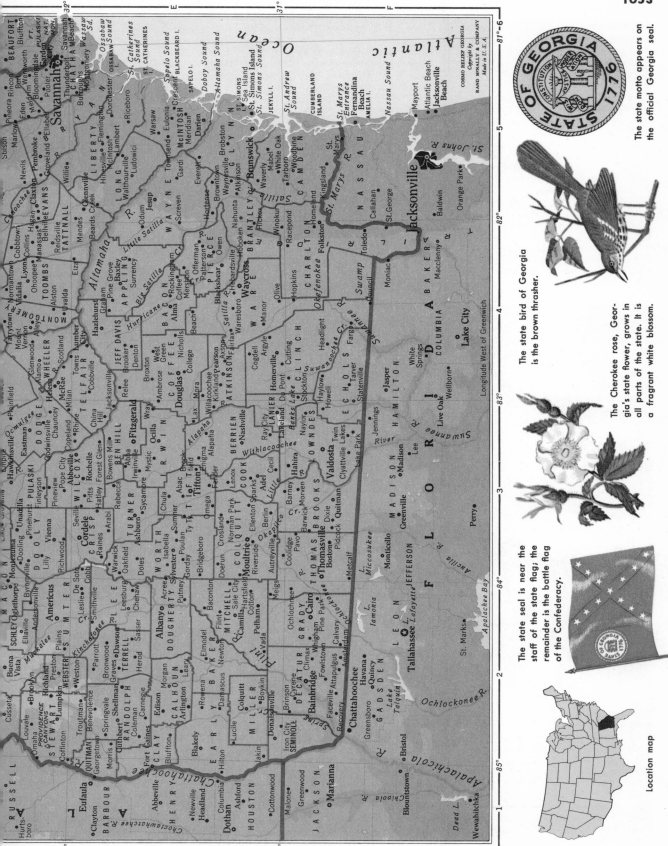

The state motto appears on the official Georgia seal.

The state bird of Georgia is the brown thrasher.

The Cherokee rose, Georgia's state flower, grows in all parts of the state. It is a fragrant white blossom.

The state seal is near the staff of the state flag; the remainder is the battle flag of the Confederacy.

Location map

GERANIUM, one of the commonest and best loved of all flowering plants. It is grown as a house plant and in gardens. In warm climates it is trained against trellises, allowed to trail over walls, or even used as a flowering hedge. The plant commonly referred to as the geranium has many varieties that are marked by a circular zone of different color on the leaf. Other varieties have highly colored leaves with the colors in various patterns. The flowers are borne in round clusters on the top of long stalks. They are of many colors but mostly pink, red, white, and rarely purple or orange. Some species of geranium have strongly scented leaves and are prized for this reason. One species has much larger flowers, usually darkly blotched and borne in great profusion. All of these geraniums are propagated by cuttings and should be given full light in the house and full or partial sun in the garden. Some species are mostly perennial garden plants and are not suitable for house plants. They are propagated by seed. The word *geranium* comes from a Greek word meaning "crane" or "stork," since the fruits when dry resemble the beak of these birds. Some species are native to South Africa; other species are native to many countries, including the United States.

The leaves of some geraniums are marked by a circular, dark-colored line.

GERIATRICS is the department of medicine that deals with the problems of aging. As the proportion of elderly people in the population increases, so do the needs for the geriatric services of physicians and hospitals. With aging, certain body changes are bound to occur, but with proper medical care and health habits much discomfort and disability can be prevented. Science is also finding out about the prevention of disability in old people.

Time itself causes wear and tear on the body, but there are also other influences that cause aging. These include injuries, infections, emotional upsets, abuses of alcohol, dietary indiscretions, and fatigue.

The rate of aging differs not only among organs but also among individuals. The most pronounced changes associated with age occur in the skin and the brain. In the aging process, changes that are to be expected include graying, baldness, wrinkles, visual defects, hearing defects, and loss of memory.

In coping with the problems of aging, much can be done by the proper use of cosmetics and attention to personal appearance. Glasses and hearing aids can correct some defects of sight and hearing. The most troublesome changes usually occur in the nervous system. These changes can cause behavior problems and serious nervous disorders.

GERM, a tiny form of life invisible to the naked eye. There are many kinds of life that can be seen only under a microscope. Those that produce disease are usually called germs. Most of the germs that cause disease enter the nose and mouth as we breathe, or they are taken in with food. Germs also enter the body through breaks in the skin caused by cuts and scratches. The body protects itself against germs in many ways. Its entrances, such as the nose and throat, are lined with mucous membranes. These membranes are moist and tend to check the growth of germs. Also, fine hairs in the nostrils and the bronchial tubes tend to block the germ-carrying dust. Once the germs get into the body, there are further protections. The digestive juices of the stomach have strong acids capable of killing germs. If they get into the blood, the white blood corpuscles may kill them. The body also manufactures special protective substances in the blood known as antibodies. These persist long after the germs are destroyed and protect the body in the event of future invasions of the same kind of germs.

GERMAN is a member of the Germanic branch of the Indo-European family of languages. German is closely related to English, Frisian, Dutch, and Flemish and only a little less closely allied to the Scandinavian languages and the extinct Gothic tongues.

Traditionally there are two relatively distinct German dialect groups. These two forms are High German and Low German. With a few exceptions, these terms were originally geographic in application. Low German referred to the characteristic pronunciation of the people living on the plains of northern Germany, especially the coastal region. High German referred to the dialect spoken in the highlands and the more mountainous regions of southern Germany. The two dialects eventually lost their geographic limitations, and High (Standard) German is now the literary language.

German is one of the major languages of western civilization. About 100 million people use it as their native tongue. Most of them live within pre-World War II German boundaries, plus Austria, Luxembourg, Liechtenstein, and parts of Switzerland, Hungary, Poland, the U.S.S.R., and Czechoslovakia. German is the vehicle for a significant literature and culture.

For a long time the *Fraktur*, or Gothic alphabet, was used. Later the simpler roman style, in which such languages as English and French are written and printed, in most instances replaced it.

GERMANIC LANGUAGES, or Teutonic languages, a sub-family of the Indo-European family of languages. They include Dutch, English, German, the Scandinavian languages, and several extinct languages.

The Germanic languages are commonly grouped according to linguistic similarities into three branches— the East, North, and West Germanic branches. The East Germanic group consists of the language of the Goths. Now extinct, Gothic survives in parts of a 4th-century translation of the Bible. The North Germanic, or Scandinavian, languages include Swedish, Danish, Norwegian, and Icelandic. See SCANDINAVIAN LANGUAGES.

The West Germanic languages are divided into two groups—High German and Low German. The principal High German language is modern German, also known as Standard German. (See GERMAN.) The surviving Low German languages are Dutch, Flemish, Frisian, and English. Dutch is the language of The Netherlands; and Flemish, or Belgian Dutch, is spoken in northern Belgium. More than half of the Belgian population speaks Flemish, although French is current throughout the country. Frisian is spoken by people on the coast and coastal islands of the North Sea, particularly in the north Netherlands province of Friesland. Frisian differs considerably from Dutch and is nearest of the Germanic languages to English. English, the most widespread of the world's languages, is considered to be an offshoot of an Anglo-Frisian dialect that must have been fairly widespread before the Germanic tribes invaded England. See DUTCH; ENGLISH.

No common parent of the Germanic languages survives, but linguists refer to the hypothetical ancestor as primitive Germanic or proto-Germanic.

GERMAN LITERATURE is the literature of the German-speaking peoples of central Europe. As such it includes the writings not only of German citizens but also of Austrians, German-speaking Swiss, and the large German-speaking minorities that at one time lived in Poland, Czechoslovakia, and other countries of eastern Europe.

THE MIDDLE AGES

The earliest literary form in a language that can properly be called German is the heroic ballad. Heroic ballads are long narrative poems that were sung by traveling minstrels, and of the few that have survived *The Lay of Hildebrand* is the best. It exists only as a fragment, but in style and content it resembles the Old English *Beowulf*. (See BEOWULF.) Another famous medieval heroic poem is *The Song of the Nibelungs*, which was composed by an unknown south German minstrel about 1200. See BALLAD.

During the late Middle Ages German heroic poetry was gradually replaced by chivalric romances written in the manner of the courtly epics of the French troubadours. The most noteworthy German examples of these romances are Hartmann von Aue's *Poor Henry*, Wolfram von Eschenbach's *Parzival*, and Gottfried von Strassburg's *Tristan and Isolde*.

The chivalric ideals of courtly love also inspired the highly complex and artificial lyric poetry of the minnesingers, outstanding among whom was Walther von der Vogelweide. Others were Neidhardt von Reuental and Tannhäuser.

Verse forms gradually grew more ornate and complicated, and by the 15th century the minnesingers of the courts had been replaced by the Meistersinger (mastersingers) of the towns. The Meistersinger, who organized themselves into medieval craft guilds, were principally concerned with the technicalities, rather than with the substance, of poetry. The most famous among them was the shoemaker-poet Hans Sachs.

Martin Luther, the great religious leader, translated the Bible into German. This portrait is by Lucas Cranach.

RENAISSANCE AND REFORMATION

The first decades of the 16th century are among the most important in the history of German literature. The Renaissance reached Germany from Italy and, although somewhat tempered by the severer German outlook, provided the leading ideas for an important group of writers. (See RENAISSANCE.) The German humanists, among the most important of whom were Ulrich von Hutten and Johann Reuchlin, wrote almost entirely in Latin, which was at that time the international language of intellectuals. *The Ship of Fools*, a humanistic satire by Sebastian Brant, achieved fame throughout Europe—the first German work to do so—after it had been translated into Latin. The preoccupation with Latin unfortunately led to the neglect of German and eventually therefore to a severe decline in the quality of most German literature.

The Reformation, the revolt against the authority of the Roman Catholic Church begun in 1517 by Martin Luther, had a much better effect on German writing. (See REFORMATION.) Luther's superb translation of the Bible into German is of supreme importance to German literature, for it established a standard written version of the German language that could be read and understood wherever the many greatly varied dialects of German were spoken. Luther also wrote many prose tracts in support of the Reformation, and his hymns (the most famous of which is "A Mighty Fortress Is Our God") are among the finest religious lyric poems ever written.

The Reformation ushered in a series of religious wars that culminated in the Thirty Years' War (1618-1648), which left Germany almost a wasteland. The wars, together with the vogue for writing in Latin, effectively stifled German literature for two centuries. Only H. J. C. von Grimmelshausen's *Simplicissimus*, a novel of the Thirty Years' War, stands out as a literary masterpiece.

THE 18TH CENTURY

In the early years of the 18th century the sorry state of German literature was improved somewhat by a number of writers who followed the established rules of French classicism. Eventually, however, writers came to view the rules as hindrances to German literary production. The revolt against these rules, begun by Klopstock, Wieland, and Lessing, ushered in the greatest period in the history of German literature.

Friedrich Gottlieb Klopstock (*The Messiah*) and Christoph Martin Wieland (*Oberon*, and the novel *Agathon*) were poets who, in their principal work, simply ignored the

Gotthold Ephraim Lessing, an 18th-century German writer, achieved an international reputation as a dramatist and a critic.

"The Lorelei" is the lyric by which the 19th-century poet Heinrich Heine is best known.

prevalent styles and instead turned to English poets and Greek culture for their inspiration. In several essays Gotthold Ephraim Lessing attacked the reliance of the German theater on French models and advocated instead modeling German drama on that of Shakespeare and the ancient Greeks. His essay "Laokoön" is a classic in the history of European aesthetic and literary criticism. Lessing put his principles into practice in such plays as *Miss Sara Sampson*, the first German domestic tragedy; *Minna von Barnhelm*, the most important German comedy of the 18th century; *Emilia Galotti*, a stirring social tragedy; and *Nathan the Wise*, a philosophic drama whose themes are universal brotherhood and religious tolerance.

Toward the end of the 18th century a group of young writers revolted against Lessing and the faith in reason that he represented; instead, they took their inspiration primarily from the romantic French author Jean Jacques Rousseau and the German philosopher-critic Johann Gottfried Herder. The revolt took the name *Sturm und Drang* (Storm and Stress) because of the emotional violence and exaggerated sentimentality of its members, most of whom carried irrationality to such extremes that their work soon passed into oblivion. *Sturm und Drang* is remembered today principally because of its influence in their youth on Germany's two greatest poets, Goethe and Schiller.

Goethe first attracted attention with his historical drama *Götz von Berlichingen* and his novel *The Sorrows of Young Werther*, both of which are permeated by the violent emotionalism of *Sturm und Drang*.

Goethe soon realized the excesses of these works. Inspired by the example of ancient Greece and by his friendship with Schiller, Goethe in his later works emphasized serenity, clarity, harmony, and service to fellow man in place of his earlier emphasis on rebellion, power, originality, and individualism. Among his important works are the dramas *Egmont*, *Iphigenia in Tauris*, and *Torquato Tasso;* the narrative poem *Hermann and Dorothea;* the novels *Wilhelm Meister* and *Elective Affinities;* and the autobiography *Poetry and Truth*. Goethe's *Faust*, the writing of which occupied almost his entire adult life, is considered the greatest poem in German literature.

Schiller, Germany's greatest dramatist, was also greatly influenced in his youth by *Sturm und Drang;* his first drama, *The Robbers*, contains all the excesses of the movement. As Schiller matured, his plays became more restrained. The principal characteristic of all his work is a passionate concern for every man's right to freedom and dignity. This theme permeates all his great plays: *Don Carlos, Wallenstein, Maria Stuart, The Maid of Orleans, The Bride of Messina,* and *Wilhelm Tell*. Of his lyrics the best known outside Germany is "An die Freude," the "Hymn to Joy" of the finale of Beethoven's Ninth Symphony.

THE 19TH CENTURY

The early decades of the 19th century were dominated by romanticism, which inherited the qualities of *Sturm und Drang* and to them added a love of beauty and art, a new concern for religion, mysticism, and the supernatural, and a striving toward an ill-defined, unattainable ideal. The romantic movement in Germany was somewhat more violent than its counterparts in England and France. See ROMANTICISM.

The principal romantic poets were Friedrich Hölderlin, the brothers August Wilhelm and Friedrich von Schlegel, Novalis (Friedrich von Hardenberg), Ludwig Tieck, Joseph von Eichendorff, Ludwig Uhland, Clemens Brentano, Eduard Mörike, and Nikolaus Lenau. Important prose writers included the novelist Jean Paul (Friedrich Richter), the short-story writer E. T. A. Hoffman, and the brothers Jakob and Wilhelm Grimm, compilers of the famous collection of German folk tales. Among dramatists the most important are Heinrich von Kleist (*The Prince of Homburg*) and Franz Grillparzer (*The*

Ancestress, Sappho); others are Dietrich Grabbe (*Don Juan and Faust*) and Georg Büchner.

Heinrich Heine, the greatest of the romantic poets and, after Goethe, the greatest lyric poet in German literature, broke away from the sentimental and self-pitying excesses of much of German romanticism. Heine called himself the last of the romantics; others have named him the first of the moderns, for he was among the first to recognize, and come to grips with, the problems presented by the Industrial Revolution and the resulting social and political changes.

The second half of the 19th century was dominated by an increasing trend toward realism, which directed its interest and emphasis to economic and social problems and to accuracy in depicting the lives and problems of ordinary people. The realistic approach to literature is best served by fiction, which flourished at this time. Among the important figures are the novelists Gottfried Keller (*The Green Henry, The People of Seldwyla*), Karl Immermann (*Münchhausen*), Gustav Freytag (*Debit and Credit, The Ancestors*), Theodor Fontane, and Wilhelm Raabe and the dramatists Otto Ludwig and Friedrich Hebbel. Important poets were Paul von Heyse, Conrad Ferdinand Meyer, Detlev von Liliencron, and Richard Dehmel. Theodor Storm, a poet-novelist, was the author of the very famous short novel *Immensee*. Romanticism experienced a late revival in the music dramas of the poet-composer Richard Wagner.

At the end of the century the most flourishing literary movement was naturalism, a revolt against the escapism of some of the writers of the previous generation. (See NATURALISM.) The principal theorist of the movement was the poet Arno Holz; its most important members, the playwright Gerhart Hauptmann (*The Weavers, The Sunken Bell, The Beaver Coat*) and the playwright and novelist Hermann Sudermann (*Dame Care; Honor; Heimat,* or *Magda*).

THE 20TH CENTURY

The 25 years preceding the outbreak of World War I (1914) saw a remarkable revival of lyric poetry. The outstanding poets were Stefan George, Hugo von Hofmannsthal, and Rainer Maria Rilke (*The Book of Hours, Duino Elegies, Sonnets to Orpheus*). Important dramatists were Arthur Schnitzler (*Flirtation, The Green Cockatoo, Professor Bern-*

Bertolt Brecht is one of Germany's most outstanding modern playwrights and poets.

hardi) and Frank Wedekind (*Spring's Awakening, The Earth Spirit, Pandora's Box*).

The greatest German novelist of the 20th Century was Thomas Mann, whose work reflects a consciousness of a declining society, a preoccupation that dominates his first great novel *Buddenbrooks*. In several short novels, most notably *Tonio Kröger* and *Death in Venice*, he examined problems relating to the function of the artist in society; he continued his emphasis on decadence and death in the long symbolic novel *The Magic Mountain*, his most widely read and probably his greatest novel. Mann became somewhat less gloomy in his later masterpieces, most notable of which are the *Joseph* tetralogy (four novels) and the *Confessions of Felix Krull, Confidence Man*.

For about ten years, roughly from 1914 to 1924, the dominant movement in German writing was expressionism, another revival of the romanticism that is always near the surface of German literature. The most important expressionists were the playwrights Georg Kaiser and Ernst Toller and the novelist Jakob Wassermann. The poet, novelist, and playwright Franz Werfel (*The Song of Bernadette, The Forty Days of Musa Dagh*) abandoned expressionism in his later and better works. Hermann Hesse, who was only partially identified with the expressionist movement, was the most important new novelist of the period. He eloquently summarized the predicament of man in the 20th century in such novels as *The Wolf of the Steppes, Death and the Lover, Magister Ludi*, and *Peter Camenzind*.

The most influential and, with the possible exception of Mann, the greatest writer in German in the 20th century was the Austrian novelist and short-story writer Franz Kafka. Kafka suffered terrifying loneliness. His horrible sense of isolation in the middle of a great city is the principal subject matter of such novels as *The Trial, The Castle*, and *Amerika* and the short stories "The Penal Colony" and "The Metamorphosis." Because of his acute perception and presentation of the problems faced by modern man, Kafka's works have exerted a tremendous influence on many writers in France, Britain, and the United States.

In the 1920's expressionism was superseded by a short-lived neorealism movement whose most notable members were the novelists Arnold Zweig (*The Case of Sergeant Grischa*), Hans Fallada (*Little Man, What Now?*), and Erich Maria Remarque (*All Quiet on the Western Front*) and the dramatist Bertolt Brecht (*The Threepenny Opera, Galileo, The Good Woman of Setzuan, Mother Courage*).

In 1933 the National Socialist (Nazi) party gained control of Germany, and five years later Nazi Germany annexed Austria. The Nazis stifled virtually all literary activity; although many important writers emigrated and continued writing, German literature during the 12 years of Nazi rule suffered a blow from which it has yet to recover. Since 1945 the most important of the few voices to be heard in Germany have been the poets Gottfried Benn, Hans Egon Holthusen, and R. A. Schröder; the novelist Ernst Jünger; and the poet and novelist Wolfgang Borchert.

This encyclopedia contains separate entries on several of the authors mentioned here.

Erich Maria Remarque is best known for his war novel *All Quiet on the Western Front*.

GERMANY is a country of central Europe located between the North and Baltic seas on the north and the Alps on the south. Since 1949 it has been divided into two distinct parts, each with its own government—the non-Communist west, known as the Federal Republic of Germany, and the Communist east, known as the German Democratic Republic. The German border with Poland, along the Oder and Neisse rivers, has not yet been established as final. With abundant supplies of coal and other resources, Germany is one of the great industrial nations of the world. Germany's major industrial regions are the Ruhr and the Saar, where most of its iron and steel are produced.

Berlin is its largest city, and the Communist part of the city is the East German capital. Bonn is the capital of West Germany. Hamburg and Bremen are the chief German seaports. West Germany covers about 96,000 square miles and has about 54,000,000 people. East Germany's area is about 42,000 square miles, and its population is about 18,000,000.

The southern part of Germany is mountainous. Here the Zugspitze in the Bavarian Alps rises to more than 9,700 feet, the highest point in the country. Central Germany is varied with hills and tablelands, and the northern part is flat. There are numerous mineral springs, most of them used for medicinal purposes in the many watering resorts. About one-fourth of the country is forested. Pine and spruce forests predominate. The scenic Black Forest is in the southwest, and the Bohemian Forest is in the southeast.

Northwestern Germany has cool summers and mild, cloudy winters. As one moves eastward, the climate becomes more continental. Winters are longer and colder, but the short summers are warmer. Because of the higher elevation of mountainous southern Germany, the climate there is also cooler. In general, January temperatures in Germany average about 32° F.; July temperatures, about 64° F. Rainfall, adequate everywhere, is greatest in the northwest and in the mountains.

The German people show both Nordic and Alpine characteristics. The Nordic type (tall, light haired, and blue eyed) is more common in northern Germany. The Alpine type (shorter and darker) predominates in the south. About half the people are Protestants. Most of the rest are Roman Catholics, concentrated in southern and western Germany.

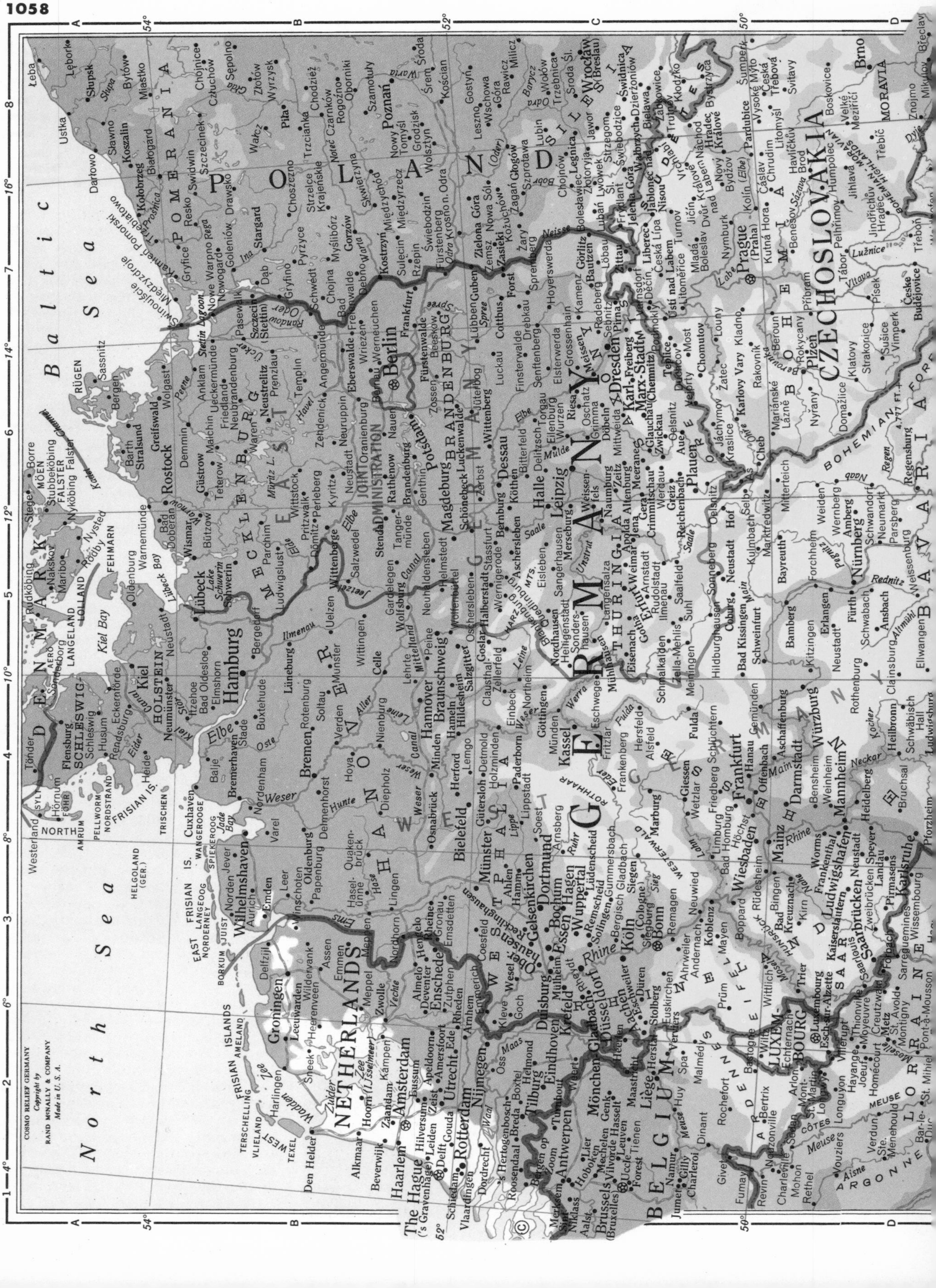

POLAND

GERMANY

EAST GERMANY

CZECHOSLOVAKIA

MORAVIA

BOHEMIA

BAVARIA

THURINGIA

BRANDENBURG

MECKLENBURG

POMERANIA

DENMARK

SCHLESWIG-HOLSTEIN

NETHERLANDS

BELGIUM

LUXEMBOURG

WESTPHALIA

HANOVER

SILESIA

Baltic Sea

North Sea

Kiel Bay

Berlin

Hamburg

Bremen

Hannover

Braunschweig

Magdeburg

Leipzig

Dresden

Prague (Praha)

Plzeň

Brno

Nürnberg

Frankfurt

Mainz

Wiesbaden

Mannheim

Karlsruhe

Köln

Bonn

Düsseldorf

Essen

Dortmund

Wuppertal

Bochum

Münster

Bielefeld

Kassel

Rostock

Lübeck

Wismar

Stettin

Poznań

Wrocław (Breslau)

Amsterdam

Rotterdam

The Hague ('s Gravenhage)

Haarlem

Groningen

Brussels (Bruxelles)

Antwerpen

Liège

Luxembourg

Saarbrücken

COSMO RELIEF GERMANY
Copyright by
RAND McNALLY & COMPANY
Made in U.S.A.

GERMANY, AUSTRIA AND SWITZERLAND

1 Inch = 63 Statute Miles

⊗ National Capital

● Size of symbols and type
indicates relative population

Miles 25 0 25 50 75

Conic Projection

RELIEF

Feet
5 000
2 000
1 000
500
Sea Level
500
5 000

Below Sea Level

West Germany's coat of arms consists of a black eagle on a golden field. This symbol can be traced from medieval Germany. Rastatt Castle, pictured on the stamp, is in Baden, a former German state. During the Allied Occupation, after World War II, Baden was under French administration.

The black, red, and gold color combination of the German flag dates from the time of the Napoleonic Wars, when it was sought to unify Germany into one kingdom. But the colors, not widely popular, were used only intermittently. During Hitler's regime they were replaced by the swastika flag.

Location map

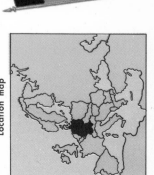

Large-scale movement of refugees since World War II, however, has greatly changed the traditional pattern of population distribution.

The ancient Germans were divided into many tribes. Brave and warlike, they fought hard against the Romans, who tried repeatedly but unsuccessfully to conquer them. In the 8th century the German tribes were united under Charlemagne. When Charlemagne's lands were divided in 843, Germany became part of a loosely knit empire of various duchies. For centuries the German kings were also the Holy Roman emperors. Practically all of Europe was at one time or another under German influence.

German history has been marked by wars of expansion, religious troubles, changes in ruling families, conflict between emperors and popes, and strife among the duchies, cities, and the central authority. In 1517 the Protestant Reformation began in Germany under Martin Luther. The bloody Thirty Years' War (1618-1648), which grew out of religious rivalry between Protestants and Roman Catholics, left Germany cut up into many small states.

In the 18th century one of these, Brandenburg, gradually expanded into the kingdom of Prussia. After the Napoleonic Wars the German Confederation was set up. Because Austria was jealous of Prussian power in Germany, the confederation could be only loosely organized. But the German people wanted a closer union. This was brought about in 1871 by Otto von Bismarck, who united Germany again in an empire under the Prussian king, leaving out Austria.

Germany expanded rapidly in power and acquired colonial possessions. After its defeat in World War I it became a republic. It lost its colonies and some of its own territory. Heavy reparations payments demanded by the victorious nations brought severe inflation and financial ruin to the country. In 1933 Adolf Hitler came to power and soon established a dictatorship. His conquest of neighboring nations ignited World War II in 1939.

With Germany's defeat, the country was divided into British, French, U.S., and Soviet occupation zones. In 1949 the British, French, and U.S. zones were organized into a West German republic. The Soviet zone became a separate Communist republic. Parts of Germany were absorbed by Poland and the Soviet Union, but the Western nations do not accept these incorporations.

A. Modl

Behind this village in southern Germany rises the Zugspitze, the country's highest peak.

GERMANY

Area: West Germany, 96,000 sq. mi. —East Germany, 42,000 sq. mi.

Population:
West Germany, 54,000,000
East Germany, 18,000,000

Capital: Bonn (West Germany)—Soviet sector of Berlin (East Germany)

Largest cities: Berlin, Hamburg, Munich, Cologne, Essen, Düsseldorf, Frankfurt am Main, Dortmund, Stuttgart, Leipzig

Highest mountain peak: Zugspitze (more than 9,700 feet)

Chief rivers: Rhine, Ems, Weser, Elbe, Oder, Danube

Chief lake: Constance

Climate: Cool summers and mild and cloudy winters in northwest —warmer summers and colder winters in east—south also colder because of higher elevation—adequate rainfall everywhere

National flag: Three horizontal stripes of black, red, gold

National anthem: West Germany— third verse of *Deutschland über Alles* (Germany Above All)

Form of government: Republic (West Germany)—Communist people's republic (East Germany)

Unit of currency: Deutsche mark

Language: German

Chief religions: Lutheran, Roman Catholic

Chief economic activities: Manufacturing, agriculture (including livestock raising), forestry, fishing

Chief manufactures: Machinery and vehicles, iron and steel, electrical equipment, chemicals, textiles, cameras and optical instruments, glass and chinaware, cutlery, leather goods

Chief minerals: Coal and lignite, potash, iron ore

Chief crops: Rye and other grains, potatoes, sugar beets, wine grapes, fruits

Chief exports: Machinery and vehicles, iron and steel, chemicals, electrical equipment

Chief imports: Processed foods, various raw materials

The countryside cross pictured below is in Bavaria, a large state in southern Germany.

Artha Hornbostel

Alfons Preindl—Shostal

Impressive Neuschwanstein is one of Bavaria's famous castles.

At the left is the marketplace of medieval Rothenburg, Germany.

The Black Forest, shown below, lies in southwestern Germany.

Wolff and Tritschler

Artha Hornbostel

Germany's Ruhr Valley is a great mining and industrial region.

Monkmeyer

GERMINATION, the growth and emergence of a plant embryo from a seed. Germination is commonly called sprouting.

A plant embryo is a minute living plant enclosed within a seed. After a seed has matured and fallen to earth, the plant embryo within it usually rests awhile before germinating. This period of rest is called dormancy. The seeds of many Temperate Zone plants mature and fall to earth during autumn, remain dormant during winter, and germinate during the following spring.

Seeds lying beneath the soil will not germinate until the temperature of the air has become warm and unless they have sufficient water and an abundance of oxygen. Upon beginning its growth an embryo absorbs water and oxygen from the soil and digests food that was stored within its cotyledons or within the endosperm of the seed. At one end of the embryo is a tiny structure called a hypocotyl, which breaks through the softened seedcoat and grows downward through the soil. The hypocotyl develops into a primary root that may remain either permanently or temporarily. A little later at the other end of the embryo another tiny structure called epi-

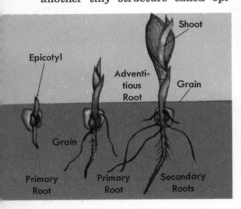

After a grain of corn has germinated, the roots of the young plant grow downward, and the shoot grows upward into the air.

cotyl, or plumule, breaks through the seedcoat and grows upward through the soil and into the air. The epicotyl develops into the stem of the young plant. The prior growth of the root enables it to absorb from the soil the minerals and additional water that are required by the growing plant. The tender young plant subsists upon food stored within the cotyledons or endosperm until it develops leaves, which can then manufacture food by means of photosynthesis.

Many seeds can germinate and grow for several weeks in darkness because their sprouts subsist entirely upon food stored in the cotyledons or endosperm. However, after the stored food has been consumed, the sprout will stop growing and will die unless it is transferred from darkness to sunlight. See SEED.

Photo Courtesy of Herb Glass

Geronimo

GERONIMO (1829-1909), American Indian chief of the Chiricahua band of the Apache tribe, was born in southern Arizona. His Indian name was Goyathlay, or One Who Yawns, but Geronimo, his best known name, was given to him by Mexicans.

Opposed to living on reservations, Geronimo and his men started a series of terror raids on ranches and settlements in Arizona and New Mexico. Fleeing to Mexico, the Indian chief remained in hiding until 1883, when General George Crook captured him. He escaped but surrendered to General Nelson Miles in 1886 at Camp Bowie in Arizona.

Geronimo demanded that he and his men be allowed to live with their families in St. Augustine, Fla. The Army agreed, but through an error in orders the Indians were moved to Fort Pickens at Pensacola, Fla. In 1888 they were resettled in Alabama, but because of the climate they were sent to Fort Sill in Oklahoma. There they became prosperous farmers.

This odd bird is a gerrymander, the result of redistricting Massachusetts in 1812. One legend says that the artist Gilbert Stuart added the head, wings, and claws.

GERRYMANDER, in politics, the redistricting of voting areas so as to give the greatest advantage to one political party over another. If a political party has a minority of voting strength in two election districts, it is possible by redrawing the boundaries to concentrate its voting power in a single district, thereby assuring the election of at least one official. By the clever (and unscrupulous) use of the gerrymander a political party can assure itself of a majority of members in a state, city, or federal assembly. A modified version of the gerrymander is the constitutional or legislative device used in some states to afford the rural population a greater representation in assemblies than the urban population. Sometimes this sort of gerrymander is the result of simply leaving the old districts as they were and neglecting to redistrict in accordance with the shift of population into the city.

The device was named after Elbridge Gerry, governor of Massachusetts in the early 19th century. By a process of redistricting Gerry was able to give the Jeffersonian Republicans the greatest possible representation in the state Senate. So strangely were the district boundaries drawn on the map of Massachusetts that the new districts resembled a salamander. Political opponents seized the notion and named the districts a gerrymander to relate them to the governor's name.

In 1842 Congress passed an act requiring that single member districts for the House of Representatives be compact and contiguous. Legal action and the referendum may also prevent flagrant gerrymanders.

Brown Brothers

George Gershwin

GERSHWIN, GEORGE (1898-1937), American composer and songwriter, was born in Brooklyn, N.Y. At an early age Gershwin developed an interest in music. Although he had many instructors, his talents were mainly self-developed.

He first worked as a song plugger for J. H. Remick and Company in Tin Pan Alley. He was a rehearsal pianist for a Florenz Ziegfeld musical. At 21 years of age he wrote his first successful song, "Swanee," which was introduced by Al Jolson.

He wrote the scores for many musical comedies, including *George White's Scandals, Lady Be Good, Strike Up the Band, Funny Face, Girl Crazy,* and *Of Thee I Sing.* The last was the first musical to win a Pulitzer prize.

As a serious composer Gershwin was best known for his use of jazz rhythms. Among his compositions were *Rhapsody in Blue,* Piano Concerto in F, *An American in Paris,* and the opera *Porgy and Bess.* This opera, considered his greatest work, was written with broad strokes of realism blended with touches of poetry.

GESTAPO, the Nazi secret police during the Adolf Hitler regime in Germany (1933-1945). Gestapo was an abbreviation of *Geheime Staatspolizei,* or secret state police. Formed by Hermann Göring in 1933, it was later headed by Heinrich Himmler, who assumed control of all police organizations in 1936. Organized on military lines, the Gestapo had two military branches and one political. It was noted for its terrorism, brutality, and extrajudicial activities. The Gestapo administered the concentration camps. Its members constituted a greatly feared elite. At the Nuremberg trials in 1946 it was declared a criminal organization.

GESTATION, the development of an embryo within the maternal uterus from the fertilization of the ovum to birth. The term *gestation* is also employed to designate the total period of time required for embryonic development.

The length of the period of gestation varies greatly in different mammals. The length of the gestation period of some mammals is as follows: opossum, 13 days; mouse, 21 days; rabbit, 30 days; cat, 63 days; dog, 63 days; pig, 120 days; man, 252 days or 36 weeks; cow, 41 weeks; horse, 48 weeks; whale, 20 months; elephant, from 20 to 22 months. As a general rule, the length of the period of gestation varies directly with the size of the animal. An exception to this rule is the fact that the opossum, which as an adult is much larger than the adult mouse, has a shorter period of gestation than the mouse. Because of its short period of gestation a newborn opossum is only about $\frac{1}{2}$ inch long and by comparison with many other animals is born very prematurely. The term *gestation* is applied to embryonic development only when such development occurs within the body of the mother and not within eggs that are extruded from her body before they are hatched.

GESTURE, a movement of the body that conveys an idea or an emotion. There are a few known systems of communication that consist entirely of gestures. Usually, gestures supplement a spoken language.

Some gestures have practically the same meaning among all peoples. A smile and a frown of despair are such gestures. Most gestures, like most of the sounds in a spoken language, are learned rather than natural. In Africa the Uduk people snap their fingers together with another person to indicate friendliness. Many social scientists find that the gestures of a group of people yield as much information as the words of their language.

GETTYSBURG, BATTLE OF, one of the most important battles in the Civil War. General Robert E. Lee, with an army of about 80,000 well-trained soldiers, crossed the Potomac River and marched across Maryland into Pennsylvania, intending to take Harrisburg and Philadelphia and cut off Washington, D.C., from the rest of the North, if not actually to capture it. Neither Lee nor George G. Meade, the Union commander, had intended to fight at Gettysburg, but a Confederate foraging party was caught by Union forces there, and the battle began on July 1, 1863. It lasted three days. On the first day the Confederates were successful, driving the Union army out of Gettysburg. The Unionists fell back to Cemetery Hill, a low ridge about a mile south of Gettysburg, while Lee drew up his men on Seminary Ridge, which is separated from Cemetery Hill by a valley. Lee's effective fighting forces numbered about 75,000 men, some 15,000 less than Meade's. For two more days these forces fought with varying success. On the last day Lee ordered a grand charge across the valley and up Cemetery Hill. This was made by about 15,000 men under General George E. Pickett and is called Pickett's Charge. After a desperate hand-to-hand struggle, the Confederates were driven back with terrible loss. During the three days they had lost more than a third of their army in killed, wounded, and prisoners, and the Union loss was hardly less severe. On the night of July 4 the Confederates retreated to the Potomac, which they crossed nine days later, thus ending the great invasion of the North.

General George Pickett leads his Confederate troops in the futile charge that climaxed the Battle of Gettysburg, a decisive engagement of the Civil War. Defeat at Gettysburg, coupled with the simultaneous fall of the Confederate stronghold at Vicksburg, Miss., marked the war's turning point.

U.S. Army Photograph

Abraham Lincoln's memorable Gettysburg Address is one of history's great speeches.

GETTYSBURG ADDRESS, a speech delivered by President Abraham Lincoln at the dedication of Gettysburg National Cemetery, Gettysburg, Pa., on Nov. 19, 1863. Though delivered in less than three minutes, the address is a classic of oratory. One version of the text, of which there are a number, is as follows:

Four score and seven years ago our fathers brought forth upon this continent, a new nation, conceived in liberty, and dedicated to the proposition that all men are created equal.

Now we are engaged in a great civil war, testing whether that nation or any nation so conceived and so dedicated, can long endure. We are met on a great battlefield of that war. We have come to dedicate a portion of that field, as a final resting-place for those who here gave their lives that that nation might live. It is altogether fitting and proper that we should do this.

But in a larger sense, we cannot dedicate—we cannot consecrate—we cannot hallow—this ground. The brave men, living and dead, who struggled here, have consecrated it, far above our poor power to add or detract. The world will little note, nor long remember, what we say here, but it can never forget what they did here. It is for us the living, rather, to be dedicated here to the unfinished work which they who fought here have thus far so nobly advanced. It is rather for us to be here dedicated to the great task remaining before us—that from these honored dead we take increased devotion to that cause for which they gave the last full measure of devotion—that we here highly resolve that these dead shall not have died in vain—that this nation, under God, shall have a new birth of freedom—and that government of the people, by the people, for the people, shall not perish from the earth.

GEYSER, a hot spring that at intervals spouts steam and hot water into the air. Geysers occur in areas of volcanic activity. The natural pipe from which the water shoots extends deep into the earth to an area of hot igneous rocks. Although all the details of a geyser eruption are not known, it is thought that when water in the bottom of the pipe is heated to the boiling point, steam is formed, which expands and pushes the overlying water upward, reducing the pressure on it and causing it to boil. This forces steam and water into the air in a geyser eruption. The cone of a geyser is made of minerals that have been dissolved and thrown onto the surface by the hot water. As they cool they form a rock wall around the opening of the geyser.

The most noteworthy geysers are those in the Yellowstone region of the Rocky Mountains in the United States, those in southern Iceland, and those in the provincial district of Auckland, New Zealand.

The most famous of all geysers is Old Faithful in Yellowstone National Park. Old Faithful erupts regularly about every hour and shoots about 15,000 gallons of water to a height of approximately 120 feet. Iceland's geyser region is near the volcanic mountain Hekla. The region centers around a hot spring named Geysir, from which the word *geyser* comes.

This longitudinal section of a geyser shows underground channels that fill with ground water. Eruption occurs when water near the bottom gets hot enough to change to steam.

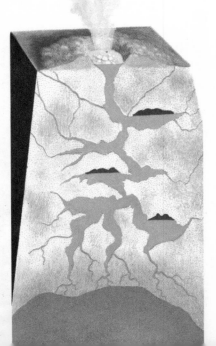

GHANA, an African republic that became independent of Great Britain on Mar. 6, 1957. It is located on the southern coast of the western bulge of Africa, between Togoland and the Ivory Coast. The capital is Accra; other chief cities are Kumasi, Sekondi, Takoradi, and Cape Coast. Ghana has an area of 91,843 square miles and a population of about 5,000,000.

The coast is flat, and the interior is rolling and covered with tropical forests of valuable mahogany and other hardwoods. In the north are large areas of tropical grasslands. The climate is tropical—hot and wet in the southwest and central portions and hot and dry in the north. The eastern coastal area is the most temperate part of the country.

Cacao beans, exported in large quantities, constitute Ghana's most important product. Other important agricultural crops are millet, durra, rice, yams, and cassava. Ghana is rich in minerals, especially gold, diamonds, manganese, and bauxite. In 1957 a large dam for the Volta River was planned to provide electricity for the manufacture of aluminum from the bauxite. Railroad and highway transportation is being constantly expanded.

The people of Ghana represent many different tribes (Fanti, Ashanti, Dagomba, and others), each living in its own area and with its own chief and subchiefs. Since the tribes all speak different languages, the proceedings of the central government are conducted in English. In religion most of the people still worship their old native gods, although there are also many Christian and Moslem groups. People in the towns wear Western clothes during the day, but for holidays and during evenings they wear colorful native garb. Inhabitants of the countryside usually wear native dress at all times.

Before Ghana became independent, it was known as the Gold Coast. Under this name its history dates from 1471, when the first Europeans arrived. These were Portuguese traders who landed on the coast at Elmina. Before this, the area, known by its present name, had enjoyed a long and brilliant history. The kingdom of Ghana was apparently founded about A.D. 300, after which it expanded until it eventually reached from the Niger River in the east to the Atlantic coast in the west. Its northern boundary was the Sahara. By the 10th century the Ghana Empire was at its height. Its capital, also known as Ghana, was large and well built, boasting a population clad in woolen, cotton, silk, and velvet clothes. The empire itself engaged in a lucrative trade in textiles, dates, copper, jewels, armor, and weapons of gold and silver. So wealthy was this state, it was the envy of both Africans and Arabs, the latter of whom then held all of Africa north of the Sahara. In 1020 an African and Arab coalition attacked the empire, but they were driven back. For another half century Ghana struggled and stood, but in 1076 it fell before the overwhelming force of the Almoravides, a North African Moslem dynasty. Thereafter, the territory that was once Ghana passed to a succession of empires—Islamic, African, and finally European. During the 17th century the Dutch took over the territory, at least the coastal part of it, from the Portuguese. A few years later the English built a fort there called Cape Coast Castle. During the 18th and 19th centuries trading companies of several nations developed within the territory a large commerce in gold and slaves. The English gradually expanded their control and in 1871 purchased the Dutch forts. The territory now became wholly a British possession. In 1957 it became the independent state of Ghana within the British Commonwealth. When Ghana adopted a republican form of government in 1960, Prime Minister Kwame Nkrumah became its first president. For a map of Ghana see ALGERIA.

Todd Webb—Photo Library

These muscular men, stripped to the waist, are unloading cargo at Accra, Ghana. The ocean ships arriving from foreign ports anchor offshore, and the merchandise is transferred to canoe-shaped boats that are paddled through the Gulf of Guinea's heavy surf to the shore.

Charles May—Shostal

The picture at the left shows the Supreme Court buildings of Ghana. Many people are surprised to find such modern buildings in Africa.

The man below is inspecting cacao pods on one of his trees to see if they are ready to harvest. From the dried seeds in these pods chocolate is made. Ghana is the chief grower and exporter of cacao. The United States is the main customer.

Richard Harrington—Annan Photo Features

This flag, with red, gold, and green stripes and the black star in its center, is the national flag of the republic of Ghana. Below it is the African nation's coat of arms.

W. Fredericks

Enthusiastic crowds line the streets to watch political parades in Ghana, formerly a British possession called the Gold Coast.

GHANA

Area: 91,843 sq. mi.
Population: 6,000,000
Capital: Accra
Largest cities: Accra, Kumasi, Sekondi-Takoradi
Chief river: Volta
Climate: Tropical—two rainy seasons in most of country
National flag: Three horizontal stripes of red, gold, green—black star in center
Form of government: Independent republic within the British Commonwealth
Unit of currency: Pound
Languages: African tribal languages, English
Chief religion: Animist
Chief economic activities: Agriculture, mining, forestry
Chief crops: Cacao, yams, cassava, durra, millet, rice, peanuts, coconuts, oil palms
Chief minerals: Gold, manganese, diamonds, bauxite (aluminum ore)
Chief exports: Cacao, timber, gold, manganese, diamonds
Chief imports: Textiles, foodstuffs, machinery and vehicles, petroleum products

GHETTO, a section of medieval cities to which Jews were confined by law. The ghetto was once characteristic of most cities of Europe. Its effect on Jewish life was to foster the growth of a self-contained society. The word *ghetto* is often used in a wider sense to refer to the special economic and social conditions that prevail in any section of a city to which members of a certain race or class are confined.

In order to maintain religious observances, the Jews of the Christianized Roman Empire tended to gather voluntarily into communities within Roman cities. The first conscious effort to establish ghettos by law occurred in Speyer, Germany, and in Spain from the 11th to the 14th centuries. Originally, ghettos were established to protect the Jews from persecution. Gradually, the ghetto became a place of confinement and generally included the most unhealthful sectors of the city. Juan II of Castile in Spain had walls built around the ghettos in 1412. In the 15th century the Jews of Italy were forced to live in ghettos, and the practice spread throughout Europe.

In spite of the congestion, the restrictive regulations, and the often unsanitary conditions (the ghetto in Rome was established where the Tiber River overflowed each year), the ghettos were not necessarily drab. The ghetto at Prague, for example, was noted for its Talmudic schools, its town hall, and its cultural and religious life. Charitable institutions, schools, and synagogues were founded, and holidays, weddings, and births were times of spiritual exuberance.

The spread of the political ideals of the French Revolution—liberty, equality, and fraternity—caused the gradual abolition of ghettos in Europe. By the 20th century ghettos seemed to be a thing of the past. However, at the beginning of World War II the Nazis reintroduced in Poland the old medieval-type ghetto with enclosing walls. These ghettos were completely destroyed in the fighting in the final months of the war. The only ghettos existing today in the Western world are those corresponding to the more general sense of the word.

GHIBERTI, LORENZO (1378?-1455), Italian sculptor, goldsmith, and painter, was born at Florence. His ancestors were distinguished goldsmiths. He was a pupil of his stepfather, Bartolo Michele. Because of the plague Ghiberti left Florence. Later, he submitted a model for one of the bronze doors of the baptistry of San Giovanni in Florence. His model was accepted, and he completed this north door after 21 years of labor. The east door was done in a period nearly as long. During this period Ghiberti also completed his statue "John the Baptist" and other works for the façade of Or San Michele and the bronze reliquary of St. Zenobius for the cathedral of Santa Maria del Fiore in Florence, together with some excellent paintings on glass.

GHOST. One of the subjects of many stories, tales, and legends is the appearance of ghosts, apparitions of something no longer living. The skeptic says that they are produced by a too active imagination, yet very critical people have observed strange, apparently unexplainable phantoms. Explanations of ghosts and haunted houses include telepathy, "unconscious ventriloquism," and the appearance of things outwardly that a person only imagines in his mind. In any case, the subject of ghosts seems assured a permanent place in literature.

Some authors specialize in stories of ghosts or the supernatural. The Welsh writer Arthur Machen has written tales about ghosts that range from the delightful to the terrifying. The American writer Edgar Allan Poe touched again and again on the supernatural in his stories, and the "Legend of Sleepy Hollow" by Washington Irving is a favorite tale for lovers of ghost stories. The old legend of the *Flying Dutchman*, a phantom ship said to appear in stormy weather off the Cape of Good Hope, furnished Richard Wagner with the story for his opera *The Flying Dutchman*. Captain Frederick Marryat also wrote a novel about the *Flying Dutchman*, called *The Phantom Ship*.

Great Britain seems to abound in ghosts for some reason; there few old houses or castles lack ghostly visitors. Sorrow in life or violent death seems to give rise to some hauntings. The unfortunate wives of Henry VIII of England have been said to haunt the Hampton Court Palace. Jane Seymour, dressed in white and carrying a lighted candle, is supposed to pass through one of the palace galleries and down the stairs at night. And the Tower of London has had visitations, so it is said, from poor Anne Boleyn; for it was there that Henry VIII had her beheaded in 1536. There is a tale told in Devonshire, England, of the phantom appearance of Sir Francis Drake, who rides in a black coach drawn by headless horses. Behind the coach run a pack of ghostly hounds, and woe to the earthly dogs that hear the baying of these apparitions!

GIANT, a huge man, animal, or bird. Giants play an important part in many myths, legends, and folk tales. Goliath, in the Bible story of David and Goliath, and the giant in the story "Jack and the Beanstalk" are two of the best known. The American Indians and Eskimos told of many giants. The Shawnee Indians believed that one of their goddesses had four giant sons who could smell human beings from miles away. The Indians of the Southwest feared a giant bird called Big Owl. On the northern Pacific coast the Indians told of a giant woman. They believed that she had been burned to death and that her ashes had become mosquitoes.

In ancient Greek and Roman mythology the giants were a group of huge monsters. They had long hair and beards, and their feet were serpents' tails. Other giants of mythology include the enormous one-eyed Cyclops and three monsters who each had 100 hands.

Real cases of giantism, or gigantism, in human beings are growth disturbances caused by improper functioning of the pituitary gland. Rapid skeletal growth, increase in muscular development, and increase in the size of the internal organs are characteristic of giantism. The height ranges from 6½ to 8 feet, although the tallest man in medical annals, Robert Wadlow of Alton, Ill., was 8 feet 9½ inches tall; he died in 1940 at the age of 22. Treatment is not satisfactory, although X-ray radiation of the pituitary gland has been tried to depress the gland's activity.

GIANT GROUND SLOTH, an extinct animal that once lived in South America and the southern part of North America. It was up to 20 feet long, larger than the largest present-day elephant. Giant ground sloths ate leaves, and it is believed that the huge beasts uprooted and pushed over trees to get the tender

The giant ground sloth bit off tree leaves.

green shoots at the top, just as elephants do in Africa today. Some authorities say that the ground sloth lived about 500,000 years ago, but some of these animals may have survived into the days of the early men. In an extinct volcano in the southwestern United States the body of a bear-sized sloth was discovered. It was so well preserved that it probably died not more than 2,000 years ago.

GIANT HUNTER, THE (constellation). See ORION.

GIBBON, EDWARD (1737-1794), an English historian, famous for his *Decline and Fall of the Roman Empire*. He was born in Putney-on-Thames. Very sickly as a child, he received little formal education. He, however, read voluminously. He attended Magdalen College, Oxford, for a year, but his father withdrew him on his conversion to Catholicism. He was sent to Lausanne to live and study and while there re-accepted Protestantism, only to desert it later for skepticism. In 1757, the same year he met Voltaire, he fell in love with Suzanne Curchod, but his father objected to his marriage and called him back to England. In 1764 on his tour of the Continent he visited Rome, where "musing amidst the ruins of the Capitol . . . the idea of writing the decline and fall of the city" first came to his mind. He returned to England the next year and devoted the rest of his life, with few interruptions, to study and writing, although for several years he was a member of Parliament. The six volumes of Gibbon's *Decline and Fall of the Roman Empire*, published in the years 1776-1788, met with immediate success. It was both greatly praised and blamed, the greatest controversy centering around this interpretation of the role of Christianity in the empire's history. In 1783 Gibbon returned to Lausanne, where he wrote his *Memoirs of My Life and Writings*. He died in London.

GIBBON, a tailless anthropoid ape. The habitat is the densely forested regions of India and the East Indies. Gibbons are smaller than chimpanzees, orangutans, and gorillas—the other anthropoid apes—and seldom exceed 3 feet in height. They are also the least manlike of the anthropoids and have the smallest cranial capacity. They are predominantly arboreal in their habits and swing from tree to tree with

Gibbons hang by their arms from tree limbs.

great agility, a feat made possible by their very long arms. Certain species are reputed to be able to clear a gap of 40 feet. The walking posture of gibbons when they are on the ground is erect. Gibbons are the only anthropoids with hairless callosities on the buttocks. In this respect they are like the Old World monkeys.

The number of distinct species is variously reckoned as eight or ten. The common gibbon, or lar, is native to the Malay Peninsula. The hoolock lives in the region of Assam, India. The siamang, the largest of all the gibbons, inhabits Malacca and Sumatra.

Martin S. Klein

The Rock of Gibraltar, near the entrance to the Mediterranean Sea, rises to 1,396 feet.

GIBRALTAR is a British crown colony consisting of a strongly fortified peninsula of rock near the southern tip of Spain at the eastern end of the Strait of Gibraltar. A low, narrow isthmus connects it with the European mainland. The fortress is very important because a fleet stationed there, supported by the great guns of the rock, can keep ships from entering the Mediterranean Sea. A little more than 2 miles long and less than 1 mile wide, Gibraltar has an area of about $2\frac{1}{4}$ square miles and a population of about 25,000.

Gibraltar was taken from the Moors by the Spaniards in 1462. The Spanish so fortified it that they thought it never could be conquered. But in 1704 an English and Dutch fleet captured it, and since then it has always been in British possession. It was officially given to Great Britain by the Treaty of Utrecht in 1713.

GIDE, ANDRE (1869-1951), French novelist and critic, winner of the 1947 Nobel prize for literature, was born in Paris. Gide's parents were both Protestants, and he received a very strict religious upbringing. His father, a professor of law, died of tuberculosis in 1880; Gide himself suffered for many years from ill health.

In 1890, the year he received his baccalaureate, Gide published his first book, *The Notebooks of André Walter*. This book was characterized by an introspective, self-confessional tone that was to become one of the dominant features of his later works. Having established a small reputation as a writer and eccentric, Gide was accepted by Stéphane Mallarmé into his coterie of young writers.

In 1893 he journeyed to North Africa, where his health improved. His mother died in 1895 and left him a considerable fortune. In the same year Gide married his cousin, and they lived in Algeria. Shortly thereafter they separated, and in 1902 some of the difficulties of their relationship found expression in his great novel *The Immoralist*.

Early in 1909 the *New French Review*, destined to become the most influential literary journal in France, appeared. Gide was the guiding spirit behind it, and it was largely the result of his critical insight and efforts that such talented writers as Alain-Fournier, Jean Cocteau, Jules Romains, and Jean Giraudoux were discovered and encouraged.

The *Review* ceased publication with the outbreak of World War I, and Gide went to work in a Franco-Belgian refugee center. After the war the amoralistic hero of his book *Lafcadio's Adventures* had become a symbol to the new generation of Frenchmen. In 1924 his writings were accused of corrupting public morals, and his reputation was seriously damaged.

He left France to travel in Africa, and while he was away another of his outstanding works, *The Counterfeiters*, was published. He became

strongly critical of French colonial policies in Africa (*Travels in the Congo*), and in 1932 he openly supported communism. In 1935-1936 he visited the Soviet Union, and his disillusionment was expressed in the books *Back from the U.S.S.R.* and *Afterthoughts*. Gide supported the Loyalists during the Spanish Civil War, and he continued his opposition to the Fascists during World War II.

André Gide was a voluminous writer. His *Journals* are a multi-volume autobiographical work covering the years 1889 to 1949.

Tiny bones embedded in the gila monster's skin resemble colored beads.

GILA MONSTER, a poisonous lizard living in New Mexico, Arizona, and northern Mexico. It is the largest of the North American lizards and is sometimes nearly 2 feet in length. It has a very plump, rounded body, four short legs with five claws on each foot, and a rather long, thick, round tail. The animal is yellowish or orange, mottled with black, and has blackish rings on the tail. It looks almost as though its whole body has been made with glass beads in an Indian design. For this reason it is sometimes known as the beaded lizard.

The Gila monster lives in dry regions. Usually during daytime it lies hidden in the scant vegetation growing in the reddish sand, where its color keeps it from being seen. Its bite is fatal to small animals but seldom to man. The word *gila*, pronounced *heela*, is from the name of the Gila River of New Mexico and Arizona.

GILBERT, WILLIAM (1540-1603), an English scientist, was born in Colchester. Graduated from St. John's College, Cambridge, he was court physician under Queen Elizabeth I and James I and became president of the College of Physicians in 1600. Gilbert was the first to use the terms *electricity*, *electric force*, and *electric attraction* and to point out that

amber is not the only substance that when rubbed attracts light objects but that the same faculty belongs to the resins, sealing wax, sulfur, and glass. He also invented two instruments for finding latitude with the help of astronomical observations.

GILBERT AND SULLIVAN were a famous musical team that created a dozen memorable comic operas in the late 1800's.

Sir William Schwenck Gilbert (1836-1911), English dramatist and librettist, was born in London. After practicing law for a time, he turned his creative talents in the direction of the theater. He penned several successful romantic plays.

In 1871 he joined forces with Arthur Sullivan in creating the first of many popular comic operas. The success of *Thespis*, and following works, was attributed as much to Gilbert's urbane wit as to the charm and grace of Sullivan's music. Gilbert wrote the lyrics and dialogue for such offerings as *Trial by Jury*, *H.M.S. Pinafore*, *The Pirates of Penzance*, *Iolanthe*, and *The Yeoman of the Guard*.

Sir Arthur Seymour Sullivan (1842-1900), London-born composer and conductor, gained his reputation by the incidental music he wrote for a production of Shakespeare's *The Tempest* in the Crystal Palace. He also wrote cantatas, oratorios, and overtures.

Beside his comedy endeavors with Gilbert, Sullivan's best known works were his songs. These included "The Lost Chord," "The Arabian Love Song," and the hymn "Onward, Christian Soldiers."

Their partnership, which was highly explosive, was dissolved in 1896 after a quarter century of successful collaboration. Gilbert was temperamental and sometimes dictatorial. The break came over a carpet that Gilbert thought too expensive for the theater.

Sullivan was knighted in 1893; Gilbert, in 1907.

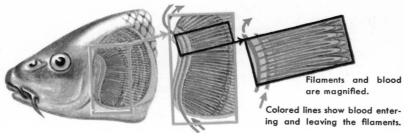

The gill filaments contain miles of thin capillaries that are exposed to flowing water.

Filaments and blood are magnified.

Colored lines show blood entering and leaving the filaments.

GILL, the respiratory organ of a fish and of other underwater animals. The gills of a fish enable it to extract oxygen from water. A true fish has four gills on each side of its head. Each gill lies between two slits that lead sideways from the inside of the mouth to a cavity that opens to the outside. Each gill consists of an ascending cartilaginous arch, from which arise two compact rows of ribbon-like appendages called gill filaments. The gill filaments are filled with capillaries separated from the water by extremely thin membranes. Water enters the fish's mouth and is forced over the gill filaments and out through the gill slits. As the water flows over the filaments, oxygen is absorbed through their thin membranes and into the blood flowing through the capillaries. Carbon dioxide contained in the blood simultaneously passes out of the capillaries, through the membranes of the filaments, and into the water.

Gills and lungs have the same function. In both organs oxygen is absorbed into the bloodstream, and carbon dioxide is discharged from it. In both organs absorption and discharge are facilitated by large areas of thin surface membranes that are packed with capillaries. The gills of fish, however, do not enable them to respire in the atmosphere; they will die of asphyxiation if kept out of water more than a few minutes. They will also be asphyxiated if the quantity of oxygen in the water becomes too low.

Crustaceans, clams, larval amphibians (tadpoles), and a few insect larvae also breathe through gills.

GINKGO, a tree that is the sole surviving species of an order of gymnosperms that dates from late Paleozoic time. These trees were possibly saved from extinction by monks of Asiatic religious orders who cultivated the trees for centuries. Chinese priests had originally found them growing wild in Chinese forests and had transplanted them to their temple gardens. The gymnosperm order Ginkgoales, to which the ginkgo tree belongs, flourished about 250 to 157 million years ago. Since that time all of its members except the present-day ginkgo, or maidenhair tree, have gradually become extinct. The surviving species is sometimes called a living fossil because it is the sole survivor of a large group of plants with a long geologic past.

The ginkgo tree can attain a height of 100 feet. Its trunk can become 4 feet wide. Ginkgo leaves, which are indented to form two rounded lobes, are shaped like a fan or a wedge. The ginkgo produces foul-smelling "fruits," somewhat larger than a cherry. Recently it has been planted in yards and parks of the United States. The ginkgo is also known as the maidenhair tree because its leaves are shaped like those of the maidenhair fern. The ginkgo, however, is not related to the maidenhair fern.

GIN RUMMY. See RUMMY.

GIORGIONE, IL (1478?-1511), pseudonym of Giorgio Barbarelli, was an Italian painter, born at Castelfranco Veneto. He studied under Giovanni Bellini in Venice. Among his notable works are the great altarpiece of the cathedral in Castelfranco Veneto and facades of various Venetian palaces. Pictures attributed to him include "Three Philosophers," "Sleeping Venus," and "The Judgment of Solomon."

GIOTTO (1266?-1337) was a noted Italian painter, who broke with tradition and painted human figures and portraits in a realistic manner.

Giotto was born in Vespignano, north of Florence. According to some scholars, he studied under the painter Cimabue, but others dispute this story. Giotto worked in and near Florence throughout his life. His leading works included a series of frescoes in the Arena Chapel at Padua and such paintings as "The Death of the Virgin" and "Madonna and Child." Some scholars believe that he painted a series of frescoes showing scenes from the life of St. Francis. These frescoes are in the church of St. Francis at Assisi. As an architect and sculptor, Giotto helped design and decorate the bell tower of the cathedral in Florence.

GIRAFFE, an even-toed, herbivorous, cud-chewing mammal that has an extremely long neck and long, slender forelegs. It used to be called a cameleopard because it seemed to combine something of the general shape of the camel with the spotted coat of the leopard. The giraffe, which ranges in height from 16 to 20 feet, is the tallest of living animals. The head is crowned with a pair of skin-covered horns. Some kinds have a third horn in front of the usual pair. The tongue, which is rough and sometimes 18 inches in length, can be stuck out so far that it is useful in picking off the leaves of trees for food.

The giraffe is timid and inoffensive. Its only means of defense is kicking, but it uses its hoofs with such skill and force that it often drives away lions and leopards. When it eats grass, it is obliged to straddle its front legs far apart in order to reach the ground. It has to do the same in drinking. It is swift of foot, running over the country at a rapid rate and changing often from a trot to a gallop. The word *giraffe* is from the Arabic and means "one who walks swiftly."

The giraffe formerly roamed in large herds over much of Africa south of the Sahara but is now found only in central and southern Africa. It is hunted chiefly for its skin and its flesh, of which some African peoples are very fond and even eat it raw. The long tendons of the legs are used by the Arabs for sewing leather and for guitar strings.

The long-necked giraffe can eat tree leaves.

Shown above is the official Girl Scout pin. It is worn by all members of the girl scouting movement except Brownie Scouts. The first Girl Scout Troop was established in Savannah, Ga., in 1912 by Juliette Gordon Low (left). At the lower left a Senior Girl Scout is instructing a Brownie Scout (center) and an Intermediate Girl Scout (right) in citizenship. The insignia at the lower right represent the various specialized programs in which the Senior Girl Scout may participate.

OCCUPATION: Girl Scout Executive
NATURE OF WORK: Working with adults who are troop leaders
PERSONAL FACTORS—ABILITIES, SKILLS, APTITUDES: Ability to work well with adult volunteers is important.
EDUCATION AND SPECIAL TRAINING: Bachelor's degree and background of group work are essential. Special Girl Scout training is required for professional workers.
WORKING CONDITIONS:
1. **INCOME:**
   COMPARED WITH OTHER CAREERS WITH EQUAL TRAINING: Favorable
2. **ENVIRONMENT:** Association with community leaders and other professional workers
3. **OTHER:** Work week averaging 40 hours; fringe benefits encouraged
RELATED CAREERS: Directing of camps; social-agency work; teaching

All photographs & emblems, Courtesy of Girl Scouts of the U.S.A.

International Friends

Wing Scout

Mounted Troop

Mariner

Trail Blazer Mountaineer

Explorer

General Program

GIRL SCOUTS, part of a worldwide association of girls with national organizations in the United States and 51 other countries. The national organizations have various names. The original group, the Girl Guides of England, was founded in 1909 by Lord Robert Baden-Powell, founder of the boy scout movement. Within a year of its beginning, Girl Guides were organized in Canada, Finland, Denmark, and South Africa. By 1914 there were similar groups in Australia, India, Sweden, Poland, The Netherlands, and the United States.

The basic aim of the Girl Scouts and the Girl Guides is to prepare girls for satisfying and useful citizenship through informal programs of work and play. Activities of the organizations include cooking, housekeeping, child care, arts and crafts, and athletics. Camping is also part of the training. In some European countries the Girl Guides performed valuable volunteer services in support of the defense of their nations during World War I and World War II.

In the United States girls from 7 through 17 years of age, regardless of race, class, or creed, are eligible for membership. Brownies are the youngest members of the Girl Scouts and are 7 through 9 years of age; these scouts wear brown uniforms. Intermediate Girl Scouts are from age 10 through 13, while Senior Girl Scouts are from age 14 through 17. There is a special uniform for Senior Girl Scouts. The same threefold division, under various names, exists in the Girl Guides and the Girl Scouts of other countries.

Scout troops are often sponsored by a school, a church, or a synagogue. Any girl of the right age is eligible to become a girl scout with the permission of her parents. Information about joining a Girl Scout Troop may be obtained from a troop leader or from the local Girl Scout office.

The World Association of Girl Guides and Girl Scouts was formed in 1930. In 1960, 32 countries were full members of the association and 20 others were tenderfoot (associate) members. The total world membership is about five million, and more than 65 percent of these are in the United States.

Brownie Scout

First Class

Senior Five Points

International World Friendship

Girl Scout

Membership Star

The Cabana (right), in Cuernavaca, Mexico, is the newest of several international centers for Girl Scouts and Girl Guides.

Senior Girl Scouts from all over the United States meet at a Girl Scout Roundup (above).

As their special service project these Senior Girl Scouts help out in a nursing home (below).

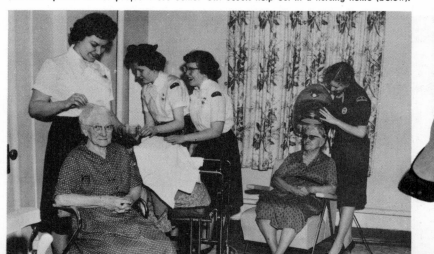

Above is a Senior Girl Scout.

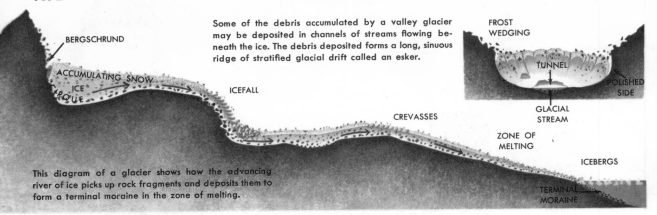

Some of the debris accumulated by a valley glacier may be deposited in channels of streams flowing beneath the ice. The debris deposited forms a long, sinuous ridge of stratified glacial drift called an esker.

This diagram of a glacier shows how the advancing river of ice picks up rock fragments and deposits them to form a terminal moraine in the zone of melting.

GLACIAL DEPOSIT. All materials brought to their present places by glacier ice or by the water from melting glacier ice are glacial deposits. Such deposits are often called glacial drift. See GLACIER.

Glaciers erode the land they pass over. The material they erode is incorporated in the moving ice and may be carried for many miles before it is deposited. Because glaciers deposit the debris they transport by many different methods, many kinds of glacial drift are formed.

Glacial drift may be without stratification and be unsorted according to particle size. Unsorted drift is called till. Till is deposited directly by glacier ice. It contains particles of all sizes—boulders, cobbles, gravel, sand, silt, and clay—mixed up together. Some drift is deposited in layers of particles sorted by size. Such stratified drift forms when rock particles released by melting ice are carried for some distance by running water before they are deposited. The water is derived from melting glacier ice.

Most till is found in moraines. Terminal moraines are long, uneven, hummocky ridges of material de-

A hummocky ground surface strewn with angular boulders is typical of till.

Ward's Natural Science Establishment

posited at the front of a glacier. A terminal moraine marks the farthest advance of the ice. When a glacier begins to retreat, the debris the ice carries tends to accumulate at the front end of the glacier, where it is abandoned as the glacier melts. If a glacier retreats very slowly, a very large pile of material is built up.

Recessional moraines are formed when a glacier is temporarily stationary during its retreat. A recessional moraine is formed in the same manner as a terminal moraine. Terminal and recessional moraines may be either large or small. Mountain-valley glaciers produce high, rather narrow, crescent-shaped terminal and recessional moraines within valleys. The ends of the moraine usually rest against the valley sides. Continental glaciers may have terminal and recessional moraines a hundred miles or more long and several miles wide.

Ground moraine is unsorted material dropped and overridden by a glacier during its advance or abandoned by a glacier during its retreat. Ground moraine does not form ridges; rather it is irregularly distributed. It may be packed into preglacial depressions. Ground moraine may be thin and scattered, or it may form a continuous blanket

over the bedrock for hundreds of square miles.

Drumlins are streamlined hills of till. They are formed when debris-carrying glacier ice overrides uneven ground moraine. Drumlins are found in groups. Many drumlins are shaped like an egg cut in half lengthwise. Different drumlins are of different sizes. The largest are more than 1,000 feet long, 300 or 400 feet wide, and more than 150 feet high. The long axis of each drumlin of a group is parallel to the axes of the other drumlins and to the direction of ice flow in the glacier.

Stratified drift is deposited in the channels of melt-water streams or in glacial lakes. Melt water is water derived from melting glacier ice. Stream deposits are called glacio-fluvial deposits. Lake deposits are called glaciolacustrine deposits.

Outwash fans or aprons are deposits of roughly sorted sands, gravels, and cobbles that are built up by streams of glacial melt water. The streams flowing from the glacier carry large quantities of sediment. The coarser sediments are soon dropped along the stream channels. The stream channels frequently shift, and eventually fan-shaped areas of sorted sediments are formed. The small end of the fan is toward the glacier. The outwash plains of continental glaciers are formed of many individual outwash fans.

Eskers are long, winding, narrow ridges of stratified sand and gravel. They are the channel deposits of streams that flowed in tunnels beneath the ice or along crevasses near the edges of continental glaciers. An esker looks something like an abandoned railway grade. Most eskers are less than 100 feet high, but they may be several miles long.

Glacial-lake sediments are deposited in several ways. Temporary lakes may be formed of water trapped between higher land and a retreating glacier front. In lakes of this type stratified deposits of fine silt and clay may accumulate. Glacial streams that flow into the lakes may build up layered deltas of coarser materials. The deltas are built where the stream enters the lake. Large stones incorporated in floating pieces of ice may be dropped as lake sediment when the ice melts. Small lakes may be quickly filled with sediment.

Kames are flat-topped mounds of stratified sediment. The sediments of kames were deposited in water trapped in the crevasses, holes, and surface depressions of stagnant, melting glaciers. When the glacier completely melted, the sediments were left in isolated mounds.

GLACIER, a thick mass of ice that tends to flow slowly downhill or to spread out under its own weight. Glaciers form in high mountain valleys in all parts of the world. In polar regions glaciers are found at low altitudes.

Glaciers form in areas where more snow falls each year than melts or evaporates. As snow accumulates, particles at the bottom of a snowfield are compressed and partially melted. The particles re-form and change to firn (small granules of ice). When a snowfield becomes large and deep enough, the firn is compressed and partially melted. Firn that is deep in the snowfield gradually becomes solid ice.

As the ice grows thicker and the snowfield becomes deeper, the ice begins to move downhill under the pressure of its own weight. It moves very slowly. The ice near the surface of the glacier is brittle and may fracture. A fracture is called a crevasse. The ice deep within the glacier is not brittle and moves and deforms readily. The ice crystals change shape by bending, by stretching out, or by breaking or melting and re-forming. Different glaciers move at different speeds. Some move a few inches a day; others move several feet a day.

The ice in a glacier always moves downstream, or away from the area of snow accumulation. The front of the glacier, the edge of the ice farthest from the source area, advances or retreats with changes of climate. The glacier front moves forward if the climate is such that ice melts or evaporates less rapidly at the glacier front than new ice is supplied from upstream. The glacier front retreats upstream if the glacier ice wastes away more rapidly than

Georgia Engelhard—Monkmeyer

A valley glacier flowing over a cliff forms an icefall. In the background is the snowfield that supplies ice for the glacier.

new ice moves toward the glacier front. If the rate of ice wasting and the supply of ice from upstream are exactly balanced, the glacier front is stationary.

The two chief types of glaciers are valley glaciers and continental glaciers. Valley glaciers are tongues of ice that move down steep-walled mountain valleys. The tongue of ice has the same shape as the valley. Valley glaciers are fed by ice that forms in permanent snowfields above the snowline. A valley glacier may extend far below the snowline. Continental glaciers are slightly domed masses of ice that cover thousands of square miles. A continental glacier is thousands of feet thick near its center. The ice moves out in all directions from the thickest parts of the glacier. A continental glacier is fed by snowfall over its entire surface. Continental glaciers are found at present only in Greenland and Antarctica.

Valley glaciers are found in many mountains. Even in low latitudes, high mountains (such as Kilimanjaro in Kenya) have valley glaciers. In the United States there are many small valley glaciers in the Sierra Nevada, the Rocky Mountains, and the Cascade Range. These valley glaciers are a few hundred yards to a few miles long and only a few hundred feet thick. The Alps of Europe are famous for small mountain-valley glaciers of about the same size. The largest valley glaciers are on the west coast of Alaska. Ice streams 30 to 70 miles long and several thousand feet thick flow from mountains toward the coast. Some glaciers reach the ocean.

The continental glacier that covers the interior of Greenland has an area of about 637,000 square miles. Much of the glacier is several thousand feet thick. The antarctic continental glacier covers an area larger than the United States.

Piedmont glaciers are formed when several valley glaciers join and spread out over a plain. The Malaspina Glacier of Alaska is a piedmont glacier that covers about 800 square miles. Icecaps are similar to continental glaciers but are much smaller. Icecaps are found in Iceland, in parts of Scandinavia, and on some of the islands of northern Canada.

Glaciers carry or drag with them large amounts of debris. Mountain-valley glaciers acquire debris in several ways. The glacier ice plucks out loosened blocks of rock from the rock walls at the head of the glacier. Avalanches that include rock and other debris fall onto the glacier from the valley walls. The debris that falls onto the glacier collects in strips along the edge of the glacier. The strips are called lateral moraines. When two valley glaciers join, the inner lateral moraines may join to form a strip of debris down the center of the combined glacier. This strip is called a medial moraine. As a glacier moves down a valley, it erodes material from the valley floor and sides and incorporates the material in glacier ice. Continental glaciers seem to obtain most of the debris they carry by erosion of the land over which they pass. Glaciers release the debris they carry when ice that reaches the front of the glacier melts.

Riders follow one of the scenic trails in Glacier Park.

Map: GLACIER NATIONAL PARK (WATERTON-GLACIER INTERNATIONAL PEACE PARK). ONE INCH EQUALS APPROX. 17 MILES

GLACIER NATIONAL PARK covers an area of nearly 1,600 square miles in the Rocky Mountains of northwestern Montana. The park's glaciers are among the few in the United States that are easily accessible. The area was set aside as a national park in 1910.

Among its high peaks are more than 50 glaciers and 200 glacier-fed lakes. Extensive forests, abundant wildlife, and beautiful waterfalls are some of the park's attractions.

GLADIATORIAL GAMES were contests between two armed opponents. The city of Rome, during the time of the Roman Republic and the Roman Empire, was the center of the gladiatorial contests. Historians record that as many as 5,000 pairs of gladiators fought there to celebrate a victory of the Emperor Trajan, A.D. 106.

Gladiators usually fought until one killed the other. Sometimes the audience allowed the defeated gladiator to live if his courage had impressed them. Some types of gladiators fought in heavy armor, using a shield, helmet, and short sword. Others fought with only a net and a three-pronged spear called a trident. Gladiators were usually prisoners of war, condemned criminals, or slaves trained especially to fight. During the empire's later years freemen, sometimes even of the wealthy classes, fought as gladiators.

GLADIOLUS, a stately cultivated plant with stiff, sword-shaped leaves and tall spikes of flowers. The word *gladiolus* comes from a Latin word meaning "little sword." The showy flowers are funnel shaped and of many different colors, ranging from pure white to pink, red, purple, orange, and yellow. Many of them are beautifully penciled or marked with other colors. The flowers keep well in water and open in succession, beginning at the bottom of the spike, so that they are in bloom for some time. This fact makes them desirable as cut flowers. The gladiolus is grown from a solid bulb, botanically a corm, which multiplies by forming new corms and tiny bulblets. The bulblets must be dug up during autumn and kept where they will not freeze during winter.

The gladiolus is native to several places, including South Africa and the Mediterranean region. Modern gladioli are the result of years of crossbreeding and are larger and showier than the original kinds. The plant belongs to the iris family.

Gladiolus varieties number several thousand.

GLADSTONE, WILLIAM EWART (1809-1898), was one of 19th-century England's greatest statesmen. The son of a well-to-do merchant, he studied at Eton and Oxford and entered Parliament in 1832. An ardent Tory, he opposed new reform bills, served as undersecretary for colonies under Robert Peel in 1834-1835, and wrote *The State in Its Relations to the Church* (1838), a defense of the Established Church. When Peel returned to power (1841), Gladstone became vice-president of the Board of Trade and, two years later, president. He resigned in 1845 but in the same year returned as colonial secretary under Peel. Throughout the following year he had no seat in Parliament; in 1847 he became the member for Oxford University.

In the succeeding years his opinions gradually became more liberal. As chancellor of the exchequer under the Earl of Aberdeen (1852-1855), he carried through numerous budgetary and university reforms. Shortly after the Aberdeen administration fell, Gladstone resigned. He spent several years studying Homer and preparing *Studies on Homer and the Homeric Age* (1858). In 1859 he returned to the cabinet as chancellor of the exchequer under Lord Palmerston. His budget of 1860 was notable for its reductions in the

William Gladstone

tariff, and during the succeeding years he sharply reduced domestic taxes. His drift to liberalism continued, and he became increasingly dissatisfied with Palmerston's foreign policy and his support of increases in naval armaments.

After Palmerston's death in 1865, Gladstone was returned from Lancashire as a Liberal and became leader of the Commons. Three years later he became prime minister and secured the disestablishment of the Irish church, the passage of the Irish Land Act of 1870, and reform in education. He abolished the purchase of army commissions, instituted the merit system in civil service, and secured various legal reforms. When the Conservatives, under Benjamin Disraeli, gained power in 1874, Gladstone retired to his classical and religious studies. Shortly afterward he returned to public life to denounce Disraeli's imperialism. In 1880 Gladstone was reelected to Parliament and again named prime minister. He concerned himself primarily with the Irish question and, although forced to undertake some coercive measures, secured the passage of a new and conciliatory Irish land act. He also carried through a redistribution of parliamentary seats and an extension of the franchise. Rising discontent over his apparently defeatist foreign policy resulted in his resignation, but after a general election he again became prime minister in 1886. He was defeated on his proposal for Irish home rule but continued to support Irish nationalism. In 1892, although more than 80 years old, he reassumed the office of prime minister and again introduced a bill for Irish home rule. With the defeat of this bill in the House of Lords, Gladstone's party was defeated, and his long career came to a close in 1894.

Gladstone had served his country for 60 years. A master of legislative and administrative procedure, he was also an able economist, one of the first serious students of colonial questions, and a defender of freedom and humanity among nations. The spotlessness of his character and his steady advocacy of reform measures earned him a large personal following.

GLAND, any organ that produces a specific secretion. Glands may be classified as endocrine, or ductless, glands and as exocrine glands, or those that discharge their secretions through a duct. A gland is sometimes both endocrine and exocrine. For example, the pancreas secretes a juice concerned with digestion into the intestine. It also has an internal secretion into the bloodstream, insulin, which helps the body to use sugar. The work of a gland in producing a secretion is to separate specific substances from the blood, to produce a new chemical substance, or to form cells.

The main endocrine glands are the pancreas, pituitary, thyroid, parathyroids, adrenals, and sex glands. The pineal and thymus glands are often classified as endocrine glands but their function is not well known. The secretions of endocrine glands are called hormones. From the arteries the endocrine glands obtain the materials for manufacturing hormones, which are discharged into the veins or the lymph vessels. Also, hormones do not directly affect the organ that produces them. Rather they influence the activity of another organ or tissue to which they are carried. Most endocrine glands are present in all orders of vertebrates, and an extract from the gland of one order exerts a specific effect when administered to a member of another order. It is this fact that makes possible the use of natural hormones in the treatment of human disease. The effects of hormones are such that if the mind and body are to be healthy and normal all the endocrine glands must pour their secretions into the bloodstream in exactly the right amounts. The hormones influence growth, use of food products, and the nervous system, including our emotions and intelligence.

An exocrine gland, or gland with a duct, may serve any of a number of functions depending upon the nature of its secretions. Sebaceous glands and sweat glands in the skin produce lubricating secretions. Glands in the digestive tract (salivary glands, gastric glands, and intestinal glands) and other glands affecting digestion (the pancreas and the liver) secrete enzymes and other products, such as bile, as well as fluids necessary to digestion.

The drawing below shows several endocrine glands, focusing especially on the adrenal glands.

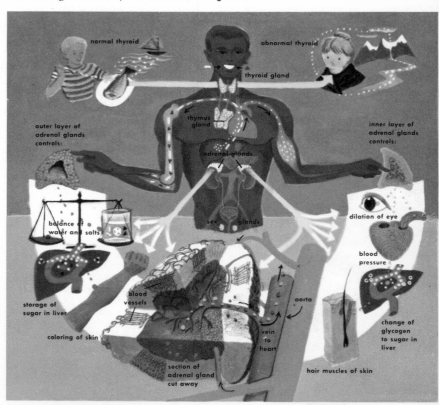

GLASGOW is the largest city of Scotland and is famous for its shipbuilding industry. It is an important port and a warehouse center for the industrial area of the Lanarkshire coalfields. Glasgow lies in the central lowland of Scotland and on both banks of the Clyde River, 22 miles from the North Channel. All except the largest seagoing ships can sail up the Clyde into the heart of the city. Glasgow and the surrounding industrial area contain the largest part of Scotland's population. The city has about 1,100,000 inhabitants.

The settlement of Glasgow dates from the Middle Ages. Between 1175 and 1178 the city became a royal borough. The Cathedral of St. Mungos dates from the 13th century, and the University of Glasgow was founded in 1450. The city became a prosperous commercial and industrial center only after the 18th century.

GLASS, STAINED. See STAINED GLASS.

GLASS AND GLASSMAKING. Glass is easily recognized as the material used for such things as bottles and windows. This material is made by heating a mixture of sand, lime, and soda until they melt and fuse. When this product of fusion cools, it becomes rigid without crystal formation, and we have glass. Glass has been made for at least 4,000 years, but in the 20th century the technology of glassmaking has advanced more than in all the previous centuries. The special properties of modern glass account for its many forms, products, and uses.

According to legend the first glass was made by accident. Some Phoenician merchants once moored their ship containing blocks of soda on

Courtesy of Pittsburgh Plate Glass Company

A long ribbon of plate glass enters a battery of twin grinders that carefully grind top and bottom surfaces simultaneously. The glass will then be cut and polished.

the banks of a river near the Mediterranean and made a fire to cook a meal. To hold their cooking pot up off the sand, they used lumps of soda from their cargo. The heat from their fire caused the soda to fuse with the sand, and the hot liquid mass flowing under the cooking pot turned upon cooling into a shining sheet of glass.

Because of impurities in the materials used, the glass made by the ancients was always colored. The first nearly colorless glass was made by the Romans about the beginning of the Christian Era. The first truly transparent glass was made in Venice in the 10th century.

In the making of glass the materials (silica sand and soda ash, limestone, and possibly other metallic oxides) are mixed in a batch. To this batch, cullet (excess glass from a previous production) is added to speed up melting. The mixture is then heated in a tanklike furnace to about 2,500° F. When the melting and fusion process is complete, the hot liquid glass is shaped. This shaping may be done by blowing, pressing, drawing, or rolling. The finished product is then moved to an annealing oven. In the annealing process the glass is reheated in a lehr (annealing oven) to remove any strains that may have been fixed in the glass during the shaping. It is then slowly cooled.

Both chemical and mechanical processes are used to finish glass. In chemical finishing the glass is etched with hydrofluoric acid. The glass is first covered with acid-resistant wax. Lines are then cut in the wax with a stylus, after which the glass is dipped in hydrofluoric acid. The acid etches the glass where the wax has been cut. In mechanical finishing the glass is ground, polished, or cut. Actually, glass is rarely cut. A diamond or some other hard material is used to score the glass. Slight pressure is then applied to the score mark to break the glass at the desired point.

As a material, glass is commonly valued for its transparency, hardness and resistance to scratching, smoothness, chemical inertness, excellent insulating and dielectric properties, optical properties, range of fine colors, high sparkle and luster, and permanency. These properties account for its varied uses as flat glass, container glass, table-

ware, cookingware, glass blocks, building panels, wire glass, heat-absorbing materials, textile fiber, and mineral wool.

There are many kinds of glass in addition to the ordinary soda-lime glass used for window glass and bottles. Ultraviolet glass transmits ultraviolet rays that are stopped by ordinary glass. In reinforced glass a network of wire is embedded in the glass while it is still hot. To make shatterproof glass a sheet of glass is placed on either side of a sheet of plastic. Glass and plastic are then placed in a hot oil bath. The plastic softens and provides a bond between the glass sheets. Colored glass is made by adding small amounts of coloring materials, usually metallic oxides, to batches of transparent glass. Optical glass is made from raw materials of the highest purity so that it may be without flaws. Photosensitive glass is a glass in which a photograph may be permanently formed.

GLASSCUTTING is not a difficult operation if one goes about it in the right way. With a little practice on some spare pieces of glass one can learn to cut glass almost as well as a glazier. Glasscutters cost only about a dollar apiece. The best has a wheel of tungsten carbide, one of the hardest materials known to science. In factories that make glass, glass is cut in continuous sheets by large electrically operated machines, but special shapes are still cut by hand.

In preparation for cutting a piece of glass, see that the glass is clean on both sides, so that the wheel of the cutter will not jump over any portion of the pane. Lay the glass on a firmly supported soft cloth or sheet of rubber. Lay your yardstick or ruler $\frac{1}{16}$ inch to the left of the line on which you wish to cut in order to allow for the overhang of the cutter. Daub kerosene on the line of cut and dip the head of the cutter into kerosene in order to get a good bite on the glass. Holding the cutter at a slight backward angle, draw it toward you in one smooth, decisive stroke, with a pressure that will produce the sound of cloth being torn. You should not go over the cut a second time. Place the line scored on the glass over the ruler and press firmly but gently. If the strip of glass to be removed is less than $\frac{1}{8}$ inch wide, pry it off with the notches on the glasscutter, but be careful to avoid inserting the glass all the way into the notch of the cutting instrument.

GLASS FIBER. Fibers of glass fine enough to be woven into textiles were first made in 1936. Such textiles have many uses, ranging from curtains to electrical insulation for wires and cables. Materials made from glass fiber may be fireproof, soundproof, heatproof, waterproof, and acid resistant. However, glass-fiber textiles are not suitable for clothing, although they may be used as insulation in special types of uniforms.

Glass fibers may be formed directly from molten glass. The force of gravity causes the glass to flow through openings in the bottom of the furnace that melts the glass. The coarse filaments of the flowing glass are then drawn onto winding devices that operate at a speed of nearly 2 miles a minute. In this way the molten glass is drawn into a fiber much finer than the openings through which it flows from the furnace.

Glass fiber is different from glass wool, which is a mineral wool made from glass. Glass wool lacks the precise uniformity in the diameter of the fibers that is characteristic of glass fiber.

The molten glass for making glass wool is drawn out as it flows from the furnace, and it is then blasted downward by jets of high-pressure steam or flame. This process forms a fibrous mass in a collecting chamber; the mass is carried away by a conveyor belt at the bottom of the chamber.

The first glass wools were used as air filters. They are now extensively used for insulation. Potentially important uses for glass wools are in the roofing and boatbuilding industries. On roofs, layers of glass-wool felt bonded with tar promise to give long life and protection from fire. Canoes and rowboats made of glass wool are light, corrosion resistant, and able to withstand heavy shocks.

GLASSWARE, articles of glass that, though useful, are primarily beautiful. Glassware is a product fashioned by the skill of craftsmen and the imagination of artists.

Although one can find in some museums large quartz crystals that have been shaped into cups and chalices, there is no such thing as rock crystal or crystal as distinct from glassware, which is made from pure sand, lead oxide, potash, and minute quantities of any one of the following: cadmium sulfide for yellow, selenium for red, black oxide of copper for a rich blue-green, and chrome for green. If the sand contains as little as $\frac{9}{100}$ of 1 percent of iron, the glassware will not be clear.

Shaping fine glass is still handwork. To make a goblet the gatherer sticks the end of his punty (a hollow steel rod 4 feet long) into the molten glass, which has a consistency of thick molasses. The cold punty picks up a blob of thick, hot glass, which is rolled onto a steel table and passed to the blower, who inflates it into a bubble. The blower drops the bubble of hot glass into a mold and rotates it there. While still hot the bubble of glass is taken out of the mold. Then the stem, which has in the meantime been blown and shaped, is applied to the bubble. The next step is to reheat the bubble with its stem to an almost molten condition and then to apply the foot to the stem. As the bubble with its stem and foot slowly cools, a cold iron cracks off the top of the bubble, and the goblet is complete, at least in terms of shape. At this stage, because of stresses within the glass, the goblet is so brittle that it will shatter on the slightest impact. The goblet must be reheated a third time for several hours.

The plain goblet may then be decorated by etching with acid, cutting with Carborundum wheels, and painting and fusing onto the glass such decorative materials as gold, silver, and enamel.

Fine glassware is of a number of different types. Venetian glass is a soft glass, noted for the beauty of its form and ornamentation and made at or near Venice. Bohemian glass is the name given to the beautiful ornamental glassware made in the 16th, 17th, and 18th centuries in Germany and noted for its clear, deep colors and delicate engraved patterns. Cameo glass is made of different colored glass. Ornamental patterns are engraved on it by cutting through the top layer to reveal the underlying one. Some of the most priceless examples of ancient glassware in museums are cameo glass. Crystal glass has a brilliant shine, especially when cut, and is mainly used for fine tableware. Cut glass is glass that is ornamented or shaped by cutting or grinding with abrasive wheels.

Good glassware should be handled with great care. If two glasses stick together, one inside the other, they should not be forced apart. Instead fill the inner one with cold water and immerse the outer one in warm water. The difference in the rates of expansion will separate the glasses without cracking. Wash and dry fine glassware on towels, one in the bottom of the dishpan, the other on the drainboard of the sink. Stack glass plates one on top of another with paper in between so that edges will not chip and decorations will not grind off. Wash all glassware in a mild solution of warm soapsuds, and rinse it in cool water. It will dry naturally to a lustrous sparkle.

GLIDER, a motorless aircraft of the airplane type that can travel forward for some distance in air as it loses altitude. When calms prevail, a glider must lose altitude to make headway, but a skillful pilot may utilize thermal air movements to maintain, or even increase, his altitude. Such craft are usually of plywood and fabric construction, are streamlined, and are fitted with skids for landing and a brake for stopping.

The dragon-stem goblet at the left was the work of a 16th-century Venetian artisan. The center goblet was produced in the factory of George Ravenscroft, noted English glassmaker of the 17th century. At the right are three contemporary pieces of Steuben crystal.

Courtesy of The Corning Museum of Glass　　Courtesy of Corning Glass Works

A soaring glider, or sailplane, once aloft, can rise with upward-moving air currents.

The first glider was designed and constructed by Sir George Cayley, a British experimenter, about 1809. The first actual glider flight was made in 1855 by Jean Marie Le Bris in a machine patterned after the albatross. The flight was made near Douarnenez, France. Other early experimenters with gliders were Otto Lilienthal, Samuel Pierpont Langley, and Albert Santos-Dumont. Later flights by the Wright brothers added much information to the science. During World War II, plane-towed gliders, carrying up to 25 soldiers, were used in the German invasions of Belgium and Crete. The United States used gliders in the invasion of Normandy and in the attack on Arnhem, The Netherlands, in 1944. Gliders were also used in the Burma campaign.

Soaring in gliders is an international sport, and annual competitions are held.

In 1954 the U.S.S.R. introduced a new type of glider with flapping wings.

GLINKA, MIKHAIL (1803-1857), Russian composer, was born in the government of Smolensk, the son of a wealthy landowner. He studied at the Pedagogic Institute in St. Petersburg (now Leningrad, Russian S.F.S.R.) and while there took up music. In 1824 he entered the Ministry of Communications, from which he resigned in 1828 to study composition. He left Russia in 1830 and in the following years studied in Italy and at Vienna and Berlin. On the death of his father, Glinka returned to Russia and began work on his first opera, *A Life for the Tsar*, which was produced in 1836. In 1838 he began work on his second opera, *Russlan and Ludmilla*, which was produced in 1842. Later works of Glinka's include *Kamarinskaya* and the overture *A Night in Madrid*.

GLOBE, a spherical model of the earth showing the true shape, relative size, and position of all countries. A celestial globe is a spherical model of the heavens indicating positions of the stars.

The use of a globe as a geographical map is widespread. Since a globe does not allow for the slightly flattened poles of the world, it is not an exact model, but for most calculations this inaccuracy is negligible. Globes are made of metal, wood, or plastic and are usually attached to a metal rod that cuts through the north and south poles. This serves as an axis around which the globe can be rotated. The surface of a globe is covered with cuts of paper, called gores, on which a map has been printed. It shows countries, seas, rivers, circles of latitude and longitude, and the like.

GLORIOUS REVOLUTION, the English revolution in 1688 that drove James II from the throne. The crown was transferred to the joint sovereigns William III and Mary II. The Bill of Rights and the Act of Toleration were also outcomes of this bloodless revolution. Most important, it ended the concept of absolute monarchy and established parliamentary sovereignty in England.

Within his brief three-year reign, James II managed to alienate almost the entire nation. He claimed the right to suspend acts of Parliament. He tried to extend religious liberty to Roman Catholics and appointed them to offices in state and church in violation of the Test Act. He granted complete freedom of worship to Roman Catholics and Nonconformists and forced his Second Declaration of Indulgence to be read in the Anglican churches. The Tories, who favored James's prerogatives, were alienated by his creation of a standing army and by the fear that their monopoly of government offices was at stake. The Whigs were furious because James ignored Parliament. His attempt to foster trade with France angered merchants, and his support of Louis XIV of France lost the support of many Roman Catholics who disliked Louis' attitude toward the pope.

James II had two daughters, Mary and Anne, who were both Protestant. The thought that they would succeed their father placated the Whigs and the Tories. The birth of a son to James's Roman Catholic wife in 1688, however, changed the prospects for the future. Both Parliamentary parties invited William, prince of Orange, and Mary (James's elder daughter) to assume the throne. William sailed with an army from Holland and landed at Brixham. The entire nation supported him, and James II, without an army, fled to France. A special session of Parliament declared that James had abdicated and granted the crown to William and Mary in 1689.

The revolution made Parliament the ultimate arbiter of decisions. Religious liberty was granted by the Act of Toleration of 1689 to all but Jews, Roman Catholics, and Unitarians. The Bill of Rights of 1689, besides declaring William and Mary king and queen, extended the power of Parliament and established the Protestant succession to the throne. The revolution was a major step toward freedom of the press. A major result of the revolution was the establishment of an independent judiciary in England.

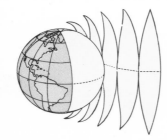

Globe maps are truer representations of earth surface patterns than are flat maps.

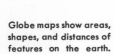

Globe maps show areas, shapes, and distances of features on the earth.

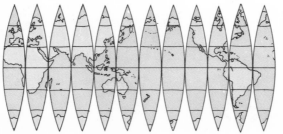

GLOVE, a hand covering, usually with separate sections for each finger, worn for warmth, decoration, or protection. Records show that gloves have been worn since earliest history. A linen glove was discovered in an Egyptian tomb dating from the 4th century B.C. The literature of the early Persians, Greeks, and Romans indicates that they wore gloves for warmth. At other times the wearing of gloves appears to have been viewed as a sign of weakness on the part of those who could not withstand the cold.

Leather gloves were being manufactured in France by the 10th century, in England by the 11th, and in Scotland by the 13th. It was the Scots, in the 18th century, who brought the glovemaking trade to America.

Gloves have had various symbolic meanings. In Europe during the Middle Ages gloves were a symbol of chivalry, high rank, and church position. High priests and emperors wore silk gloves to indicate their rank. A knight who struck another with a glove challenged him to a duel. Rulers used gloves to confer honors and privileges. As late as the time of Queen Elizabeth I gloves were a symbol used to signify rank and honor. It is said that the queen wore gloves constantly, taking them off only in the presence of a highly esteemed visitor. Her gloves, like those of others during her reign, were decorated and often jeweled and were made with a cufflike extension at the wrist.

In the Orient the glove was a symbol of property. When a seller completed the sale of his property, he handed his glove to the buyer to indicate the close of a transaction.

By the 18th century in England and France gloves had become a required part of the wardrobe. Women wore long silk gloves; men of wealth wore leather gloves. The common people wore either leather or knitted woolen gloves.

These fashions continue with some variation. Long gloves are still often worn with evening dress, and it is still the custom to keep them on throughout the evening. For inexpensive, warm gloves, wool is still the choice.

The making of gloves has changed greatly in the last 100 years. Except for a few knitted and leather gloves made by hand, most are made by machine. Cotton, rayon, nylon, rubber, and plastic have been added to the list of materials from which gloves are made.

Leather gloves are made from the

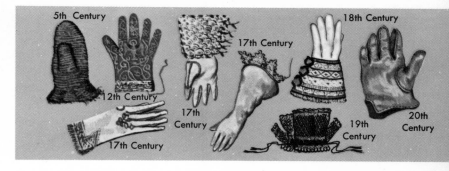

These are some of the typical glove styles that have been worn in the past 14 centuries.

hide of sheep, calf, lamb, goat, and kid. Skins dressed on the wool or hair side are called grain. Those dressed on the flesh side are called suede. Lambskin and kidskin are usually used for making suede. Mocha is usually made from goatskin but sometimes from sheepskin. (Both *suede* and *mocha* are words that describe types of finish, rather than kinds of leather.) Pigskin is made from the skin of either peccary or carpincho. Capeskin is made from sheepskin; kidskin is baby goat, or kid; chamois may be antelope, goat, or sheep; and buckskin is the skin of a buck (male deer), antelope, goat, or even a rabbit.

GLUCK, CHRISTOPH WILLIBALD (1714-1787), German composer, was born in Bavaria. He grew up in Bohemia and studied music at Prague, Vienna, and Milan. His first opera, *Artaserse*, produced at Milan when Gluck was 27, was the first of many successes that brought him increasing public attention in both Germany and Italy. When he was 40, he was appointed musical director of the Royal Opera in Vienna, and his future was assured.

Gluck's early operas, and many later ones, followed the traditions of the Italian *opera seria*, which had reached its peak in the work of Handel earlier in the 18th century. By the middle of the century the form, which emphasized spectacular singing at the expense of literary and dramatic values, consisted merely of a series of songs loosely held together by a weak plot. Gluck, inspired by the current interest in ancient Greece, began a series of reforms intended to give to opera some of the power and dignity of Greek tragedy. However, his first major work, *Orfeo ed Euridice*, was written before the new principles had been fully formulated and was produced at Vienna in 1762. Its success encouraged him to write *Alceste* (1767), the first of the "re-

form" operas. In a preface to the opera he set forth his new principles of operatic composition: Music must further the dramatic interest and emotional intensity of opera rather than simply call attention to itself by spectacular vocalizing.

During his last years Gluck spent much time in Paris, where he became involved in a famous controversy about his new style of opera. For Paris he composed several fine operas, including *Iphigénie en Aulide*, *Armide*, and *Iphigénie en Tauride*. He then retired to Vienna, where he died. Although no major composers fully adopted the principles of Gluck's reform, he nonetheless exercised considerable influence upon those who followed him. See OPERA.

GLUCOSE is a simple sugar occurring naturally in ripe fruits, most vegetables, and honey. Its chemical formula is $C_6H_{12}O_6$. Glucose is also known as dextrose, corn sugar, and blood sugar. It is rarely found in solid form and is less sweet than sucrose (table sugar).

Glucose is one of the chemicals into which more complicated carbohydrates and 58 percent of proteins are broken up during the process of digestion of food. The human body absorbs glucose through the walls of the intestine; it is a normal component of human blood. Glucose is an important source of energy for the body.

The body of a person with the disease diabetes is unable to oxidize and use the glucose in the bloodstream. Excess glucose collects in the blood and the urine. Diabetes can be diagnosed by analyzing the urine for excess glucose.

Glucose is used commercially in making candies, jams, baked and canned goods, and wines from fruit juices. It is also used as a food in intravenous feeding. Large amounts of glucose are manufactured from cornstarch.

GLUE, a protein product made from the bones and hides of animals. Relatively small amounts of glue are also made from the skins, bladders, and bones of fish. Glue cannot be made from the horns or hoofs of any animal. From tanners and meatpackers the bones and hides go to the glue manufacturer, where they are cleansed, chemically treated, and heated with water to give a glue solution. The dilute solution is concentrated by evaporation and is then dried and ground to give a granular product.

Although animal glue was used extensively by the Egyptians and Romans and was manufactured on a commercial scale in the United States as early as 1808, intensive study of it began only a generation ago. The molecular structure of glue is still unknown.

The user sifts the dry glue into an amount of cold water suitable for his specific needs. The glue is allowed to swell for about one hour and is then melted at 140° F. in a water-jacketed tank. It is used warm for most commercial applications.

Cold liquid glue is generally made from dry glue by the addition of water and special chemicals. Cold glues are more convenient for household use and possess excellent strength. Flexible glues are available in gelled cakes composed of dry glue, water, and such agents as sugar and glycerin.

Hundreds of common products are made of glue or with the aid of glue. As an adhesive, glue is used in the manufacture of wood furniture, sandpaper, gummed tape, fancy paper boxes, bookbindings, and paratrooper kits. It is used to size writing paper, currency paper, textiles, and gaskets. Match heads, hectographs, and the cork linings in the caps of soft-drink bottles are made with glue compositions.

Three unusual uses of glue indicate the power and usefulness of this common product. Glue is so strong that when it is spread on a glass panel, it can chip off the surface as it dries and thus etch a name or a design.

Glue, used two parts per million when added to sewage and industrial waste waters, causes the impurities to settle out rapidly so that the clarified water may be returned to a pure stream. An excellent foundation finish for wood is obtained by sizing the wood surface with a dilute solution of animal glue. After drying, the wood area is sanded, and the sanding produces a glasslike surface that readily accepts stains and other finishes.

GLYCERIN is the commercial name of the chemical glycerol, also known as 1, 2, 3-propanetriol. It is one of the most important industrial chemicals.

Glycerin, $CH_2OH\text{-}CHOH\text{-}CH_2OH$, is colorless and nearly odorless when pure. It is a liquid at room temperatures and is completely miscible with water and with alcohols. Many organic and inorganic compounds are soluble in glycerin.

Glycerin can be obtained by breaking down animal and vegetable fats and oils, which are esters of glycerin. (See ESTER.) The processes of making soap from natural fats and oils and of making fatty acids from fats and oils yield glycerin as a byproduct. The fermentation of sugar also yields glycerin. Most of the glycerin produced in the United States is synthetic and is made from propylene that is obtained by cracking petroleum.

Glycerin is used to preserve a moist condition in tobacco and fruits, since it attracts and holds water. It is used in antifreeze solutions and in many cosmetic and skin preparations. Glycerin can be assimilated by the human body as food and is used as a solvent or a moisturizer in foods and beverages.

Glycerin is the starting chemical for the manufacture of many commercially important products. The two best known products are the alkyd resins and nitroglycerin. (See NITROGLYCERIN.) The alkyd resins are used in paints, enamels, varnishes, and other coatings.

GLYCOGEN is a carbohydrate occurring generally in animal cells and is called animal starch. It is built up from molecules of D-glucose, which may be converted into glycogen by the animal cell and stored for future use. It is the supply of glycogen that sustains life in a hibernating animal, and there is a theory that man's second wind is derived from the glycogen stored in his system. Unlike plant starch, which turns dark blue when mixed with iodine, glycogen—when mixed with iodine—becomes reddish-brown. It forms an opalescent colloid when mixed with water. In pure form it is a white powder.

GNATCATCHER. See KINGLETS AND GNATCATCHERS.

GLUE AND OTHER ADHESIVES

TYPE	USES AND PROPERTIES
Glue	Most effective with wood, paper, leather, textiles; not very effective with metal, ceramics, rubber. Adversely affected by moisture and high humidity.
Casein	Best with wood; also good with paper, leather. Not recommended for use with glass, ceramics, rubber.
Vegetable and Gum Resins	Paper, textiles, leather, and so on. Limited strength.
Natural and Synthetic Rubber-Based	Both porous and nonporous materials. Especially recommended where joint will be subject to flexing. "Contact" types used to bond plastic materials to wood. Satisfactory resistance to heat, cold, moisture.
Cellulose	Paper, leather, some types of repairing and modelmaking. Tends to break down on contact with water, get brittle with age.
Vinyl Resin	Formulas with acetate recommended with wood, paper, textiles, leather, glass, ceramics, metal. Polyvinyl chloride types for use in patching wading pools and other vinyl chloride plastic products.
Urea Resin	For use with wood, paper, textiles, leather. Strong, moisture-resistant.
Resorcinol	Especially suited for sports equipment, boats, outdoor furniture. Also good with paper, textiles, leather. Tough, waterproof bond.
Epoxy Resin	Effective on many materials—wood, glass, porcelain, plastics, metal. Extremely high strength, but not recommended for joints subject to flexing. Excellent resistance to temperature and moisture.

GNEISS, a common type of rock of coarse texture and crude banding. The parallel arrangement of the layers is sometimes well defined. Gneisses are metamorphic rocks formed from pre-existing igneous rock or sedimentary rock. These rocks are found in a wide variety of colors, depending on the kind of mineral that makes up the largest portion of the mixture. See IGNEOUS ROCK; METAMORPHIC ROCK.

Gneiss permeated by igneous materials during its formation is called injection gneiss.

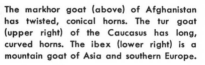

The markhor goat (above) of Afghanistan has twisted, conical horns. The tur goat (upper right) of the Caucasus has long, curved horns. The ibex (lower right) is a mountain goat of Asia and southern Europe.

GOAT, an herbivorous, cud-chewing, horned mammal that belongs to the same family as cattle and sheep. The horns of the goat curve backward, and those of the male are very long. The male—and sometimes the female also—has a beard. The ibex, or wild goat, belongs entirely to the Old World and is found chiefly in mountain regions, where it climbs to almost inaccessible heights. The mountain goat ranges through the mountains of western North America from Alaska to Montana and Idaho. This goat is an excellent climber and jumper. Except for mountain goats, goats have been domesticated since early times. They are pictured in the sculptures of ancient Egypt and are mentioned in the Bible.

Milk goats are raised in parts of Europe and Asia. In Switzerland their milk is used in making choice cheeses. In Mexico also much cheese is made from goats' milk. In the United States there are comparatively few herds of milk goats, and the milk is used largely for supplying babies who do not do well on other kinds of milk or on baby food.

Angora, or mohair, goats came from Asia Minor. Their fleece is long, silky, and curly and is used for making mohair, a fine woolly fabric. Many flocks of these goats are raised in western and southwestern states and in British Columbia for their wool. Cashmere goats are raised mostly in Tibet. Their fine underwool is used for making the famous cashmere shawls, sweaters,

and scarves. The skin of goats is made into leather or sometimes into parchment. That of young goats, called kids, is used largely for kid gloves.

GOBI DESERT, an immense tract of desert country, extending over much of southern Mongolia and northern China. Surrounded by mountains, the Gobi is a sand-and-gravel plateau, ranging from 3,000 to more than 5,000 feet above sea level. Ages ago it was probably a great inland sea. Stretches of short grass occur on its edges. The short summers are very hot, while the winters are clear and very cold. Only a few nomads live in the desert. They wander about, using tents for shelter. The western extension of the Gobi is called the Taklamakan Desert. Estimates of the Gobi's area range between 300,000 and 500,000 square miles.

GOD, any being that is worshiped as divine, or as having more powers than man. The ancient Greeks were polytheistic, which means that they worshiped many gods. Since they lived mainly by agriculture or hunting, they were dependent on the forces of nature, such as rains, winds, rivers, and the seasons. Because man seemed to have no control over these forces, the people of Greece believed them to be controlled by gods, to whom man could appeal. Zeus was thought of as the god of the sky; Apollo became the protector of flocks; and Poseidon, who ruled over the sea, was also the creator of earthquakes and horses.

The gods of Greece supposedly lived on snow-covered Mt. Olympus, which was the most inaccessible height in Greece. They were considered to be immortal, exempt from pain or sorrow, givers of good, and punishers of evil. Occasionally, they

	Sumeria	China	Egypt	Vedic India	Greece	Rome	Germanic Tribes	Mexico	Japan
Creator									
Sun									
Moon									
Earth									
Sea									
Dawn									
Thunder									
Birth									
Love									
Death									
Agriculture									
War				(plural)					
Wisdom									
Healing									
Evil									

KEY

Male

Female

Male and Female

Indra, God of Thunder (India)

Osiris, King of the Dead (Egypt)

Athena, Goddess of Wisdom (Greece)

Huitzilopochtli, Aztec War God (Mexico)

walked in disguise among men. In the poems of Homer they are shown taking an active part in the Trojan War. Even among the gods, family strife, war, and mutiny were common. By the time of Socrates, however, the belief in these gods was not so firm among some thinkers as it once had been. Plato and his pupil Aristotle, for example, began to work out other ideas of divinity.

The belief in a single, all-powerful God developed in the Near East. This belief, however, has also been found among primitive groups, such as tribes of the Australian aborigines before the arrival of the missionaries. Among the Assyrians in the Near East the god Ashur eventually became foremost in their religion. Ashur was warlike and was believed to be responsible for the victories of Assyrian armies. He was pictured as standing on a winged disk (the sun), from which he shot arrows.

The firmest believers in one God, however, were the Hebrews. Among the other polytheistic tribes in the Near East the Jews held to their idea that God was one. Now and then they wavered in their belief, as when Moses returned from Mt. Sinai to find his people worshiping a golden calf. Yet, throughout the Old Testament, which relates the efforts of the Hebrew prophets to understand him, the belief in one God was maintained. He was conceived to be all-powerful in wisdom, righteousness, and goodness.

The New Testament repeated most of the moral attributes of God mentioned in the Old Testament. Jesus stressed God's goodness and his willingness to forgive the im-perfections of men. This Christian-Jewish idea of God continued to develop, and men attempted to study the revelations of God and his nature in that branch of study called theology. Theologians sought out the meanings that were contained in Jesus' teachings.

During the Middle Ages men also began to study Plato and Aristotle, finding in these philosophers certain supports for the Christian-Jewish idea of God. A form of thought called scholasticism developed. The great scholastics, such as St. Anselm, Abelard, and St. Thomas Aquinas, believed that man's reason was given him in order to verify his faith in God. Even the buildings of the Middle Ages, with their tall, pointed spires, were a part of this scholastic belief. The Reformation and the Protestant theologians changed some of the ideas about man's relation to God, but the religious concept of him remained basically the same. See CHRISTIAN-ITY; GODS AND GODDESSES; GREEK MYTHOLOGY; JUDAISM; REFORMA-TION; RELIGIONS OF THE WORLD.

GODS AND GODDESSES. Many peoples and nations throughout history have believed in superhuman beings called gods and goddesses. Certain peoples, such as the ancient Greeks, Romans, Germans, and Norsemen, believed that their gods and goddesses had human form. Often the major difference between the gods and human beings was that the gods were immortal. However, the gods and goddesses of such peoples as the Egyptians, Babylonians, and Hindus often did not re-semble human beings. For further information, see the separate entries on many of the Greek and Roman gods. The articles appear under the Roman names. See GREEK MY-THOLOGY; NORSE MYTHOLOGY; ROMAN MYTHOLOGY.

GOETHALS, GEORGE WASHING-TON (1858-1928), an American army engineer, was born in Brooklyn, N.Y. He was engaged in work at Muscle Shoals, Tenn., before being appointed chief engineer of the Panama Canal Commission in 1907. In 1914 he became first civil governor of the Canal Zone. In 1919 he voluntarily retired from active service to set up a consulting engineering practice.

George W. Goethals

GOETHE, JOHANN WOLFGANG VON (1749-1832), German poet, dramatist, and prose writer, was one of the geniuses of European literature. He was born in Frankfurt am Main, the son of a councilor of state. The autobiographical material left by Goethe—letters, the novel *The Sorrows of Young Werther,* and *From My Life: Truth and Poetry*—provides much information about the writer's literary development, love affairs, emotions, and ideas. He received no formal early education but studied under tutors. His love for the theater began when he had access to many French productions in Frankfurt. His father sent him to study law at the University of Leipzig. His health failed, and he returned to Frankfurt, where he spent a year and a half before recovering sufficiently to go to Strasbourg for further legal study. There he delved into anatomy and chemistry and was introduced by Johann Herder to the works of William Shakespeare and Oliver Goldsmith. In 1772 Goethe went to live in Wetzlar, where he practiced law. During this period he finished his first important drama, *Götz von Berlichingen,* and wrote *The Sorrows of Young Werther.* The latter was the first forceful expression of the *Sturm und Drang* movement, a term meaning "storm and stress" and applied to the impetuous writings of young Germans of the period. His other plays were *Clavigo, Iphigenie auf Tauris, Egmont,* and *Torquato Tasso.*

In 1775 Goethe moved to Weimar at the invitation of its young duke. While there Goethe was made a minister of state, interesting himself particularly in agriculture and mining. He also formed a close friendship with Schiller. This lasted until the latter's death in 1805. Each writer stimulated the other, and they collaborated on the satires *Die Xenien* and ballads published in the *Musen Almanach.* Alone, Goethe produced studies of optics and color, the novel *Wilhelm Meister's Apprenticeship,* the poem *Hermann and Dorothea,* and the novel *The Elective Affinities.*

Goethe remained active until the end of his life. His last works included his autobiography, *From My Life: Poetry and Truth;* the oriental poems in *West-Eastern Divan; Wilhelm Meister's Travels;* and a series of *Daily and Yearly Journals.* Above all his other works, however, towered the great dramatic poem *Faust,* published in two parts, in 1808 and 1832. The idea for *Faust* was conceived in Goethe's early 20's, but the work was not completed until he was 83 years old. From a simple story of the tragic love affair of Faust and Gretchen, the poem developed into a probing attempt to discover the value of knowledge, the nature of beauty, and the meaning of man's relation to his fellow men and to God. The work is considered one of the greatest in German literature.

GOGOL, NIKOLAI (1809-1852), Russian novelist and playwright, was born on his family's estate in the Ukrainian province of Poltava. After completing his education he went to St. Petersburg (now Leningrad) determined to become an actor, but failure in that field forced him to become a clerk in a government office. He turned to writing, and first achieved success with the two volumes of *Evenings on a Farm near Dikanka,* a reworking of Ukrainian folk tales. In 1836 his comedy *The Inspector General,* a hilarious satire of Russian officialdom, was the cause of a considerable controversy. Gogol, whose political opinions were very conservative, found himself praised by liberals for exposing the vices of the Russian government. In 1842 he published the first part of his masterpiece, the novel *Dead Souls,* another satire, which created as great a furor as had *The Inspector General.* Thoroughly shaken by the controversy, Gogol began work on the second part of *Dead Souls,* in which he hoped to justify rather than satirize Russian institutions. The task was impossible; Gogol suffered a nervous collapse and burned most of the manuscript, so that only fragments remain. He died a bitterly unhappy man.

Gogol's works are a combination of realism and fantasy, profound sympathy and riotous humor. Because of the emphasis he placed on discussing the problems and exposing the faults of the Russia of his day, Gogol is considered the first of the great Russian realists; but he usually tended toward hilarious exaggeration, so that his characters and situations are generally caricatures rather than mirrors of reality. Gogol wrote a great number of short stories, but he is best remembered for three works: *The Inspector General, Dead Souls,* and *The Overcoat.* The latter is a short novel that strangely combines realism and the supernatural.

GOITER. See THYROID.

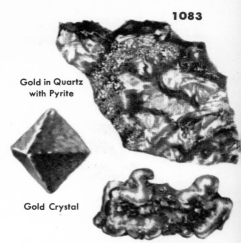

Gold in Quartz with Pyrite

Gold Crystal

Gold Nugget

Gold, pyrite, and quartz may occur together in gold-bearing mineral veins. Rarely, octahedral gold crystals are found in veins. Nuggets may be found in placer deposits.

GOLD, symbol Au, a heavy, soft metal used as the basis for money and in jewelry. It is found in quartz veins, usually combined with silver. It varies from pale yellow to golden yellow. Gold is usually so scattered among other minerals that it cannot be seen in gold ore. Some commercial veins produce only 0.1 ounce of gold for each ton of rock. When gold-bearing veins are eroded, some of the gold may be washed into streambeds and later be found as flakes or grains and, rarely, as nuggets. It was in such stream beds that gold was first discovered in the famous California gold strike of 1849.

The largest gold-producing areas are the Witwatersrand region of South Africa, the U.S.S.R., Canada, the United States, Ghana, Rhodesia, and Australia.

This diagram of a gold atom shows how the 79 electrons (−) are arranged around a nucleus of 79 protons (+) and 118 neutrons. Gold has atomic number 79; the atomic weight of the only stable isotope is 197. Chemically, gold is an unreactive element.

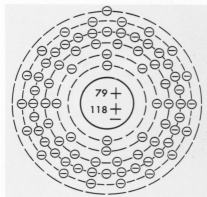

79 +
118 +

Goldenrod pollen at times causes hay fever.

GOLDENROD, a coarse, weedy herb usually bearing many small, yellow flowers. It is one of the commonest of American wild flowers, found in almost all parts of the country. The goldenrod is one of the plants that has frequently been proposed as the national flower, and it has been adopted as the state flower of Alabama, Kentucky, and Nebraska. It grows 1 to 7 feet tall and blooms in late summer and fall. Its leafy, often rough and hairy stem sends up spikelike clusters of yellow flowers. These are usually bright golden yellow, although some species have light greenish-yellow or cream-colored flowers. The branching flower clusters are made up of a multitude of little flower heads. Each flower head, in turn, is made up of tiny individual flowers, just as is the blossom of the daisy, to which the goldenrod is related.

GOLDFISH, a small fish of reddish-gold hue. Its beautiful color and its lively, graceful movements make it a popular fish for home aquariums and outdoor pools. Young goldfish are silvery; the golden-red hue

Goldfish with fanlike tails have been developed by selective breeding.

does not appear until they are six weeks or more old. The fish turns first dusky and then gold, all within a very few days. Sometimes it turns milky white instead of gold, and sometimes it remains silvery.

A native of China and a close relative of the carp, the goldfish was introduced into Europe in the 17th century and from there into the United States late in the 19th century. There are fancy goldfish varieties with double tails, fringed tails, or fan tails or with unusual color markings or shapes. Many of these have been developed in Japan. When the goldfish escapes from artificial ponds and establishes itself in rivers and lakes, as it has done in the eastern states, its offspring may revert to an olive bronze, which apparently was its original color. In the wild the goldfish grows to a length of 6 to 12 inches.

HOW TO KEEP GOLDFISH

Goldfish can easily be kept at home in a glass bowl or aquarium. Fish breathe oxygen that is dissolved in water, and care must be taken that the oxygen supply is sufficient. If too crowded in a bowl, the fish will exhaust the oxygen from the water and die. In order to keep them safely it is wise to allow at least 1 gallon of water for each goldfish 2 inches long. If water plants are grown in an aquarium, they will release oxygen to ensure the fishes' safety.

About 1 or 2 inches of sand or of small pebbles should be placed on the bottom of the aquarium to provide a hold for the plants. Goldfish, which are hardy, can live in near-freezing water. Their water should be disturbed as little as possible but should be changed when it becomes dirty. Goldfish should be fed specially prepared and packaged food. At intervals of two or three days they may be fed as much food as they will eat at one time. At intervals of two or three weeks the sediment that collects in the bottom of the aquarium should be siphoned off with a rubber hose. See AQUARIUM.

Minnesota Historical Society

Few of the tens of thousands of adventurers who streamed to the world's newly discovered goldfields during the 19th century ever got rich. This daguerreotype pokes fun at the young gold hunters eager to "strike paydirt."

GOLD RUSH, a hastening to newly discovered goldfields. One of the world's most spectacular gold rushes occurred in California in 1849 after quantities of the yellow metal had been found near Sutter's Fort. This was the first of a series of gold rushes that helped populate not only distant wildernesses on the North American continent but also sparsely populated territories in Australia and in South Africa. For example, just two years after the forty-niners rushed from all parts of the world to California, gold was discovered in Australia at Ballarat, Victoria. Another worldwide rush of people took place, as is indicated by the rise in Victoria's population from 77,000 in 1851 to 333,000 in 1855. South Africa's Transvaal was the scene of a similar event after gold was found there on the Witwatersrand in 1886. Within weeks the city of Johannesburg was laid out, and soon it had a population of approximately 100,000 inhabitants.

These three events were probably the world's most colorful gold rushes, but they were not the only colorful ones. As the supply of easily mined gold diminished in California, men in search of the yellow metal wandered eastward through the Sierra Nevada into the Rockies. In 1858 and 1859 they found it in Colorado and Nevada and farther north in British Columbia. However, the miners who rushed to Colorado to the chant of "Pike's Peak or Bust" discovered so little gold that few of them remained in the territory. Those who went to Nevada were more successful. They found some gold, but far more important was their discovery of the fabulous Comstock Lode, which contained some gold but mainly silver. Between 1860 and 1864, gold finds sent miners streaking to the Snake River valley in Idaho and also to Montana, Washington, and Canada. Eleven years later General George A. Custer reported gold in the Black Hills of South Dakota. The resulting invasion of miners angered the Sioux Indians there and contributed to a Sioux uprising and to the Battle of the Little Big Horn, during which Custer made his famous "last stand." The last of the major gold rushes occurred in 1896, when the prized metal was found in the Klondike River valley in the Yukon, Canada. See FORTY-NINERS; KLONDIKE GOLD RUSH.

Chicago Hist. Soc.

Oliver Goldsmith

GOLDSMITH, OLIVER (1728-1774), Irish writer, was born in either Pallas or Elphin, the son of a clergyman. He was educated at Trinity College, Dublin, and later studied medicine at Edinburgh, Scotland, and Leiden, in the Dutch Republic. In 1756 he reached London and there supported himself as a doctor and as a writer for the *Monthly Review*. In 1759 he published his first notable work, his *Enquiry into the Present State of Polite Learning in Europe*. During the next years he wrote for various publications and in 1762 republished his "Chi-

nese Letters" in his book *Citizen of the World*.

In 1761 Goldsmith met Samuel Johnson and, along with Johnson, Edmund Burke, Sir Joshua Reynolds, James Boswell, and others, was a founder of The Club. Goldsmith's novel *The Vicar of Wakefield* was sold by Johnson for £60 to meet Goldsmith's debts. It was published in 1766. During the next few years Goldsmith occupied himself with literary hackwork. He published a life of Voltaire, a memoir of Beau Nash, a life of Bolingbroke, and an English history.

In 1768 Goldsmith's comedy *The Good-Natur'd Man* was produced with moderate success. "The Deserted Village" appeared in 1770. Goldsmith's second play, *She Stoops to Conquer*, was produced in 1773 and was immensely successful. At Goldsmith's death The Club had a monument erected to him in Westminster Abbey.

GOLDSMITH, originally and primarily an artisan who made objects of gold and who decorated objects with gold. To understand the art of the goldsmith one must remember that gold has three remarkable qualities: It is soft, it is stable, and it combines in useful and beautiful ways with many other metals and compounds, such as glass. Gold-leaf can be hammered out to $\frac{5}{1,000,000}$ inch and still maintain its rich gold color.

In Egypt 5,500 years ago goldsmiths were casting, chasing, soldering, hammering, and plaiting gold. They made bracelets of cast-gold flowers and beads held together by bands of hair and of gold thread as fine as the hair itself. They made vases of gold, beaten over wooden cores, and then inlaid the gold with lapis lazuli.

During the Roman Empire goldsmiths embellished shields and corselets of officers and provided gold dishes for nobles. Some of these gold dishes have been found in the ruins of Pompeii.

During the Middle Ages goldsmiths worked in the service of the church. Besides making the initialed letters of the illuminated manuscripts, they made chalices for the churches and decorated vestments for the priests. As the Middle Ages waned and merchants and kings became powerful, goldsmiths turned to decorating tableware for them. Benvenuto Cellini, the great Italian bronze worker and goldsmith of the 16th century, made a gorgeous salt-cellar for King Francis I of France.

Reinecke Vam Dressche (about 1484)

Wenzel Jamnitzer (1508-1588)

John Belton (about 1525)

Ludwig Krug (1510-1559)

Charles Louis Auguste Spriman (about 1775)

Henry Clavel (about 1780)

Alexandre de Roussy (1758-1784)

Goldsmiths, like craftsmen working in other mediums, generally stamped their finished products with an identifying mark. Several well-known goldsmith marks are shown above.

About the same time gold in vast quantities began to flow into western Europe from Mexico and South America, where goldsmiths had worked for many centuries. Many of these treasures were melted down by European goldsmiths to be the gold of commerce, and so goldsmiths became bankers rather than artisans. In London the Company of Goldsmiths grew to be a rich monopoly that hired poor goldsmiths. It survives as a historic relic to this day.

GOLD STANDARD, the foundation of a monetary system in terms of gold as the recognized measure of value. The gold standard has four varieties: the gold-specie (coin) standard, the full gold-bullion standard, the qualified gold-bullion standard, and the gold-exchange standard. All these varieties have, in practice, a basic monetary unit with a legally fixed value in a specified fineness of gold. However, under a qualified gold-bullion standard this amount of gold cannot be ob-

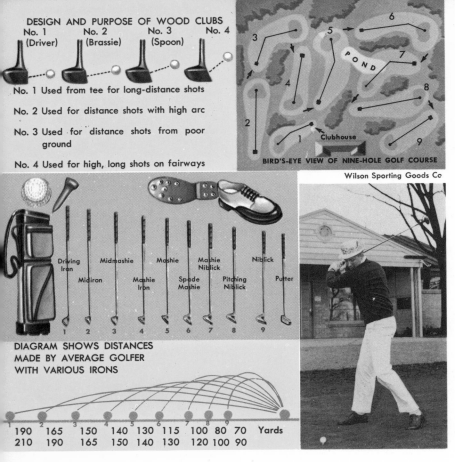

DESIGN AND PURPOSE OF WOOD CLUBS

No. 1	No. 2	No. 3	No. 4
(Driver)	(Brassie)	(Spoon)	

No. 1 Used from tee for long-distance shots

No. 2 Used for distance shots with high arc

No. 3 Used for distance shots from poor ground

No. 4 Used for high, long shots on fairways

BIRD'S-EYE VIEW OF NINE-HOLE GOLF COURSE

POND

Clubhouse

Wilson Sporting Goods Co

Driving Iron   Midmashie   Mashie   Mashie Niblick   Niblick

Midiron   Mashie Iron   Spade Mashie   Pitching Niblick   Putter

DIAGRAM SHOWS DISTANCES MADE BY AVERAGE GOLFER WITH VARIOUS IRONS

1	2	3	4	5	6	7	8	9	Yards
190	165	150	140	130	115	100	80	70	Yards
210	190	165	150	140	130	120	100	90	

tained for general circulation. For example, before the United States abandoned the gold-specie standard in 1933, the yellow metal circulated as coin, with every dollar having a value of 23.22 grains of fine gold. After the adoption of a qualified gold-bullion standard in 1934 no gold circulated, but the dollar continued to have a fixed value in gold: 13.71 grains.

Other aspects of the gold-specie standard are unlimited coinage of gold, free and unlimited melting of gold coin, free interconvertibility of gold money and all other types of money at parity, and free import and export of gold. The main difference between the gold-specie standard and the full gold-bullion standard is that, with the latter, gold coins are withdrawn from circulation and converted into gold bars. These become legal tender for all financial obligations, both private and public. Of course, with this standard only the very wealthy can acquire the valuable gold bars. Under a qualified gold-bullion standard, such as the United States has had since 1934, not even the rich can purchase gold, for the principal feature of this standard is that while a fixed quantity of gold supports every monetary unit, the gold can never be obtained for ownership by

the country's citizens. The fourth type of gold standard is the gold-exchange standard. Under this system the country's monetary unit is fixed in terms of some foreign currency, which is, in turn, fixed in terms of gold.

GOLF, a popular outdoor sport. It is not certain where or when golf was originated, but most authorities believe it began in Scotland in the 15th century. The Scots were the first to develop the game, and in 1744 the first golf club was founded in Edinburgh, Scotland. The English formed a golf club near London in 1766 and soon afterward introduced the game into India. The first golf club on the Continent was established in France in the 1850's.

Golf was established in the United States with the founding of the St. Andrew's Golf Club in 1888 in Yonkers, N.Y. By 1900 there were more than 1,100 courses in the United States, and this number has now increased to more than 5,000.

The game of golf is played with a ball and clubs. The first golf balls were small bags of thin leather stuffed with feathers. In 1848 the guttapercha golf ball was invented. It soon replaced the feather ball because it was easier to hit long distances and was less expensive. The

rubber-cored ball replaced the guttapercha ball during the 1900's.

A golf club (the implement with which the ball is struck) is a long, thin shaft with a small head for striking the ball. The total length of each club ranges between 3 and 4 feet; the head must be longer than it is wide. The shafts, originally made of wood, are now usually of steel. Types of club include 5 with wooden heads and 11 with metal heads; they vary also in the degree of slant of the surface (of the head) with which the ball is hit. The clubs are numbered, except for the shortest metal-headed one, known as the putter. A player is allowed a maximum of 14 clubs for any match.

The golf course is the large, grass-covered area within which the game is played; it is often purposely placed on hilly, undulating terrain to increase the difficulty of the game. Most major courses are comprised of 18 holes, but many have only 9 holes. Each hole is surrounded by a smooth, well-tended area of grass known as the green. Each fairway (the terrain between the tee and the green) ranges in length from 100 to 600 yards. An 18-hole golf course is usually 6,500 to 7,000 yards in length. In addition to such natural obstacles as hills, trees, streams, and lakes, artificial pits of sand (called sand traps or bunkers) are constructed to make the course even more difficult.

RULES

The rules of golf are based mainly on the principle that a player may not touch or move his ball (without penalty) except by hitting it with a club. The only exception is in placing the ball on the tee at the start of play for each hole (the tee is the peg used to support the ball the first time it is hit on each hole). If a player decides his ball is unplayable because it is in water, behind a tree or other obstruction, or under bushes, he may pick it up and drop it over his shoulder in a playable spot (but not nearer the hole); the player is then penalized two strokes.

A game is begun by striking the ball with a club toward the first hole. The ball is progressed, by the use of various clubs, until it is in the cup (hole) on the green. The players proceed in this manner from hole to hole around the course. Each player tries to use as few strokes as possible at each hole. If five strokes are taken to play the ball from the tee to the green and into the cup, a score of five is recorded for the player for the hole.

There are two methods of scoring a game—match play and stroke play. In match play the game is won by the player or team winning the greater number of holes. The player who wins the first hole will be "one up." If his opponent wins the second hole, the match will then be even. When each player, or team, takes the same number of strokes on a hole, the hole is said to be halved, and neither side scores. In stroke play the total number of strokes taken to complete the round or match is the player's score.

A match may be played as singles, as a foursome, or as a four-ball match. Singles consists of a match between two players; a foursome is between two pairs, each pair using one ball, which each of the pair strikes alternately. A four-ball match is contested between four players playing in pairs, each one playing his own ball; the better ball of the pair (that is, the one going farther) is used for each subsequent stroke.

GOMPERS, SAMUEL (1850-1924), American labor leader and president (1886 to 1924) of the American Federation of Labor. Gompers was in a large measure responsible for the direction and the success of the early U.S. labor movement.

Gompers was born in London, the son of a workingman. He attended a Jewish free school in his youth, but at the age of ten he went to work. Gompers was apprenticed to become a cigarmaker, like his father. The family moved to New York in 1863, settling on the East Side. Young Gompers joined the Cigarmakers' Union in 1864. At 17 years of age he married a working girl, Sophia Julian.

Gompers was possessed of great energy, and he took part in every activity, social and educational, open to an immigrant boy. At the cigar shop he engaged in debates and often read aloud the editorials of Charles A. Dana in the New York *Sun*. A fellow worker, Ferdinand Laurrell, gave Gompers insights into the labor movement and its literature in Europe. A strike in 1877 proved a disaster to the cigarmakers' unions. Gomper's friend Adolph Strasser became head of the weakened International Cigarmaker's Union, and in 1881 Gompers was made president of his old local, 144. Together, Gompers and Strasser increased the power of the international officers, built a sizable fund, and prepared to adopt a plan of unemployment and sickness bene-

Brown Brothers

Samuel Gompers was responsible for the policies that made the AFL a successful union.

fits. They made the Cigarmakers' Union a model. In 1881 the Committee on Constitution, headed by Gompers, created the Federation of Organized Trades and Labor Unions of the United States of America, which became the American Federation of Labor (AFL) in 1886. Until his death, Samuel Gompers was president of the AFL except in 1895, when the more radical members elected John McBride. Gompers steered the AFL successfully through the many crises of the early labor movement.

During President Wilson's administration Gompers was a member of the Advisory Commission to the Council of National Defense. He toured Europe in 1918 to stimulate loyalty toward the Allied war effort. Gompers died a few days after participating in a joint Mexican and American labor conference in 1924. His autobiography, *Seventy Years of Life and Labor*, is an introduction to the history of the labor movement in America.

GOOD FRIDAY, the Friday before Easter, observed by Christians as the anniversary of the Crucifixion of Jesus. See JESUS.

The custom of observing Good Friday probably originated among early Christians, who gradually transformed the Passover celebration into an observance of the Crucifixion. (See PASSOVER.) Good Friday has always been marked by fasting and usually by church services somewhat simpler than those of any other day of the year.

In the Roman Catholic Church Good Friday and the following day, Holy Saturday, are the only days of the year on which the entire Mass is not celebrated. The service centers around the Mass of the Presanctified, so called because the liturgy is omitted, and the Mass is celebrated with elements consecrated the day before, preceded and followed by prayer and reading of passages from from the Bible. The altar and the priest are draped in black. The organ remains silent throughout the service. In addition to this service, special devotional services often take place in the afternoon and evening.

Protestant observances of Good Friday vary. In many churches it is a special day for Communion. In others the principal emphasis of the service is on a sermon. Sometimes churches are draped in black and the organ is silenced, as in the Roman Catholic Church. A few denominations have no special observances of Good Friday.

The term "Good Friday" (probably originally "God's Friday") is used only in English-speaking countries. Elsewhere the day is known as Holy Friday, Sorrowful Friday, or Long Friday.

GOOD NEIGHBOR POLICY, the U.S. policy toward Latin America adopted during the presidency of Franklin D. Roosevelt. The Good Neighbor Policy, which actually had its beginnings during the Harding, Coolidge, and Hoover administrations, aimed at winning the friendship of the southern republics by treating them as equals of the United States rather than as naughty children. The administrations of Theodore Roosevelt, Taft, and Wilson had aroused the resentment of Latin American countries by intervening in their affairs whenever a local revolution or bankruptcy threatened U.S. interests.

President Franklin D. Roosevelt and Secretary of State Cordell Hull, convinced that Latin-American friendship would be a better guarantee of United States security than would United States control in Latin America, inaugurated the Good Neighbor Policy in 1933. The United States cemented good relations with the countries to the south by signing a mutual nonaggression and nonintervention pact with them at the Pan-American Conference at Montevideo, Uruguay, in 1933; by renouncing U.S. rights to intervene in the internal affairs of Cuba, Haiti, the Dominican Republic, and Panama; and by withdrawing U.S. troops from Haiti. When Mexico nationalized its oil lands in 1936, Secretary of State Cordell Hull limited U.S. action to negotiation for fair compensation for U.S. oil holdings, despite pressures in some quarters for intervention. The United States also sought to foster friendly relations within the Western Hemisphere by encouraging trade. The first reciprocal trade agreement was signed with Cuba in 1934, providing for mutual reduction of tariffs by the two countries.

GOODYEAR, CHARLES (1800-1860), an American inventor, was born in New Haven, Conn. He failed as a hardware merchant in 1830. In 1834 he turned his attention to india rubber, the manufactured products of which had hitherto proved failures because of their tendency to soften in the heat of summer. He perfected a process for vulcanizing rubber and discovered so many new uses for the product that it required 60 patents to secure

The Goodyear Tire & Rubber Co.

Perfection of the vulcanization process by Charles Goodyear marked the beginning of the modern rubber-manufacturing industry.

his inventions. He received medals at London (1851) and Paris (1855) and also received the Legion of Honor. He lived to see his material being applied to nearly 500 uses and giving employment to thousands of people in England, France, Germany, and the United States.

GOOSE. See DUCKS, GEESE, SWANS.

GOOSEFLESH is a roughness of the skin caused by contraction of smooth muscles attached to hair follicles. It is usually a reaction to

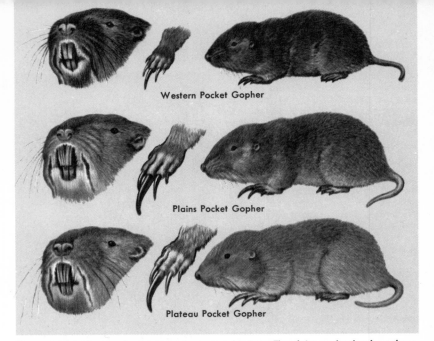

Western Pocket Gopher

Plains Pocket Gopher

Plateau Pocket Gopher

The western gopher has short claws and ungrooved incisors. The plains gopher has long claws and double-grooved incisors. The plateau gopher has long claws and single-grooved incisors.

The map shows the ranges of the western pocket gopher, the plains pocket gopher, and the plateau pocket gopher. Each of these types constitutes a genus. Pocket gophers dig burrows with their sharp claws. They gnaw roots and stems with their long, sharp incisors.

Western

Plains and relatives

Plateau

the coldness of the skin and may be produced by exposure of the skin to cold or to a disturbance that limits the circulation of blood. The muscles producing gooseflesh, or goosepimples, are involuntary and are controlled by the sympathetic nervous system. The stimuli that may bring about this condition may be an emotional reaction (such as fear), exposure to cold, or a disturbance of the circulation of blood to the skin.

GOPHER, a gnawing, burrowing underground rodent that belongs to the same family as squirrels, chipmunks, and prairie dogs. The North American pocket gopher is about as long as a small rat but is much thicker. In the skin of each cheek it has a big pouch, which opens not into the mouth but onto the surface beside the mouth. It ranges in color from almost white through all intermediate hues to coal black.

The pocket gopher is seldom seen because it lives underground and only rarely comes to the surface—then usually only to poke its nose out of its tunnel. It digs tunnels about a foot below the surface of the earth in order to reach and eat the roots of shrubs, trees, and grasses. It often destroys young fruit

trees by eating their roots. The tunnels that the animal makes are usually connected with each other and with a shaft that goes down 3 or 4 feet to a large living chamber lined with soft grasses. In this chamber the gopher stores roots, seeds, and nuts, which it collects in its pouch as food for winter. A tunnel system is occupied by only one animal; even a mated male and female do not occupy the same system. A female's chamber contains a nest lined with fur from her own body. In the nest she brings forth five to seven young during spring.

GOPHER SNAKE. See BULL SNAKE.

GORDON, CHARLES GEORGE (1833-1885), English soldier and colonial administrator, known as "Chinese" Gordon, was born in Woolwich. He served in the Crimean War, and on an expedition to China participated in the capture of Peking. In 1863 he was in command of the Chinese force that suppressed the Taiping Rebellion. In 1873 Gordon served in Egypt under the khedive. As governor of the equatorial provinces he established numerous posts, explored the region, and suppressed the slave trade. In 1877 he was named governor general of the Sudan. There he continued to suppress the slave trade and tried to make peace between Egypt and Abyssinia. He served for a time on Mauritius. After spending a year in Palestine studying biblical history, he was sent to the Sudan to quell a rebellion of the Moslem Mahdi. He was surrounded at Khartoum, a badly fortified town, and held out for almost a year. Two days before the arrival of a relief expedition Khartoum was finally taken, and Gordon was killed.

GORGAS, WILLIAM CRAWFORD

(1854-1920), surgeon general in the U.S. Army and internationally known expert on sanitation, was born near Mobile, Ala. Gorgas' education, interrupted by the Civil War, was completed at the University of the South, at Sewanee, Tenn., from which he was graduated in 1875. In 1879 he was graduated from Bellevue Hospital Medical College, New York, and the following year was appointed to the Medical Corps of the U.S. Army.

Early in his career he contracted yellow fever and built up an immunity to it. This enabled him to serve in disease-infested areas. In 1898 he was placed at the head of a yellow-fever camp at Siboney, Cuba. Shortly afterward he became chief sanitary officer of Havana. After Walter Reed and his associates identified the carrier mosquito of yellow fever, Gorgas managed to rid Havana of the disease within a matter of months.

From 1904 to 1913 Gorgas held the post of chief sanitary officer of the Panama Canal Commission. Work on the canal was virtually impossible because of the high incidence of yellow fever among the workers. The campaign against yellow fever was not nearly so successful as it had been in Cuba. Heavy criticism was leveled at Gorgas and his associates. However, with the support of President Theodore Roosevelt the task was completed. By controlling yellow fever

William Crawford Gorgas

in the canal area the major obstacle blocking the completion of the Panama Canal was removed.

In 1914 Gorgas was appointed surgeon general of the U.S. Army with the rank of brigadier general. He was later promoted to major general. In the closing years of his career Gorgas did important work in conjunction with the Transvaal Chamber of Mines and the International Health Board. Gorgas retired from the U.S. Army in 1918.

Courtesy Ryerson Library, Art Institute of Chicago

Benvenuto Cellini's sculpture "Perseus with the Head of Medusa" is one of the most famous artistic reproductions of this legend.

GORGONS,

in Greek and Roman mythology, were three sisters named Stheno, Euryale, and Medusa, daughters of the aged sea god Phorcys. They were frightful to behold, having snakes for hair, brass hands, bodies covered with hard scales, huge gold-colored wings, and teeth as long as the tusks of a wild boar. They could turn to stone all who looked at them. Two of them, Stheno and Euryale, were immortal, but Medusa could be killed. In the Greek legend Perseus cut off Medusa's head while she was asleep. Even after Medusa's death whoever looked upon her head was turned to stone. Perseus used the head to overcome several enemies. Then he gave it to Minerva, who placed it on her aegis.

The gorilla is the largest anthropoid ape. It is surpassed in intelligence by no other animals except the chimpanzee and man.

GORILLA, an anthropoid ape of the same primate family as the chimpanzee and the orangutan. The gorilla is a very strong, fierce-looking, ugly-tempered animal. In bodily structure it and the chimpanzee are more like man than any other higher ape. The gorilla, when standing, is about 5 feet tall. Its body is heavier and bulkier than a man's. Its hair is coarse and black or grizzly gray. The forehead is sloping, the eyes are sunk deep in the head, and the chin is short and receding. The chest is thick, the shoulders are wide, and the arms and legs are powerfully developed.

The gorilla lives in the dense, jungle-like forests in the region of the Congo River in western and central Africa. Though fitted for climbing, the gorilla spends most of its time on the ground. Grown males are seldom seen in trees, probably because of their great weight. The animals generally travel through the woods in troops consisting of a male and female with their young. They make beds of branches on the ground or in the trees, usually occupying them only a single night. Their food includes bananas, plantain, and juicy vegetables. They seem very much afraid of man and keep as far away from him as possible. As a rule they will not attack unless cornered or wounded, but then they are terribly ferocious.

It is supposed that the "wild men" that Hanno, a Carthaginian navigator, discovered on the west coast of Africa in the 5th century B.C. were gorillas. Three females were captured, but they bit and scratched so wildly they had to be killed. Their skins are said to have been preserved in the temple of Astarte in Carthage.

A scene from Maxim Gorky's play *Enemies*

GORKY, MAXIM (1868-1936), Russian writer, was born in Nizhni Novgorod, a city that has since been renamed Gorky. His real name was Alexei Peshkov; Gorky is a pseudonym meaning "bitter" or "miserable." He grew up in extreme poverty and received almost no formal education; rather he was forced to go to work at a very early age. His occupations ranged from ragpicker to stevedore and included a period as pantry boy on a Volga River steamship, at which time he was taught to read by an old cook. Much of Gorky's later writing was based on the experiences of his unhappy childhood.

In 1898 Gorky became famous overnight with the publication of a collection of his stories, and for almost 40 years thereafter he remained an important figure on the Russian literary scene. The first Russian to have risen from the lower classes to a position of literary eminence, he emphasized the suffering of the oppressed lower classes in his writing. His early works on this theme include some excellent short stories, most notably "Twenty-six Men and a Girl." When Gorky became associated with the revolutionary Bolshevik party, however, his plays and novels became instruments of propaganda. The most successful of these works was the play *The Lower Depths*, which was first produced at the Moscow Art Theater and later enjoyed a tremendous vogue in western Europe.

After the unsuccessful revolt of 1905 Gorky was forced to take refuge abroad, where he stayed until the Russian Revolution. During these years he wrote his best works, a number of autobiographical volumes of which *My Childhood* and *Recollections of Tolstoi* are outstanding. In 1917 he returned to Russia, and during the turbulent years that followed he did much to preserve the best of the old Russian culture and also helped many writers keep from starving. In 1921 Gorky left the Soviet Union, but he returned in 1928; eight years later he died under mysterious circumstances.

GOTHS were Teutonic tribesman of unknown origin who lived along the lower Danube in the 3d century A.D. They were dispersed in the 8th century.

The Goths were divided into the East Goths, or Ostrogoths, and the West Goths, or Visigoths. In 410 the Visigoths conquered Rome under their famous king Alaric. Under the successor of Alaric they went into Gaul and across the Pyrenees and founded an empire comprising the southern part of Gaul and the northern part of Spain. In the beginning of the 6th century they lost the northern part of their kingdom to the Franks, but they prospered in Spain and part of Gaul until they were routed by the Saracens in 711. Then their empire was broken up.

About 490 the Ostrogoths, under their king Theodoric, overthrew Odoacer, the first barbarian king of Rome. Theodoric thus became the sole ruler in Italy. After Theodoric's death the Byzantine emperor Justinian broke up the Ostrogothic Empire in Italy.

GOUNOD, CHARLES (1818-1893), a French composer, was born in Paris. He studied at the conservatory under Jacques Halèvy, Jean Le Sueur, and Ferdinando Paer. Awarded the first prize in 1839, he was able to complete his musical education in Rome, where he devoted himself to religious music. Returning to Paris, he wrote his *Solemn Mass*, which brought him into general notice. He served part of the novitiate for holy orders but discarded the idea of becoming a priest.

Sappho, produced in 1851, was his first opera. His comic opera, *The Physician in Spite of Himself*, a great success, was followed by *Faust* in 1859, which gained him world recognition. It was followed by such works as *Romeo and Juliet*, quantities of church music, and many lyrical songs.

Charles Gounod

Gourds

Gourds are of many shapes and colors. A gourd is a fruit that contains seeds. When a dry gourd is shaken, its seeds will rattle.

GOURD, the fruit of a vine closely related to the pumpkin, melon, and cucumber. The plant grows wild in Asia and Africa and is cultivated in most parts of the world. Gourds are of many sizes, shapes, and colors. Some are almost round; some bulge at the center and are narrowed at the ends; some bulge at the ends; some have necks; others are like long tubes. The varieties of form seem almost numberless. In color gourds range from white to green, orange, and brown, often marked or streaked with other colors or shades.

When dried, gourds are used for many different purposes. They serve as table ornaments or can be fashioned into bowls, dishes, water jugs, or rattles. In pioneer days they were used in these ways much more extensively than now. The Indians used them a great deal, and it is said that they often shaped gourds to their liking by tying bandages of cloth on the young fruits. Gourd vines are annuals, the seed being planted every spring. Sometimes the vines are allowed to run over the ground, and sometimes they are trained over porches and trellises.

GOVERNMENT. The word *government* comes from a Latin word meaning "to steer." This is a good definition, for a government is actually a body of men whose task is to steer society. The duties of government range from installing a city sewer to handling the defense and foreign policies of a nation. Differences of opinion often exist as to how much government should do for its citizens, especially in the economic realm. For example, supporters of conservative capitalism may differ with socialists, who would increase the power of government in the economic sphere. Only anarchists, and not all of them, think that man can do away with all government.

No one knows how governments originated. Ancient societies developed legends about a single wise lawgiver who founded their governments. Athenians thought that the laws of their city-state were framed by Solon. Spartans believed that their government was the work of Lycurgus. Following the Renaissance, new theories of the origin of government were devised. Jean Jacques Rousseau's social contract was among these. It argued that men voluntarily agreed to form governments. Whether Rousseau thought that men gathered in a clearing at some time in the distant past and formally agreed to the social contract is doubtful. Later historians disagreed with the explanations of both the ancients and Rousseau and tried to trace the growth of government from the primitive family. The head of the family might have become the head of a tribe. The tribe, which is similar to a government, might later have become a sort of monarchy.

Although there is much disagreement on the origin of government, there has been general agreement on the types, or forms, of government. These forms were described by Aristotle in his *Politics*. They are monarchy, aristocracy, and democracy. Monarchy is the government of one person. Aristocracy is the government of a small number of persons. Democracy is the government of many persons. All these

UPI

This is a meeting of the Governors' Conference, an organization founded in 1908 to foster interstate cooperation and to allow an interchange of views among governors.

forms of government are in the public interest. But monarchy, according to Aristotle, could turn into tyranny, or government in the interest of one person. Aristocracy could turn into oligarchy, or government in the interest of a minority. And democracy could turn into mob rule.

Aristotle's terms for these forms of government are still used, but his ideas have been largely abandoned. Aristotle also advanced the idea that government should concern itself with service to all citizens. This was a great advance over the primitive idea that government is only power over others.

In modern constitutional governments fundamental laws guarantee and protect individual rights and provide for assemblies of popular representatives to make laws. See ANARCHISM; ARISTOCRACY; DEMOCRACY; DICTATORSHIP; FEDERALISM; MONARCHY; PARLIAMENT; STATE AND LOCAL GOVERNMENT IN THE UNITED STATES; UNITED STATES GOVERNMENT.

GOVERNOR, in the United States, is the head of the state government. He is elected for either a two-year or a four-year term. Some states limit the number of terms he can serve.

The governor is responsible for seeing that all the parts of the state government are well run. However, he does not have as much control over the various departments of the state government as the president has over the federal government. The governor, unlike the president, usually does not appoint the heads of the various departments of government. They are usually elected. He usually cannot threaten to remove them if they do not do their work properly. However, the governor can investigate any department he suspects of being badly run.

The governor also influences legislation. In his messages to the legislature he recommends laws he thinks should be enacted and warns against those he thinks should not be. He also criticizes or approves previous actions of the legislature. The messages are widely published and help obtain public support for the governor's program. The legislatures also rarely pass laws over the governor's veto. Frequently the threat of a veto is enough to prevent passage of a bill.

The governor is responsible for the maintenance of law and order in the state. In time of emergency, riot, or rebellion he may call out the state police or the National Guard, request troops from the national government, or declare martial law.

The governor, as first citizen of the state, performs many ceremonial functions. He receives visitors, dedicates buildings, lays cornerstones, and attends university graduation ceremonies.

This is a scene from a town meeting held in Wenham, Mass., in 1945. The town meeting is a form of democratic local government characteristic of New England.

Wide World Photos

GOYA, FRANCISCO (1746-1828), famous Spanish painter, was born in Fuendetodos. He began his art studies in the academy at Saragossa and continued them at Rome. By the age of 30 he had settled in Madrid. His first important commission was a series of designs for royal tapestries.

In 1786 he was appointed court painter, and the likenesses of all the great figures of Spain, including four monarchs, appeared upon his canvases. Goya's main interest, however, was in the common people, of whom he had intimate knowledge.

In his etchings called "Caprices" he caricatured contemporary Spanish society and its vices. He revealed his true sympathy for the peasants in a set of etchings "Disasters of War." This recorded French atrocities committed in the invasion of Spain. Other etchings depicted incidents of bullfighting.

Goya spent his last years in France, where he produced a set of lithographs "Bulls of Bordeaux." The "Maja Nude" has been ranked as his most celebrated work. Many people believed that the model was his friend the Duchess of Alba, who later was banished from the Spanish court. Goya followed her into exile.

GRACCHI were two Roman brothers who were politicians. As leaders of the people's party, the *populares*, they introduced numerous reforms. They were killed by henchmen of the aristocratic party, the optimates, which opposed the Gracchi and which controlled the government through the Roman Senate.

Tiberius Gracchus (163?-133 B.C.), became tribune, or representative of the people in the Senate, in 133. The republic of Rome, then engaged in successful wars, was governed by this body, whose prestige lay in the successful conduct of military operations. While pursuing their imperialistic schemes, the senators and other members of the aristocracy acquired great estates at home and accumulated much private wealth. The free small farmers, who had once been the backbone of Rome's legions, were rapidly disappearing in Italy. In order to restore this class Tiberius Gracchus enforced again the old agrarian law, which limited the number of acres of land owned by one person. But this was an action against the interests of the Senate, and the optimates murdered him.

Gaius Gracchus (? -121 B.C.), younger brother of Tiberius Gracchus, became tribune in 123 B.C. He renewed the land law passed by his

Courtesy of The Metropolitan Museum of Art, The Jules S. Bache Collection, 1949

This is a famous oil painting, by Francisco Goya, entitled "Don Manuel Osorio."

brother. Gaius was a great speaker and was a better statesman than Tiberius. His other laws, particularly the grain law (which provided that the state should sell a fixed puantity of grain at half price to citizens of Rome), were designed to help the poorer classes. When Gaius insisted that the people of the provinces be given citizenship, and when he tried to reduce the power of the Senate in the provinces, he was killed by the optimates.

GRACKLE. See BLACKBIRDS, GRACKLES, COWBIRDS.

GRADUATION. In high schools, universities, and colleges the day of graduation is always a day of interesting ceremony. Graduation, or commencement, signifies that a person has completed successfully the studies necessary to obtain a diploma or a degree. And, after four years of application to notes and books, even the most blasé of students feels proud on commencement day.

Commencement in colleges is an affair for the whole family: grandparents, aunts, and uncles, as well as parents and brothers and sisters. The schedule differs slightly in various colleges, but Friday night usually brings with it the senior prom. On Saturday afternoon there may be a baseball or basketball game with a neighboring school or with a group of former graduates. On Saturday night, graduates from previous years sometimes put on a show,

Graduation is a time of customs and traditions. Here, as a final gesture, graduated cadets of the United States Military Academy throw their hats into the air.

UPI

which is often followed by a parade. Sunday brings the more serious aspect of commencement week. The graduates-to-be attend the baccalaureate service with their families and close friends. Commencement day itself arrives on Monday, and the graduates assemble for the formal conferment of the degrees.

The graduating seniors usually wear caps and gowns. This graduation apparel dates from the Middle Ages, when the square, flat cap was worn by the clergy or other persons of note, such as lawyers or judges. The cap is commonly called the mortarboard. The hood, usually worn now by persons with advanced degrees, was very useful to students in medieval Europe. It could be pulled over the head for warmth in the cold, drafty halls of the unheated monasteries.

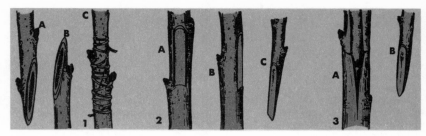

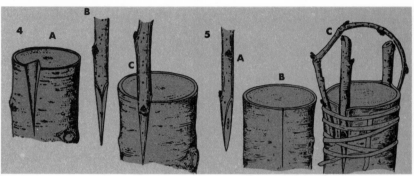

1. In splice grafting the scion, **1A**, and the stock, **1B**, are tied together. **2.** In side grafting the end of the scion, **2C**, is fastened to the trimmed portion of the stock, **2A**. **3.** In shield grafting the bark of the stock, **3A**, is cut, and the scion is inserted. **4.** In whip grafting a notch is cut in the stock, **4A**, and the scion, **4B**, is inserted, **4C**. **5.** In cleft grafting the stock, **5B**, is cut on opposite sides and a scion, **5A**, is fastened, **5C**, into each cut.

Courtesy of Wadena High School, Wadena, Minn.

Cap-and-gowned high school graduates burst out the door after graduation exercises.

GRAFTING is a method of plant propagation in which parts of two plants are joined so that they will grow together permanently to form one plant. A graft is composed of stock and scion. The scion is the piece of stem containing several buds; it is inserted into the stock. Budding is a type of grafting in which the scion is only a single bud. The scion and stock are joined so that their cambium layers are in intimate contact. The cambium is the thin layer of actively dividing cells that lies just under the bark. Union of stock and scion is accomplished by the growing together of the cambium tissue of the two plants.

Grafting is used to propagate plants that do not root readily from cuttings, do not come true from seed, or are seedless. Grafting may be used to change the habit of growth somewhat; trees can be dwarfed by grafting scions of a vigorous variety onto a less vigorous stock. Damaged trees can often be repaired by grafting. Roses are grafted to put the scion on a more vigorous or hardier stock or to speed up the growth of the scion.

Most fruit trees, grapes and roses, many evergreens, and certain ornamental trees and shrubs are commonly propagated by grafting. Soft-wooded plants such as tomato, chrysanthemum, and dahlia can be grafted but usually are propagated more easily by other means. Grafting is successful only if scion and stock belong to closely related species. For example, successful grafts can be made between different varieties of apples, between plum and peach, and between tomatoes and potatoes. However, successful grafts cannot be made between apple and orange trees, between tomatoes and chrysanthemums, or between potatoes and roses. Grafting is not a method of hybridizing or breeding to produce new varieties of plants. The scion retains the characteristics of the plant from which it was taken. The stock also retains its characteristics and provides the scion with a different root system.

GRAHAM, MARTHA (1900?-   ), American dancer, was born in Pittsburgh, Pa., and was reared in California. After being graduated from high school, she entered the dance studios at the Denishawn School in Los Angeles. Three years after her first lesson she starred in Ted Shawn's Aztec ballet *Xochitl*.

Following her break with the school in 1923, Martha Graham next appeared as a solo dancer in the *Greenwich Village Follies*, which she left to teach dancing at the Eastman School of Music in Rochester, N.Y. At her New York debut in 1926 she introduced many new steps she had learned from Ruth St. Denis and Shawn.

As the years passed, her dances became more revolutionary. In the 1930's she rooted her work in American Indian folklore. In the 1940's she turned to more theatrical forms. Among the works of this period are *Appalachian Spring, Letter to the World, Punch and the Judy,* and *Deaths and Entrances*.

In some of her dance productions Martha Graham wove the spoken word into the dance action. Many of her musical scores were written by leading composers, such as Paul Hindemith, Aaron Copland, and Lehman Engel.

Martha Graham's purpose was to give physical substance to things people felt, such as hate, passion, bigotry, and fear. With her own company, she created such outstanding productions as *Clytemnestra* and *Alcestis*, based on Greek myths.

GRAIN AND GRAIN PRODUCTS.

A grain is the seed or seedlike fruit of any of the cereal grasses. These plants were the first crops cultivated by man. The most important food grains today are wheat, rice, sorghum, corn (maize), rye, barley, and oats. Buckwheat, though not a member of the grass family, is similar in composition and use to the cereals and is usually classified with them. Grains are used chiefly in producing food for human beings, feeds for livestock, and various industrial products.

All of the important food grains, except rye and possibly oats, seem to be very ancient. No one knows when or where any of them was first domesticated. Stone Age hunters probably gathered wild grains before they learned to cultivate them in fields, but in all excavations of the earliest habitations grains are found as cultivated crops.

All of the major cereal grains developed in Asia with the exception of the larger ones—maize originated in the tropical or warm, temperate parts of the Americas, and sorghum originated in Africa. All the small grains except rice seem to have developed on the treeless steppe plateau of west-central Asia. Rice had its origins in the coastal swamps of southeastern Asia.

PRINCIPAL GRAINS

The cereal grains adapt to a wide variety of soils and climates, yield well with minimum labor of cultivation, and store easily and keep well for long periods.

Wheat, the most important of the food grains, is grown on more of the world's acreage than any other crop. It adapts to a wide range of soils and climates and can be grown extensively throughout the world, except in the tropics. The great grasslands and steppe areas of the world are especially suited for wheat production because of the moderate climates and the clear and level land that permits use of large machines in seeding and harvesting. Such conditions are found in the central plain of North America, the central steppe of Europe and Asia, and the smaller plateaus of Argentina, Australia, and northern India. See WHEAT.

Rice is the chief food of probably one-third of the human race. It gives high acre yields on fertile land with abundant water and warm climate. Except in countries, such as the United States and Australia, where rice is grown by mechanized methods, cheap labor is required for the transplanting by hand of the rice plants from underwater seed beds to the fields. Favorable growing conditions and an abundant supply of cheap labor make rice the staple food in the Orient. See RICE.

Sorghum is the principal food grain in Africa and a staple food, with rice, in Asia. Like corn, but unlike the small grains, sorghum grows on large stalks and, in some areas, is planted in widely spaced rows and cultivated. Sorghum, like corn and rice, is suited to the tropics, but it can withstand more heat and drought than any other common cereal grain. It competes with corn for industrial use because of similarities in composition and because it contains more protein and is cheaper on the open market than corn. See SORGHUM.

Corn, or maize, was not known to the Old World until the discovery of the Americas. It seems to have been very old in origin; it had spread throughout both Americas by the time the Europeans arrived. Today it is the most important food grain in Latin America. See CORN.

Rye, the most recently developed of the important food grains, will grow in colder and more exposed places and on poorer soil than will wheat. However, rye flour is generally considered markedly inferior to wheat flour for baking. Rye is second in importance to wheat in continental Europe but is little used in other lands. See RYE.

Barley remains an important human food only in certain limited areas, notably the Mediterranean fringe of northern Africa and parts of northern Europe. It is the only grain that equals wheat in climatic adaptability. See BARLEY.

Oats are especially suited to cool, moist climates. Once an important food grain in central and northern Europe, they have been important as human food in recent times only in Scotland and the Scandinavian countries. See OATS.

Buckwheat is grown largely in Europe and North America. It is particularly adapted to nonproductive lands. In good soils it is less productive than other grains. See BUCKWHEAT.

A grain elevator and the world's ten most important grains, which include wheat, rice, corn, oats, rye, and barley, are illustrated below.

Courtesy of Massey-Ferguson, Inc.

Grains have the advantage over other foods of lending themselves easily to transportation and storage in large quantities. Under modern conditions storage facilities have grown enormously and prevent shortages.

Tony Chapelle—Monkmeyer
In India much wheat is still harvested by means of sickles.

In the United States corn is picked and husked by machine.
Courtesy of Massey-Ferguson, Inc.

Ernst A. Heiniger
In Japan much rice is cultivated by hand in flooded paddies on hillsides.

On Australia's plains vast wheatfields are sown and reaped by machine.
Courtesy of Australian News and Information Bureau

GRAIN PRODUCTS

Grains furnish the principal food for human beings and the principal feeds for some of the animals upon which human beings depend. Grains are generally the cheapest sources of food energy. They are also the sources of many important industrial products.

Ancient men probably first ate wild grains whole, later learning to cook them to make them more palatable. Even today several grains are eaten whole or nearly whole. Brown rice and parched whole kernels of corn are examples of whole grains, while white rice, hominy, pot barley, and pearl barley are examples of foods produced by polishing away outer portions of the kernels. Rolled oats and oatmeal, produced by flattening or grinding the kernels, are essentially whole-grain foods.

Every one of the cereal grains may be ground into flour for use in baking. (See BAKERY PRODUCTS.) Some flour is used in making breakfast foods, or cereals. (See CEREAL.) Semolina and farina, the purified middlings of hard wheat, are the ingredients of spaghetti and macaroni. (See MACARONI PRODUCTS.) Most buckwheat flour is used as pancake flour.

The cereal grains are the principal raw materials in the production of beer, ale, and distilled alcoholic beverages. The starch in the grains must be converted to sugar during the brewing process. This is accomplished by the action of an enzyme in malt, another grain product. Malt is produced by germinating a cereal grain, usually barley, under proper conditions. See BREWING.

A large portion of most of the grain crops is used to feed livestock. For example, in the United States, where about 60 percent of the world's corn crop is grown, only 6 to 8 percent is processed for food and industrial uses. About two-thirds of the buckwheat is used on the farms. Barley and oats are used chiefly as livestock feed.

Principal industrial uses of wheat are for the production of industrial alcohol, starch, gluten, pastes, and core binder. Corn is a more important source of starch, and it also produces corn oil. Sorghum is now being used to produce products similar to those obtained from corn. Oat hulls are an important byproduct of the milling of oats because they are a source of furfural, a chemical used in oil refining, the purification of wood rosin, and the production of synthetic resins, such as bakelite. Buckwheat leaves and flowers are one of the important sources of rutin, a compound used medically in controlling hemorrhage.

GRAIN ELEVATOR, a building designed for the reception, storage, and transshipment of wheat, corn, and other cereals. It is a tall, massive structure situated alongside the waterfront or railroad right-of-way. Usually built of steel-reinforced concrete for protection against fires and vermin, elevators consist essentially of numerous storage bins, towers containing the elevating and conveying equipment, and the unloading and loading machinery. Loading spouts and unloading conveyor legs at intervals along the sides of the structure make possible the handling of several cargoes simultaneously. Screw or bucket conveyor mechanisms, lowered into loaded railroad cars and boats, carry the grain to the top of the structure; the grain then pours into hoppers for weighing and is finally conveyed to the storage bins to await transshipment. Loading from the storage bins is accomplished in much the same manner as unloading, many of the larger elevators having wide conveyor belts to carry the grain over considerable distances to vessels alongside the pier. By this means more than 100,000 bushels an hour may be handled in the larger plants. Many elevators with capacities in excess of 1,500,000 bushels of grain have been erected to meet the needs of leading grain-handling centers.

GRAMMAR

GRAMMAR. All languages have certain elements in common. All languages have sounds, letters, syllables, words, and sentences. These elements are the materials that make up the study of grammar. By analyzing these basic elements of a language, grammarians, or specialists in grammar, set up a system of rules for the proper use of the language. These rules are the "do's" and "don'ts" about pronunciation, spelling, word selection, and the proper arrangement of words in sentences.

After a person has learned to read, he is usually taught elementary rules about pronunciation and spelling. These include rules about the number of syllables in a word, the length of vowel sounds, and the position of the accent, as well as the spelling rules for doubling the consonants.

Next the student may be introduced to what are now generally considered the eight basic parts of speech in English. Nouns and verbs are studied first, since they are the fundamental parts of a sentence. The other parts of speech—pronouns, adjectives, adverbs, prepositions, conjunctions, and interjections—are all studied in turn. See ADJECTIVE; ADVERB; CONJUNCTION; INTERJECTION; NOUN; PREPOSITION; PRONOUN; VERB.

Syntax, or the arrangement of words in a sentence, is especially important in English grammar because the meaning of a word in English is often determined by its position in a sentence. Thus, in the two sentences "Love is a simple thing" and "I love you" we know that *love* is a noun in the first sentence and a verb in the second sentence, even though the word is the same in both instances. It is the syntax of the sentences that tells us this, since in English the placement of words in a particular order is a way of indicating their functions and therefore their meanings. We decide on the meaning of a word by examining its place in the sentence as a whole. The normal word order of an English sentence is subject first, verb next, and object last. See SYNTAX.

GRANADA. Both the province of Granada and the city of Granada are situated in a region of southern Spain called Andalusia. The province of Granada has the highest peak in Spain, the 11,411-foot-high Mulhacèn in the Sierra Nevada. The province, with the exception of small coastal plains opening to the

Spanish Natl. Tourist Dept.

The Palacio de Generalife at Granada was the summer residence of the Moorish kings.

Mediterranean, is mountainous. Sugar production and olive-oil processing are the chief industries of the province.

Until 1492 the city of Granada was the capital of the Moorish kingdom of the same name. It is situated at the foot of the Sierra Nevada, surrounded by beautiful scenery. The city, with a population of about 170,000, is divided by the Darro River. On the right bank of the Darro River is the historic hill Albaicín. Here are the Sacramonte caves, where gypsies dance before big audiences—one of the great spectacles in Spain. The Albaicín is full of narrow, winding streets, little squares, and old Moorish houses, with gardens adorned by roses, cypresses, and fountains. The modern town is below the Albaicín.

The left bank is dominated by the world-famous Alhambra, a Moorish palace and fortress built on top of a hill. (See ALHAMBRA.) Granada is also the site of a Renaissance cathedral from the 16th century—one of the most beautiful in all Spain. Adjoining the cathedral is a Gothic chapel, within which are the marble tombs of King Ferdinand and Queen Isabella.

Granada has changed little since medieval times. Its main exports are still based upon the old trades of fine ironwork, copperwork, and leatherwork and the weaving of tapestries. The valley below the city is fertile, and cereals, wine grapes, and tropical fruits are grown there.

GRAND CANYON NATIONAL PARK includes part of the great gorge of the Colorado River in northwestern Arizona. The canyon walls are fantastically eroded and highly colored. The canyon is about 217 miles long, is 4 to 18 miles wide, and has an average depth of about 1 mile. Approximately 105 miles of the canyon are included in the park, which covers more than 1,000 square miles. It was established in 1919.

About 500 ruins of ancient Indian pueblos have been discovered in the canyon and on its rim. Today the Indians in the Grand Canyon region belong to three tribes—Navaho, Hopi, and Havasupai. The Havasupai live in the western part of the national park. The Navaho and Hopi live on reservations east of the park.

A striking panorama of the Grand Canyon and the surrounding country is seen from a point near Cape Royal on the North Rim. A highway ends at Cape Royal and winds through a magnificent forest and along the rim.

Union Pacific Railroad Colorphoto

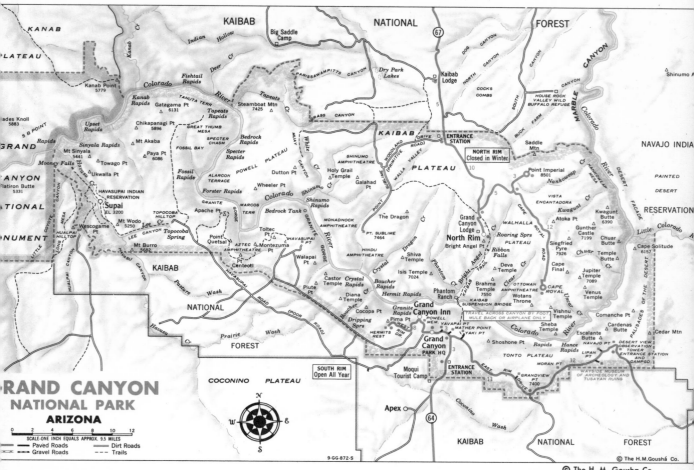

© The H. M. Gousha Co.

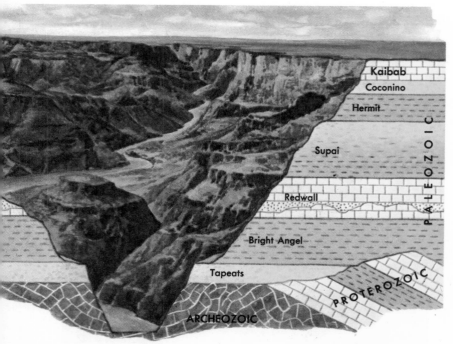

This is a cross section of the Grand Canyon, which has been formed by the work of running water as the region has been slowly elevated. The exposed rock strata represent a vast geologic time. Some of the oldest rocks (from the Archeozoic era) known to geologists are in the lower part of the canyon. Tilted rock layers of the second geologic era (Proterozoic) are found in the lower section. The rock strata on the upper canyon walls are of the Paleozoic era.

GRAND NATIONAL STEEPLECHASE

is the name of a famous horserace. It takes place every spring over a $4\frac{1}{2}$-mile course at Aintree, England. In common with all steeplechases, the Grand National is run over a course containing many obstacles. These include approximately 30 jumps over bushes, fences, rails, and water. Because of the difficulty of the course, horses are often injured in the race. The Grand National is the best known steeplechase and one of the most popular sporting events in England. It is attended by crowds of more than 250,000 persons.

GRAND TETON NATIONAL PARK

includes the most impressive part of the Teton Range in northwestern Wyoming. This spectacular glaciated region was once a noted landmark of Indians and mountain men. The park, covering approximately 485 square miles, was established in 1929.

GRANGE, RED

(1903-   ), the nickname of Harold Edward Grange, an American football player. He grew up in Wheaton, Ill. In high school he won 16 letters in football, baseball, basketball, and track.

He entered the University of Illinois in 1922 and made a spectacular football record. In three years he played 20 games, scored 31 touchdowns, and gained over 2 miles of ground. His greatest year was 1924. In the first 12 minutes of a game against Michigan Grange handled the ball five times—and made four touchdowns.

After leaving Illinois in 1925, the "Galloping Ghost" became a football star of the Chicago Bears. In 1931 he was named all-professional halfback. He was praised for his punting, passing, blocking, and especially for his broken-field running.

Grange retired from professional football in 1935 to devote his life to broadcasting the game. In 1950 he was elected a trustee of the University of Illinois.

GRANGER MOVEMENT

was a political movement among U.S. farmers. It opposed the owners of grain elevators and railroads, who charged the farmers exorbitant rates for storage and transportation of their produce. The movement began with the founding in 1867 at Washington, D.C., of the Patrons of Husbandry, an organization for the teaching of better methods of farming. The name Granger Movement came from the member clubs of this organization, which were called granges. The movement grew, particularly in the Middle West, where in addition to opposing high freight and storage rates, the granges organized cooperative grain elevators, creameries, and general stores. Political action by the grangers and other farmers caused various midwestern states to pass in the 1870's laws regulating the railroads. The Granger Movement lost its power at the end of the 1870's, but the National Grange of the Patrons of Husbandry remained one of the largest farmers' organizations in the United States.

GRAND TETON
NATIONAL PARK
WYOMING

SCALE - ONE INCH EQUALS APPROX. 10 MILES

Paved Roads — Dirt Roads
Gravel Roads --- Trails

© The H. M. Gousha Co.

GRANITE

GRANITE is a granular intrusive igneous rock composed mainly of feldspar and quartz. It is very common and is present on all the continents in large quantities.

Granite is a light-colored rock, usually white, gray, pink, or light red. Granite often has a speckled appearance. Some of the minerals in the rock are dark, and some are light. The individual mineral crystals in the rock are large enough to be seen without a magnifying glass.

The size of all the particles is about the same. Unweathered granite is a hard, firm rock. A newly broken piece has a jagged surface.

Most of the feldspar in a granite is potassium feldspar. Usually some sodium-calcium feldspar, plagioclase, is also present. Mica, either biotite or muscovite, or both, is found in many granites. Some granites contain grains of hornblende,

Potassium feldspar makes granite red.

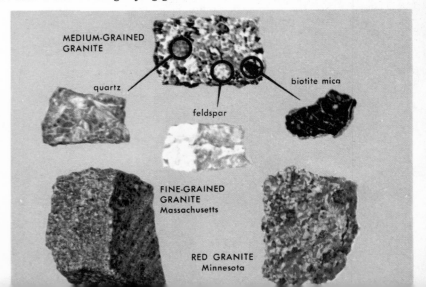

MEDIUM-GRAINED GRANITE

quartz

feldspar

biotite mica

FINE-GRAINED GRANITE
Massachusetts

RED GRANITE
Minnesota

a dark, prism-shaped mineral. Other minerals may be present in small quantities.

Large masses of granite are found at the cores of many mountain ranges. Granites are also found where erosion has exposed rocks that were once far beneath the earth's surface.

Granite is used as a building stone. It is strong and durable. Granite can be given a high polish and is used as an ornamental stone in the interiors of buildings and in monuments.

Ulysses S. Grant

GRANT, ULYSSES SIMPSON (1822-1885), American general and 18th president of the United States, was born in Point Pleasant, Ohio, Apr. 27, 1822. He was graduated from West Point in 1843, entered the Regular Army, and served with distinction in the Mexican War. In 1854 he resigned from the Army and, after engaging unsuccessfully in a number of occupations, became a clerk in his brothers' leather store at Galena, Ill. After the outbreak of the Civil War Grant was made colonel and then brigadier general of volunteers and was put in command at Cairo, Ill.

In 1862 he invaded Kentucky and, by a series of rapid movements aided by naval forces, surrounded and then captured Fort Henry and Fort Donelson. The loss of these strongholds forced the Confederates to abandon western Kentucky. In his next battle, at Shiloh, in Tennessee, Grant displayed poor generalship. He took no precautions against an attack, was surprised by Albert S. Johnston's army, and was saved from defeat only by the arrival of reinforcements. In March, 1863, after a brilliant campaign, he

surrounded Vicksburg, Miss., and in July the city was surrendered. With the capture of Port Hudson, La., ten days later, the entire Mississippi River fell under Union control, and the South was cut in two. Later in the year, in the Chattanooga campaign, Grant defeated Braxton Bragg and drove the Confederates out of eastern Tennessee.

In March, 1864, President Lincoln made Grant a lieutenant general and commander of all Union armies. In this capacity he devised the strategy that resulted in Confederate defeat and himself directed the Army of the Potomac. Although he failed to outmaneuver or defeat Robert E. Lee in the Wilderness, at Spotsylvania, Va., and at Cold Harbor, Va., his overwhelming strength enabled him to wear down the enemy. For several months Grant besieged Lee at Petersburg, Va., and in April, 1865, Philip Sheridan's victory at Five Forks, Va., forced Lee to evacuate the city. A few days later Lee surrendered his army on the generous terms allowed by Grant. In 1866 Grant was given the rank of full general, the first U.S. Army officer to be given this rank since George Washington.

From 1869 to 1877 Grant served two terms as president of the United States. He pursued a sound monetary policy and supported the foreign policy of his able secretary of state, Hamilton Fish. He was a poor administrator, however, and his reputation was tarnished by the actions of disreputable politicians and financiers with whom he associated.

A few years after his retirement from the presidency he went into business. The failure of his brokerage firm threw him into bankruptcy, and to earn some money he wrote his *Personal Memoirs*, which have become a historical and military classic. A few days after finishing the work he died of throat cancer. His tomb is a granite mausoleum on Riverside Drive in New York.

Courtesy of Ford Motor Company

Hicks grapes are improved Concord grapes.

GRAPE, an edible berry that usually grows on a vine but sometimes on a shrub or tree. Grapes are grown for table use and for making raisins, unfermented juice, jellies, and wines. They are raised chiefly in France, Italy, Spain, and other Mediterranean countries. In the United States they are grown commercially in 19 states, California, New York, Michigan, Washington, Pennsylvania, and Ohio being the leading growers. Other states have small areas that specialize in grape culture, and many home gardens have a few grapevines.

There are many kinds of grapes: blue, red, white, or black; large or small; sweet or sour; seedy or seedless. Some of the grapes grown in America have been developed from various native wild grapes. Others are foreign grapes, many of them grafted onto American roots. The well-known blue Concord grape originated from a chance seedling grown by a man in Concord, Mass. The seed was planted in 1843 and bore fruit in 1849. The wild grape is a woody vine that climbs by means of tendrils. In the woods it is found growing up tall trees or running over fences. Its fruits are usually smaller than those of the cultivated varieties and are quite tart.

The effect of proper fertilization on sweet green grapes is illustrated here (right).

Courtesy of Ford Motor Company

GRAPEFRUIT, also known as pomelo, a large cultivated citrus fruit of the same family as the orange and the lemon. Most of the world's grapefruit is grown in Florida, Texas, California, Arizona, and the West Indies. Florida, the first state to raise the fruit, began to grow it on a commercial scale about 1880 and has since been its largest producer. The big yellow fruit usually grows in bunches of 3 to 15 on a small, handsome tree. The tree has large oval leaves and big white blossoms.

Grapefruit is thought to be a native of Asia, but not much is known about its early history. There is a story that the first grapefruits in the Western Hemisphere grew from seeds brought from the Orient to the West Indies prior to 1696 by the commander of an East Indian ship. However, no tree just like the American grapefruit has been found in the Orient. It probably originated as a chance sport of the coarser shaddock, a pear-shaped fruit that grows in India, China, and the East Indies. The grapefruit tree was brought to Florida early in the last century merely as an ornamental tree and was slow in being used as a fruit crop. Since the time when its culture began in the United States, many new varieties have been developed. Their skins are thinner, and their pulp is sweeter and finer-grained; some varieties are nearly seedless.

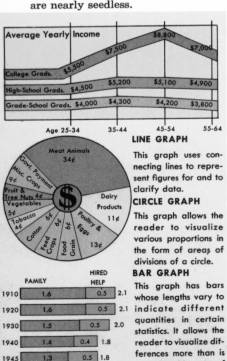

Average Yearly Income

	Age 25-34	35-44	45-54	55-64
College Grads.	$5,500	$7,500	$8,800	$7,000
High-School Grads.	$4,500	$5,200	$5,100	$4,900
Grade-School Grads.	$4,000	$4,300	$4,200	$3,800

Circle graph: $ — Meat Animals 34¢, Govt. Payment 9¢, Misc. Crops 4¢, Fruit & Tree Nuts 4¢, Vegetables 5¢, Tobacco 4¢, Cotton 6¢, Feed Crops 6¢, Food Grain 13¢, Poultry & Eggs 6¢, Dairy Products 11¢

	FAMILY	HIRED HELP	
1910	1.6	0.5	2.1
1920	1.6	0.5	2.1
1930	1.5	0.5	2.0
1940	1.4	0.4	1.8
1945	1.3	0.5	1.8
1950	1.3	0.4	1.7
1954	1.4	0.4	1.8

LINE GRAPH
This graph uses connecting lines to represent figures for and to clarify data.

CIRCLE GRAPH
This graph allows the reader to visualize various proportions in the form of areas of divisions of a circle.

BAR GRAPH
This graph has bars whose lengths vary to indicate different quantities in certain statistics. It allows the reader to visualize differences more than is possible with a set of figures that require study to grasp.

GRAPH, a picture of the differences between numbers. If we read that one building is 200 feet tall and another is 1,000 feet tall, we are not nearly so impressed by the difference in their sizes as we are if we see a picture showing that one building is five times as tall as the other building.

We need not draw the actual shape of two buildings if we only want to compare their heights. Instead we could draw two lines, one five times longer than the other, using a scale of perhaps 1 inch for every 100 feet of height. To make this picture into a finished graph, we would need to mark off the 1-inch intervals along the side of the picture and label them 100 feet, 200 feet, and so on, and then label the lines with the names of the buildings. The graph could easily be enlarged to compare the heights of other buildings simply by adding more lines.

Lines used this way in a graph are usually widened into bars, and the graph is called a bar graph. If, instead, the tops of the lines are connected by straight lines, the graph is called a broken-line graph. To compare a whole with its parts, a circular graph is helpful. The segments of the circle show the size of each part, and all the segments together make up the whole circle.

One of the most interesting kinds of a graph is the line graph. It is similar to a broken-line graph except that it is a smooth curve measuring a continuous number of points instead of the separated points of a broken-line graph. The changing length of a pole's shadow as the sun moves across the sky could be shown in a line graph. The line graph shows how one thing changes as another changes. Algebraic equations in two unknowns express the same idea, and graphs are frequently used to study them. See EQUATION.

GRAPHITE is one of the softest of all minerals. It is a carbon mineral, black or steel gray in color, with a greasy feel. It occurs in igneous and metamorphic rocks, such as schists and marbles. It is used as the "lead" in lead pencils and as a dry lubricant. It is also used in the manufacture of crucibles and of brushes for electric motors. A recent use has been as a material to slow down neutrons in atomic piles. Graphite is mined commercially in Korea, Ceylon, Mexico, and Madagascar and in the United States on a small scale in Alabama, Texas, Rhode Island, and New York.

GRASS, a large family of angiosperms whose members characteristically have jointed stems, sheathing leaves, flower spikelets, and a seedlike grain for a fruit. This family includes Kentucky bluegrass, rye grass, timothy, bent grass, wheat, oats, corn, rice, rye, barley, sugarcane, bamboo, and sorghum. The grass family comprises 450-525 known genera and more than 4,500 known species. The distribution of grasses is worldwide. The grass family is of great economic importance to man because it contains his food grains, his grasses for pasture, lawn, and hay, and a principal source of sugar.

Although they are of diverse form, size, and habitat, most grasses have certain common characteristics. The stems of most of them are round and hollow, but the round stems of corn and sugarcane are solid. The grass leaf consists of a sheath, which surrounds the stem upward from the node, and the blade, which is the flat and usually linear part free from the stem. Like all angiosperms, grasses produce flowers, but the flowers of most of them are small and green. However, the flowers of corn and a few others are larger. Some grasses have white, red, or purple flowers. The roots of the grasses are fibrous and clustered and do not grow far beneath the surface of the soil. Some prairie grasses, though, have roots that penetrate many feet into the soil. Kentucky bluegrass and some other grasses have underground stems that are jointed. New shoots

Below is an example of graphite found in New York. The softness of graphite makes it a good lubricating and writing material.

MASSIVE GRAPHITE New York

pencils

lubricant   motor brushes

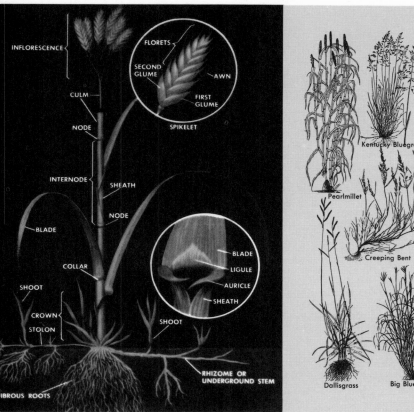

INFLORESCENCE

FLORETS

SECOND GLUME

AWN

FIRST GLUME

SPIKELET

CULM

NODE

INTERNODE

SHEATH

NODE

BLADE

BLADE

LIGULE

AURICLE

SHEATH

COLLAR

SHOOT

SHOOT

CROWN

STOLON

RHIZOME OR UNDERGROUND STEM

FIBROUS ROOTS

Pearlmillet

Kentucky Bluegrass

Creeping Bent

Dallisgrass

Big Bluestem

somites, which are termed respectively the prothorax, mesothorax, and metathorax. The prothorax bears the first pair of short, thin, jointed legs. The mesothorax bears another pair of short, thin legs and the anterior pair of wings. The metathorax bears the jointed leaping legs and the posterior wings. Behind the thorax is the worm-shaped abdomen, which consists of ten segments.

From the head arises a pair of jointed antennae that function as receptors for the sensations of touch and smell. At the base of each antenna are three small simple eyes. Behind the simple eyes is a pair of larger compound eyes. Each compound eye consists of hundreds of eyes, each with a six-sided lens. Each tiny eye sees only a part of the image, and the whole compound eye probably can see in several directions at once. The ears are large, membrane-covered cavities located on the abdominal segment next to the thorax.

The grasshopper's mouth is adapted for biting off and chewing leaves and blades of grass. The grasshopper breathes through tiny pores, called spiracles, located on the sides of the abdomen. Tiny tracheae, or air tubes, carry air from the spiracles to various parts of the body. The tracheae constitute the principal respiratory organ. The circulatory system consists of a dorsal tubular muscular heart that pumps blood through vessels to spaces in the body. This is an open circulatory system that contrasts with the closed system of heart, arteries, capillaries, and veins of vertebrates.

Besides enabling it to fly, the grasshopper's wings act as gliders

The large drawing is a diagram of a typical grass plant. The grains grow in the spikelets at the top of the plant. The sheath of each leaf surrounds the stem. New shoots grow upward from the underground stems.

grow upward from these joints, spread rapidly, and in a few years form extensive, dense sod. Bent grasses have stems that grow on the surface, and the roots penetrate the soil. The roots rise at the nodes on the creeping stem. By this means bent grass spreads and forms sod.

The fruits of grasses are called grains. Wheat, oats, corn, rice, rye, and barley produce grains that are staple foodstuffs of man. The grains of all grasses are small and dry and enclose a single seed. The grain is a seed and the adherent pericarp. The seed consists of an embryo, which is the undeveloped plant, surrounded by a quantity of stored food and the seed coat. See BLUEGRASS.

GRASSHOPPER, an insect that belongs to the order Orthoptera. The word *Orthoptera* (Greek, straight winged) refers to the fact that the wings of the grasshoppers and other insects of this order are folded straight back against the body when not being used for flight. The grasshopper is so named because hopping is one of its means of locomotion, and grass is one of its habitats. The

grasshopper can hop a distance much greater than its own length by means of its hindmost pair of legs, which are long, strong, and constructed especially for leaping.

The grasshopper has an external skeleton that covers most of its body and appendages. This skeleton is composed of a light, brittle, tough substance called chitin. The body of the grasshopper, like that of all insects, consists of a series of segments called somites. The head consists of six small fused somites. The thorax consists of three larger

The external anatomy and a diagram of the internal organs of a grasshopper are shown below.

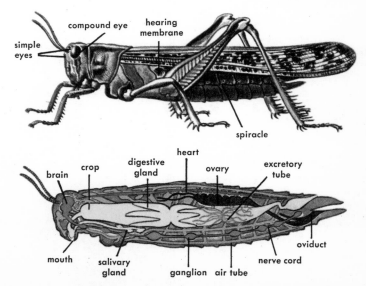

compound eye

hearing membrane

simple eyes

spiracle

heart

brain

crop

digestive gland

ovary

excretory tube

mouth

salivary gland

ganglion

air tube

nerve cord

oviduct

when the insect leaps. The male grasshopper makes a shrill chirp with its wings, either by rubbing the wing covers together or by rubbing a leg against a wing.

The female lays her eggs in earth or rotten wood, where they lie all winter and hatch during spring. Most grasshoppers live only from spring until autumn. After the eggs are hatched in autumn, grasshoppers stop eating, shrivel up, and die.

Grasshoppers are often serious pests because they eat the leaves of corn, alfalfa, and other crops. Migratory grasshoppers, often called locusts, are the most destructive. They sometimes migrate in great swarms, darkening the sky and eating every green plant before them. Historical records tell of such dreadful visitations in the past. The Old Testament mentions a plague of locusts in Egypt at the time of Moses. The so-called Rocky Mountain locust appeared in swarms in the Missouri Valley between 1874 and 1880 and did incalculable damage there. Many farmers had their growing crops entirely consumed and were reduced to starvation. Another plague of locusts attacked parts of South Dakota during the summer of 1931. Many farmers there saw their growing corn consumed within a few hours.

GRAVES, ROBERT (1895-   ), English novelist and poet, was born in London. He attended Charterhouse and served in World War I in the Royal Welsh Fusiliers. He attended Oxford University and acquired his degree in 1926. Before this time several volumes of his poetry had been published; they included *Over the Brazier*, *Country Sentiment*, and *The Pier Glass*. In 1927 appeared his *Poems: 1914-1926*. In addition to his poetry Graves early established a reputation as a scholar and critic. His *The English Ballad* was published in 1921 and *Poetic Unreason* in 1925. His fine autobiography, *Goodbye to All That*, was published in 1929 and in the following year a sequel, *But It Still Goes On*.

In 1934 Graves published the historical novel *I Claudius* and its sequel *Claudius the God and His Wife Messalina*, two works that reconstruct life in imperial Rome. Other noted historical novels by Graves' include *The Antigua Stamp*, *Hercules, My Shipmate*, and *Homer's Daughter*.

With Alan Hodge, Graves wrote a social history of life between World Wars I and II, *The Long Weekend*. Other writings include scholarly works on mythology and *Collected Poems*. In 1961 he was elected professor of poetry at Oxford University.

GRAVITATION, LAW OF. Masses of matter attract each other. This fact was known hundreds of years ago. The general mathematical law of this attraction, which we call gravitation, was formulated by Sir Isaac Newton. The story of Newton and the falling apple is well known, and it may be that by reflecting upon the reasons for the apple's fall he was led toward a general expression for the law that apparently governed the entire universe.

Newton's general law of gravitation is: Every particle of matter in the universe attracts every other particle of matter with a force that varies directly as the product of the masses and inversely as the square of the distance between them. In mathematical form this law is expressed by the following equation:

$$F = \frac{Gm_1 m_2}{d_2}$$

In this equation F stands for the attraction between two bodies whose masses are represented by m_1 and m_2, and d is the distance between them. G is the constant of gravitation, which is the same for all masses of all materials.

In general terms this law means that the greater the particles, the greater the attraction between them; and the farther apart the particles, the smaller this attraction. This law was verified in investigations that gradually extended to the moon, the planets, the moons of Jupiter, the tides, and even to comets.

Different ideas about the phenomena that Newton's law of gravitation explained were developed by other scientists. Most important in this connection was the work of Albert Einstein. See RELATIVITY, THEORY OF; SPACE.

A body's weight (the gravitational force exerted on it by the earth) varies with the body's distance from the earth's center.

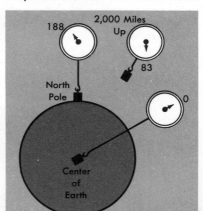

188   2,000 Miles Up   83

North Pole

0

Center of Earth

GRAVITY. The attraction that the earth has for every particle or body on its surface is called gravity. This force of gravity holds objects on the surface of the earth and prevents them from flying off into space as the earth rapidly rotates. Gravity brings back to earth a ball that is thrown in the air. Gravity makes water flow downhill, and gravity causes apples to fall to the ground when they are ripe. Some people use the words *gravitation* and *gravity* indiscriminately, as if they meant exactly the same thing, but *gravitation* should be reserved for the general force throughout the universe, and *gravity* for the pull between the earth and things on its surface. It is because of gravity that things possess weight. The weight of a thing is the force with which it is being pulled toward the center of the earth. As the pull between the earth and any article on it depends upon the product of their masses, and the mass of the earth always remains the same, it is clear that if we double the mass of the article, we double the pull, or attraction, of gravity and so double the weight. Therefore, weight depends upon mass. See GRAVITATION, LAW OF.

GRAVITY, CENTER OF. The pull of gravity, or the weight of a thing, acts along an imaginary line from its center of mass, or the point at which it would balance, straight downward toward the earth's center. Of course, if a body is exactly regular in shape, as a cube or a sphere, this point of gravity, or center through which the pull of gravity acts, will be in the geometrical center of that body. But if the body is bigger and heavier in one part than in another, or is irregular in shape, this center of mass, or center of gravity, is not necessarily the geometrical center of the body. If the body is a solid, the center of gravity will be somewhere within it. If it is hollow or curved, like a crescent or a boat, the center of gravity may lie outside it. In the case of a hollow body, such as a rubber ball, the center of gravity is in the center of the hollow space inside the body.

When a body can be set on the ground so that the line drawn from its center of gravity to the earth falls within the body, it will not topple over; however, if the perpendicular line drawn from its center of gravity to the earth falls outside the base of the body, the body will topple over if it is not adequately supported.

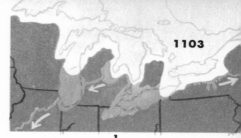

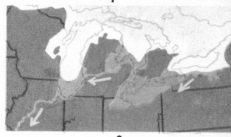

GRAY, ASA (1810-1888), American botanist, was born in Oneida Co., New York. He earned his degree in medicine in 1831, but instead of beginning practice he devoted himself to botany. In 1842 he became Fisher professor of natural history at Harvard. In 1873 he retired from the chair but retained charge of the great herbarium he had presented to the university in 1864. In 1874 he succeeded Louis Agassiz as a regent of the Smithsonian Institution. He ranked among the leading botanists of his age and became an influential supporter of the Darwinian theories of evolution. Gray was a prolific and able writer both of scholarly works and of popular books on botany. He has a place in the Hall of Fame of New York University.

GRAY, THOMAS (1716-1771), English poet, was born in London. He was educated at Eton and Cambridge. After a tour of Europe with Horace Walpole, Gray lived at Cambridge. In 1742 he published three odes: "On Spring," "On a Distant Prospect of Eton College," and "On Adversity." About this time he began working on his "Elegy in a Country Churchyard," a work finished in 1750.

In 1757 Gray refused the laureateship. In that year he published his Pindaric ode "The Bard." In 1768 he became professor of history and modern languages at Cambridge. His very fine letters were collected in 1915.

GREAT BASIN. This vast, triangular interior region is in the western United States. It includes parts of southeastern California and western Utah, most of Nevada, and parts of Idaho and Oregon. Rugged north-south mountain ranges, chiefly from 7,000 to 10,000 feet high, separate basins of interior drainage. The climate is semiarid.

GREAT BEAR, THE (constellation). See URSA MAJOR.

GREAT BRITAIN. See UNITED KINGDOM.

GREAT DIVIDE. See CONTINENTAL DIVIDE.

GREATER DOG, THE (constellation). See CANIS MAJOR.

GREAT LAKES. These are the largest group of fresh-water lakes in the world. The five connected lakes are on the border of the United States and Canada. From west to east they include Lakes Superior (the largest), Michigan (the only one wholly within the United States), Huron, Erie, and Ontario. The international boundary line crosses each lake, except Lake Michigan, near its center. They have a water surface of more than 90,000 square miles. About one-third of this is in Canadian territory. The lakes are drained by the St. Lawrence River into the Atlantic Ocean.

During their navigation season the lakes carry enormous trade. Generally, they are navigable for only seven or eight months a year, for ice and storms stop winter navigation. The Great Lakes region is a center of heavy industry in North America.

GREAT NEBULA IN ANDROMEDA. See GREAT SPIRAL GALAXY.

GREAT NEBULA IN ORION, a huge, greenish, glowing cloud of gas and dust in the direction of the constellation Orion. Its position is marked by the middle star of Orion's sword. To the naked eye it is barely perceptible on a moonless night. However, for direct viewing in the telescope it is the brightest of all nebulae. Ultraviolet radiation from nearby stars causes its material to glow. See NEBULA.

1. In 11000 B.C. an ice sheet covered most of the Great Lakes area. The lakes formed by the melting ice drained west through the Mississippi and east through the Mohawk and Hudson river valleys. **2.** By 9000 B.C. the Mohawk Valley was blocked by ice. **3.** Retreat of the ice sheet by 7000 B.C. again allowed drainage east as well as west through Lake Superior. **4.** By 6000 B.C. further retreat of the ice and rising of the land to the south caused drainage through the St. Lawrence Valley.

Shown below is the Great Nebula in Orion.

Mt. Wilson & Palomar Observatories

The Great Spiral Galaxy rotates about an axis at right angles to its plane of symmetry.

GREAT PLAINS. Located in western North America, the Great Plains form a sloping plateau measuring about 400 miles in width. The area extends eastward from the front ranges of the Rocky Mountains. The Great Plains stretch south and east from Alberta and Saskatchewan in Canada and include parts of Montana, Wyoming, New Mexico, Colorado, and Texas. Sections of Oklahoma, Kansas, Nebraska, and the Dakotas are also included.

Indians were living in the Great Plains when the first white men, Spaniards from Mexico, came in 1540. Most of the Great Plains area was part of the Louisiana Purchase of 1803. Cattle grazing spread from Texas over much of the region soon after the Civil War. The great cattle drives to better grazing land and to markets brought new settlers in the middle 1800's. The Dust Bowl of the 1930's resulted from too widespread cultivation and too close grazing.

GREAT SALT LAKE. This large inland salt lake is located in the Great Basin in northwestern Utah. It is a remnant of ancient Lake Bonneville, which was a fresh-water lake during the Pleistocene, or period of continental glaciation. It is about 75 miles long and 50 miles wide and is generally shallow. The average depth is 13 feet. The lake is fed by three rivers. It has no outlet, and evaporation causes great fluctuations in its size. The lake has no fish. Antelope Island, about 15 miles long, is the largest of several islands in the lake. The Great Salt Lake was discovered in 1824 by James Bridger.

The Great Salt Lake Desert is just west of the lake. It is a vast, arid region, which extends to the Nevada border. World speed records for automobiles have been set at Bonneville Salt Flats, a level stretch near the Nevada line.

GREAT SMOKY MOUNTAINS NATIONAL PARK contains the highest section of the Great Smoky Mountains. It is located on the crest of the high divide that forms the North Carolina-Tennessee boundary. This range, which represents one of the oldest uplands on the earth, zigzags through the park for 71 miles. The park covers approximately 800 square miles. It was established in 1930. The park is known for beautiful displays of mountain laurel, rhododendron, and other wildflowers. Park headquarters are at Gatlinburg, Tenn.

GREAT SPIRAL GALAXY, the largest galaxy in our local group of galaxies and the first to be identified as an exterior galaxy. It was formerly classed as a nebula, which explains its other name, the Great Nebula in Andromeda. You can see it with the naked eye as a hazy patch in the constellation Andromeda somewhat below the figure's extended right arm. It is the only spiral type of galaxy outside our own that you can see without a telescope. Astronomers estimate its distance at 1,500,000 light-years and its diameter as 120,000 light-years. It is known as Messier 31 in the astronomical catalogues.

GREAT TREK, a mass movement of the Boers of South Africa out of Cape Colony (now Cape of Good Hope Province) in the 19th century. The Boers had been the first to settle in South Africa, but Cape Colony had come under the control of the British. This situation gave rise to enmity between the two groups in 1834, in which year the British passed a law freeing the slaves in South Africa. The Boers, fiercely independent, determined to leave the British colony. Beginning in 1835 great numbers of Boers loaded their household goods onto wagons, shouldered their rifles, and drove their cattle and sheep before them into the interior. They established settlements that ultimately became the Orange Free State and the Transvaal republics, and they abandoned Natal when the British proclaimed sovereignty over that territory.

A simple description of the great trek cannot convey the meaning that the movement has to the Boers. It is to them what the American Revolutionary War is to citizens of the United States. Admirable fortitude was exhibited by the Boers in their journey into the unknown. The great trek also created an almost mystical bond among the Boers. To an extent the great trek still influences the relationship between the British and the Boers in the Republic of South Africa. **The Boers have retained their own language and have resisted cultural Anglicization. See AFRIKANER.**

GREAT WALL OF CHINA. Across northern China extends the greatest wall in the world. It reaches 1,500 miles from the Gulf of Chihli on the Yellow Sea in the east into Kansu province in the west.

The Great Wall divided the desert steppe in the north from the arable land in the south. The area to the south was settled by peaceful farmers, while the area northward was inhabited by fierce nomads. Sometimes the weather over a period of years caused the dry steppe to shift southward, a change that brought the warlike nomads with their herds into farming areas. At other times the rains increased, and the farmers moved north to till the soil. The Great Wall was conceived as a way of keeping the horsemen of the deserts from sweeping into China. Only local walls were built at first, but during the Ch'in Dynasty (221-207 B.C.) the walls were connected to form the Great Wall. This project was begun by Shih Huang Ti, the great builder of canals, roads, and palaces. Had the Great Wall been his only accomplishment, he would live with favor in Chinese history, but Shih Huang Ti is also remembered with dislike by Chinese scholars because he burned most of the classical writings of China. The Great Wall was continued over Manchuria by the construction of wooden palisades.

The Wall did not halt all the barbarian invasions, but for many centuries it did keep out people like Hsiung-nu, who are better known to Westerners as the Huns. Nomadic horsemen could not penetrate the

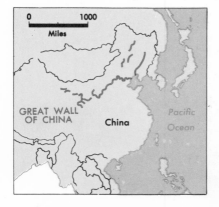

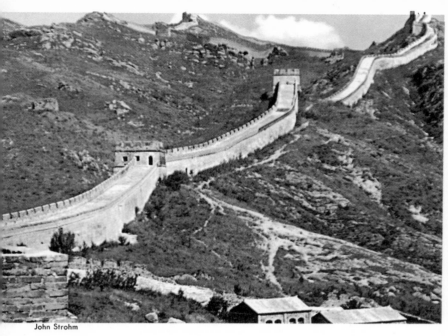

John Strohm

Some 300,000 men worked to build the Great Wall of China in the reign of Shih Huang Ti.

wall unless they captured one of its gates, destroyed a section, or constructed ramps against it. The Great Wall had four huge gateways. The westernmost gate at Kiayükwan was called the Jade Gate and was China's front door to Europe during the Middle Ages. Through the Jade Gate filed caravans carrying silk, tea, and art objects along the Silk Road of central Asia to Europe. It was through this gate that Marco Polo passed on his famous trip to the court of Kublai Khan.

GREBE, a family of ducklike swimming birds, expert in the water and famed for their diving. They are the only birds known to submerge and swim under water with the young clinging to the parent's back. They submerge so quickly and gently that they seem to disappear by magic. Sometimes only the body and neck submerge, the head remaining above the water to reconnoiter the situation. To fly they must patter along the water to gain momentum, as do many ducks. Grebes may be identified by the pointed bill, narrow head, erect neck, and tailless appearance. Their legs are narrow and

The great crested grebe is gaily adorned.

bladelike, and their feet are lobed for easy swimming. Their food, aquatic animal and vegetable matter, mostly fish, is usually secured under water.

Grebes are covered with soft, silky feathers. In an actual count of the feathers on 94 different species, it was found that grebes had the most feathers. One pied-billed grebe had a total of 15,016 feathers.

The nests are marvelous feats of engineering. Composed of light vegetation, they float on the water and rise and fall with changes in its depth; they are, however, fastened by guy shafts to nearby reeds or other vegetation so they will not float away.

Eighteen species of grebes are distributed almost worldwide. One of the best known in the Old World is the great crested grebe, which has startling black horns and other dark head decorations during the breeding season. Many other grebes have colorful breeding plumage. Young chicks are usually striped.

The six species of North American grebes range in size from the 9-inch least grebe to the 29-inch western grebe, which is noted for its spectacular mutual display at breeding time, when the pair run side by side across the water. The other North American species are the red-necked (or Holboell's), the horned, the eared, and the pied-billed.

At right is the waterfront of Salonika, a Greek seaport. Salonika is one of Greece's most important cities. Greece is rich in historic treasures, and Salonika has a great number of Byzantine monuments.

GREECE, a country at the southern tip of the Balkan Peninsula in southeastern Europe. The remains of its noble ancient civilization and the beauty of its landscapes, its bays, and its islands make Greece one of the major shrines and inspirations of the Western world. Greece is about 51,200 square miles in area. The Greek islands form approximately one-sixth of the total area. Athens is the capital; other chief cities are Corinth, Piraeus, Salonika, Patras, and Candia. The population is about 8,000,000.

Greece is mostly mountainous, with many peaks over 7,000 feet high. The highest, Mt. Olympus, is more than 9,500 feet. The mainland of Greece is a large peninsula with a very long, deeply indented coastline. The climate is moderate, with warm, wet winters and hot, dry summers. In the northern mountains there are heavy snowfalls in the winter. The country is relatively poor in natural resources. Forests that formerly covered the hills are being replanted, and some minerals are mined, including iron, bauxite, zinc, and silver.

The principal occupations are in agriculture and fishing. Only about one-fifth of the land is fit for farming, and much of the food needs have to be supplied from other countries. The chief farm products are olives, currants, grapes, tobacco, and figs. These are processed and shipped overseas. There is a little manufacturing, mostly of chemicals, textiles, tobacco products, and soap. Considerable shipbuilding is carried on, and the Greek merchant fleet is one of the largest in the world. There are few members of minority groups in Greece; these are mainly Albanians in the Peloponnesus and Turks and Bulgarians in the northeast. Most of the people belong to the Greek Orthodox Church, the established church of the country. Greece, a constitutional monarchy, is governed by a king and a parliament, whose members are elected by the people every four years.

After almost 400 years of rule by the Turks the Greeks revolted in

Ministry of Inf., Greece

GREECE
AND ALBANIA

1 Inch = 63 Statute Miles

Miles 25   0   25   50

⊛ National Capital

• Size of symbols and type
• indicates relative population

Conic Projection

RELIEF   Feet

		5 000
		2 000
		1 000
		500
Sea	Level	
		Below
		Sea Level
		500
		5 000

1 Inch = 16 Statute Miles

© RMcN & Co.

Location map

The blue color in the flag of Greece has alternated over the years between light and dark.

On the coat of arms of Greece this shield is borne by two figures of Hercules.

This is a Greek postage stamp. The inscription at the right is *Ellas* and means "Greece."

Ewing Krainin—Photo Researchers

The Acropolis, with the temple of ancient Athens, the Parthenon, overlooks modern Athens, the capital of Greece.

1821, and after a long and courageous struggle they succeeded in gaining their independence. The new nation was recognized by all the powers in 1830, and Otto, a Bavarian prince, was proclaimed King Otto of the Hellenes in 1832. He abdicated in 1862, and Prince William George of Denmark became King George I in the following year. The Ionian Islands off the west coast were annexed in 1864. In 1913 King George was assassinated and was succeeded by Crown Prince Constantine. As a result of the Balkan War Greece increased its territory to its present northern border west of Thrace. In December, 1913, Crete was annexed. During most of World War I Greece remained neutral, but she finally entered the war on the side of the Allies in 1917. At the end of the war Greece gained the Bulgarian part of the Aegean coast. A republic was proclaimed in 1925, but in 1933 a royalist became premier, and two years later the monarchy was restored. In 1940, after the outbreak of World War II, Italy invaded Greece from bases in Albania, but the Greeks pushed back the Italian forces and were forced to retreat only by a full-scale invasion by the German army. From 1945 to 1949 civil war raged in the country, carried on by Communist guerrillas in the northern mountains with the aid of the Soviet satellite states. King George II died in 1947, and his brother became King Paul. In May, 1947, the U.S. Congress voted 300 million dollars in aid for Greece as a part of the Truman Doctrine of help for anti-Communist states. An

American military mission went to Greece, and in 1949 the campaign against the Communist forces ended in success. The war and the struggle against Communist enemies destroyed the economy of the country, but with aid from the United States and hard work by the Greek people, the country recovered. By 1959 most parts of Greece were producing more than they produced before the war.

GREECE

Area: 51,200 sq. mi.
Population: 8,000,000
Capital: Athens
Largest cities: Athens, Salonika (Thessalonica), Piraeus
Highest mountain peak: Olympus (over 9,500 feet)
Chief rivers: Vardar, Peneus, Achelous, Alpheus
Climate: Hot, dry summers and mild, rainy winters along coast—hot summers and cold winters in central and northern mountains—rainfall greatest in west
National flag: Five blue and four white horizontal stripes—white cross on blue background in upper left
National anthem: *Se gnorizo apo tin kopsi*
Form of government: Constitutional monarchy
Unit of currency: Drachma
Language: Greek
Chief religion: Greek Orthodox

Chief economic activities: Agriculture (including livestock raising), mining
Chief crops: Tobacco, currants, wheat and other grains, vegetables, grapes, olives, cotton
Chief minerals: Iron, bauxite (aluminum ore), magnesite, chrome ore, zinc, lead, silver
Chief exports: Tobacco, currants
Chief imports: Foodstuffs (including meat, wheat, and flour), machinery and vehicles, various raw materials, chemical and pharmaceutical products

GREECE, ANCIENT. The ancient Greeks were one of the most remarkable peoples in history. They were the first to believe in personal liberty, to practice democracy, and to strive consciously to promote the happiness of the individual. They were also the first to look for rational explanations for the natural world, and in so doing they created their philosophy.

Ancient Greece included parts of the modern Greek mainland, the islands of the Aegean Sea, and the coastal part of western Asia Minor, called Ionia. The peoples of Ionia were the cultural leaders of the ancient Greeks before the rise of Athens.

The Greeks were an Indo-European people who wandered south from the southern steppes of what is now the U.S.S.R. These tribes, which included the Dorians, Aeolians, and Ionians, entered Greece in a number of waves after approximately 2000 B.C.

The first thousand years of Greek history are known mainly through myths and legends. The Greeks about whom Homer wrote in the *Iliad* and the *Odyssey* were an agricultural people, ruled by kings and a warrior aristocracy. They were individualistic and given to jealousy and suspicion; these were not qualities that fostered the establishment of a unified Greek nation. Rather the preferred political organization of the ancient Greeks was the independent city-state.

The instructor in this Greek school chants poetry to the accompaniment of his lyre.

The Bettmann Archive

Small city-states were gradually established by the Greeks after 1000 B.C. The city-states of Corinth, Thebes, and Athens became prosperous centers of trade and banking. Only Sparta remained primarily an agricultural and military state. After the 8th century B.C. the merchants and businessmen of the city-states founded colonies modeled after the Greek city-state, in southern Italy, in Sicily, and as far west as Spain. As a result of such colonization, the Greek language and Greek art, pottery, and coins were carried to all parts of the Mediterranean coast.

Much of what we know as the classical civilization of Greece dates from the 50-year period after the wars with Persia. In these wars Athens, the most important city-state, played a leading role in the Greek victories at Marathon, Salamis, and Plataea.

In Athens, the city-state that exemplifies the glorious period of Greek culture, democracy was the form of government. The democratic constitution of Athens was the work of two 6th-century statesmen, Solon and Cleisthenes. The day-to-day affairs of Athens were conducted by the boule, or council, which consisted of 500 citizens, chosen by lot to serve one year. No one could serve more than twice. Almost half the population of Athens was elected to the boule in one generation. However, women, slaves, and resident foreigners were excluded. The boule dealt with all aspects of government, but decisions rested with the ecclesia, which met forty times each year and included all adult males who were citizens by birth. During the 5th century, however, the most important single magistrate was the strategos. He was the commander of the army and navy and was also charged with judicial and financial duties. But when sitting as a member of the boule, the strategos had no more voice than any ordinary citizen. Pericles, the great statesman of the 5th century, was strategos every year from 443 until his death, in 429.

Even the philosophers and writers in Athens were active in the government. The whole citizenry participated in a culture in which politics, art, religion, and philosophy were considered inseparable. Every citizen attended the public festivals, where the great tragedies of Aeschylus, Sophocles, and Euripides were performed. The annual Panathenaic games drew participants from many city-states of Greece.

The Greeks, especially the Athenians, most admired the philosophers. These were the men, like Socrates, who taught people to know themselves and the world around them by viewing everything with an inquiring mind. The Athenians had a passion for beauty, simplicity, and reason. These qualities are shown in the Parthenon, in Greek statues, and in Greek philosophy. The Greeks, however, in spite of their love for ideas, had small concern for material progress. They believed that man's efforts were cut short by fate or chance, to which even the gods of Olympus were subject. While they avidly pursued knowledge, the Athenians put it to little practical use. The streets of Athens were filthy and foul smelling, owing to a lack of adequate plumbing. The first real advances in technology were made later during the Hellenistic Age.

Wars were frequent among the independent city-states, all of which claimed sovereignty and aspired to self-sufficiency. The eminence of Athens was due to her economic imperialism by which she tried to exploit the other city-states. Corinth, Megara, and finally Sparta challenged the Athenian supremacy. In the disastrous Peloponnesian Wars, which lasted from 460 to 404, Athens was defeated by a coalition under the leadership of Sparta. Later Thebes and other cities tried to become leaders. In 338 B.C. the king of Macedonia defeated the disunited city-states and occupied Greece. The kings of Macedonia, especially Alexander the Great, carried Greek culture everywhere they went, from central Asia to Egypt. This culture flourished after Athens and the other city-states lost their political independence. The Roman Empire and Christianity were greatly influenced by Greek culture. See HELLENISTIC AGE.

GREEK belongs to the Indo-European family of languages. Modern Greek is spoken by about ten million people. Outside Greece, Greek has been spoken in Asia Minor, southern Italy, Sicily, and other regions settled by Greeks.

From existing evidence ancient Greek seems to have comprised a multitude of dialects, each city-state having its own. These dialects may be divided into three groups: the Attic-Ionic; the Achaean, including Aeolic; and the dialects of western Greece, as well as Doric. Because of the literary formalism that compelled a writer to employ the traditional language of the particular genre he was writing, the dialects of literary texts were not identical with the spoken dialects. Hence, the literary dialect of the epics, which was used down to Byzantine times, was basically Ionic, but it also contained numerous Aeolic elements.

Under Macedonian rule the Koine (common) dialect, based largely on Attic Greek, became the standard language for most of Greece and, for a time, the Near East. After the breakup of the Macedonian Empire this language broke into regional forms, including the Macedonian of the Greek mainland and Alexandrian Greek, into which the Jews of Egypt translated their scriptures and in which the New Testament was composed.

In its further development the Greek language evolved, beginning with the 5th century A.D., into what is called Middle Greek, from which in the 14th to 16th centuries was worked out the contemporary Greek language (or demotic).

The tendency to preserve the Attic-Ionic dialect in its purity as a literary language existed among the early Christian writers. It flourished during the Byzantine period, particularly during the 11th and 12th centuries, and was resurrected in the 19th century after the reestablishment of Greek independence. This has led to the peculiar existence in contemporary Greece of an archaic literary language together with the new spoken Greek language. However, demotic, as the habitual spoken language, is required for instruction in the schools and is the basis of contemporary literary language.

This is the Greek alphabet. The letters are pronounced as shown in the parentheses.

A	α	alpha	a	(ă)
B	β	beta	b	(b)
Γ	γ	gamma	g	(g)
Δ	δ	delta	d	(d)
E	ε	epsilon	e	(ĕ)
Z	ζ	zeta	z	(z)
H	η	eta	ē	(ā)
Θ	θ	theta	th	(th)
I	ι	iota	i	(ē)
K	κ	kappa	k	(k)
Λ	λ	lambda	l	(l)
M	μ	mu	m	(m)
N	ν	nu	n	(n)
Ξ	ξ	xi	x	(ks)
O	ο	omicron	o	(ŏ)
Π	π	pi	p	(p)
P	ρ	rho	r, rh	(r)
Σ	σ or s	sigma	s	(s)
T	τ	tau	t	(t)
Υ	υ	upsilon	y, u	(ü, ōō)
Φ	φ	phi	ph	(f)
X	χ	chi	ch	(k, κ)
Ψ	ψ	psi	ps	(ps)
Ω	ω	omega	ō	(ō)

Jane Werner Watson

Teams of archaeologists work to uncover buildings and whole Greek cities that have been buried for centuries by earth and stones.

GREEK ARCHITECTURE in the ancient world consisted of religious and secular structures of many kinds, but the classical temple is regarded as the most typical, as well as the most beautiful, of all. It consisted of an entrance porch with columns, a main chamber containing a statue, and a room to the back surrounded by a colonnade.

The early Greeks did not care for luxurious palaces. They preferred to build temples to protect the statues of their gods and athletic heroes. These buildings were comparatively crude and boxlike, having one or two rooms with a porch in front. A few columns stood on the porch or sometimes went all round the temple. Brick and wood were used in construction, and the roofs were thatched. But already the pure geometric forms so dear to the Greeks could be discerned: square or rectangular in the floor plan, walls, doorway, and ceiling; circular columns; right angles at the meeting of columns and horizontal beams; and eventually a triangle between roof and doorway. All the basic elements of the Doric style were present in the synthesis of these mathematical forms.

As Greece carried on more trade with the East and became aware of other styles, her temples became larger and more substantial. Yet she remained faithful to her native Doric style. Temples were placed on a height to command a view of the sea and the surrounding area, for worship took place in the open. Architects worked carefully on the façade of the temple. To the Doric column they gave particular atten-

tion, continually revising the base, shaft, and capital. Stonemasons and artisans carved figures and designs in the spaces over the architrave and in the triangular area over the doorway. Afterward these figures and designs were painted in vivid colors.

As a result of experience and the refinement of architectural forms, the Greeks were led to vary certain details. Thus the Ionic style is quite similar to the Doric, its most obvious difference being the double scroll of the capital. In Ionic temples of smaller proportions the slenderer columns and thinner walls give an impression of lightness and grace; their more elaborate ornamentation, an impression of elegance. The simpler, more massive Doric style produces a feeling of disciplined strength and purity. A further variation in the design of the column led to the Corinthian style, which used the motif of the acanthus leaf and other ornamental details in the capital. The Corinthian style later became popular with the Romans. See ROMAN ARCHITECTURE.

During the classical period of Greek history, from about 500 to 300 B.C., architecture reached its peak. Stone and marble were now habitually used in building. There was a stronger coherence and unity of parts. Builders strove consciously for equilibrium in their placement of shapes and masses. They also devoted more attention to the design of the interior. The ornamental figures of the façade took on a rhythmical unity. Color was used to emphasize structural elements in the design. This was the great period of Athens in all the arts, the architectural achievements of the Parthenon and Erechtheum and of the beautiful Ionic Temple of Artemis at Ephesus.

After the defeat of Athens in her war against Sparta, Greek society splintered into various groups whose interests became more specialized and more secular. As a result there was a demand for other types of buildings—monuments to the dead, theaters, public walks, marketplaces, libraries, villas, and palaces. In a few cities Greek architects even began to experiment with town planning. At the same time the rooms of temples and secular buildings became more elaborate and the decorative parts became more literal, detailed, and realistic. But the great age of Greece was already past, and such building was not again to be seen for hundreds of years.

This modern building of Pentelic marble, in Athens, was built in the ancient Greek classic style. It became the home of the national library of Greece in 1903.

Ministry of Inf., Greece

Courtesy of The Art Institute of Chicago

This 15th-century Florentine tempera painting depicts the voyage and adventures of Odysseus, the hero of Homer's great epic the *Odyssey*.

GREEK FIRE, an incendiary material used as a weapon in warfare before the advent of gunpowder, particularly by the Byzantine Greeks. It was a semiliquid mixture, shot at the enemy through metal and wooden tubes. It passed through the air as a burning mass and set fire to the objects it struck. It was exceedingly difficult to extinguish, and water made it more dangerous.

The chemical composition of Greek fire was kept a state secret by the several nations that used it, with dire penalties set for anyone who might reveal the secret to the enemy. For this reason there is no record of its main ingredients, and it is probable that different ingredients were used at different times. Modern historians have suggested a number of components that might have been used—bitumen, sulfur, naphtha, and quicklime. Historical records indicate that resinous gums from fir and other evergreen trees were also used. The mixture was blown through the tubes by small hand siphons and large bellows. It seems that some Greek-fire mixtures were ignited by a fire at the nozzle of the hose; others (those including quicklime), when the mixture came in contact with water. The weapon was very effective, particularly in sea battles, but gunpowder and the cannonball eventually superseded it.

GREEK LITERATURE was the first to achieve order, proportion, and harmony. For the Western world it is of greatest importance. The Greeks invented many of the forms known to literature and developed most of them to a height of excellence that has seldom been equaled. To their work all later literatures have been deeply indebted, not only for models of form but also for ideas and inspiration.

The development of Greek literature can be traced roughly through three great epochs: the Homeric Age, or period of beginnings; the Periclean Age, or period of supreme achievement; and the Alexandrian Age, or period of decline.

To Homer (9th century B.C.) tradition ascribes the composition of the *Iliad* and the *Odyssey*, noble products both, in what is perhaps the noblest of poetic forms, the epic. Important both as historical and as literary documents, the two epics are remarkable for simplicity and grandeur of style, for rapidity and variety of narrative, for splendor of imagery, and for comprehensiveness in picturing early Greek life. In this Homeric period also falls the work of Hesiod (8th century B.C.), a didactic treatment of Greek mythology and country life.

The Periclean Age (about 500-429 B.C., but loosely the 5th and 4th centuries) was the golden period of Greek life, thought, art, and literature. In this period lyric poetry came into flower. The seeds had been planted earlier: Alcaeus (about 600 B.C.), Sappho (about 7th century B.C.), and Anacreon (6th century B.C.) wrote in various forms about essentially the same themes —love, friendship, wine, nature, patriotism, and the beauty and brevity of life. In Pindar (5th century B.C.), however, Greek lyric poetry reached its height. His choral odes, written for the great athletic contests, gave evidence of "the glory that was Greece." Their buoyancy, profundity, and sublimity furnished inspiration to most of the great subsequent writers of lyrics.

Among the Greek historians, three deserve mention: Herodotus (5th century B.C.), Thucydides (5th century B.C.), and Xenophon (4th century B.C.). Herodotus, so-called father of history, wrote of the Persian Wars in an easy, anecdotal style. Thucydides, in contrast, presented a rigid, scientific accuracy in his treatment of the Peloponnesian Wars. A restrained account of events, his history was also a philosophical explanation of principles underlying government. His most famous passages are those that deal with the Athenian plague and with the funeral oration of Pericles. Supplementing the accounts of Thucydides were those of the minor but influential historian Xenophon. Xenophon's *Anabasis*, famous history of the march of the 10,000 Greeks into Persia, pointed the way for Alexander the Great. Of equal importance was his *Memorabilia*, which gives an account of Socrates different from that given by Plato.

One of the greatest glories of the Athenian Age was its drama. The origin and early history of both tragedy and comedy are obscure, though probably both forms arose from religious festivals. The features of Greek drama that distinguish it most sharply from drama of the present day are the lyric element provided by a chorus, offstage performance of deeds of violence, recognition scenes, its religious nature, and its tendency toward observance of the unities of action, time, and place.

Of the world's writers of tragedy four are considered great in every way, and three of these were Greek: Aeschylus, Sophocles, and Euripides (all of the 5th century B.C.). Aeschylus excelled in the majesty of his lyrics, the grandeur of his themes and characters, and his deeply religious tone. Skillful character drawing, finished dramatic technique, and subtle use of tragic irony were characteristic of Sophocles. Least respected of the three in his own day was Euripides, but his influence on later times has been greater. The explanation of this greater influence lies perhaps in his interest in psychology, his use of melodramatic elements, and his tendency toward skepticism and rhetoric. After Euripides, tragedy declined, and of these inferior plays little remains. Later, however, the Roman dramatist Lucius Annaeus Seneca (1st century A.D.) adapted themes in Latin from these old masters. Through his work and Aristotle's treatise on

Brown Brothers

Aristophanes' comedies are among the most treasured works in Greek literature.

poetry, European dramatists came to know Greek tragedy and to imitate it.

In the form known as Old Comedy, Aristophanes (5th century B.C.) was supreme. Characterized by definite poetic form and loose plot, this comedy differs from the 20th-century comedy. The plays of Aristophanes are filled with fanciful ideas, ludicrous situations, ribald jests, and puns mingled with political comment, satire, and personal abuse of prominent citizens. All these are interspersed with choral odes, some of striking grace and charm. New Comedy of the 4th and 3d centuries B.C. was the forerunner of our modern comedy of manners. The plays of Menander (4th century B.C.) and his contemporaries were adapted and imitated by the Romans and through them have had great influence on all later comedy.

In the literature of philosophy, also, the Greeks were prolific and proficient, as a listing of names indicates: Heraclitus, Parmenides, Empedocles, Anaxagoras, Zeno, and Epicurus. It was through Socrates, Plato, and Aristotle, however, that Greek philosophy was destined chiefly to influence the world. Socrates (4th century B.C.) left no written work and is known only through the comments of his disciples. Chief among these was Plato (about 4th century B.C.), the greatest literary philosopher of all time. His investigation of the problems of knowledge and ethics, his arguments on immortality and the nature of the soul, his comments on laws and governments, and finally all his much-disputed theory of universal ideas, all these have left their mark indelibly upon literature as well as upon thought and action in general. In literature Plato's place is secured by the purity and clarity of his language and style, by the dramatic skill of his dialogues, and by his superb portrayal of the life and death of his teacher Socrates. After Plato, Aristotle (4th century B.C.), by his formulation of the syllogism, founded formal logic. His learned works treated philosophy, ethics, rhetoric, natural history, physics, political science, constitutional history, poetic theory—in fact, nearly all the knowledge of his time. His works were the final authority as late as the Middle Ages and are still extremely important in all the fields upon which they touch.

Skilled in all the arts and in many other fields, the Greeks set an example also in oratory. The eloquent Demosthenes (4th century B.C.) has served as a model for even the greatest men in the field, men like Cicero and Edmund Burke. The world has long acclaimed his fiery *Philippics* against King Philip II of Macedon and his *On the Crown*, a defense of his political life.

After the death of Alexander the Great (323 B.C.) Greek literature centered in the library of the Ptolemies at Alexandria, Egypt. The period ending with the establishment of the Roman Empire is called the Alexandrian. It was an age dominated by commentators rather than creators. Learned men were diligent in the compilation of encyclopedias, in the editing of texts, and in imitating works that they could not equal. In one field only, that of the pastoral, did the age produce a master. Theocritus (3d century B.C.), living in Alexandria, idealized the Sicilian life that he knew in his youth. Simple shepherd life in a perfect Arcadia was his theme. Virgil did not disdain going to school to Theocritus, and the pastoral tradition, thanks to this Virgilian sanction, has been strong ever since.

Greek literature under the Roman Empire continued its life through the first three or four centuries of the Christian Era. Three writers were outstanding. Plutarch (1st century A.D.) contributed his *Parallel Lives*, comparing Greek and Roman worthies. He gave personal details and anecdotes that, if not strictly accurate, have at least enlivened the pages of history and have been the source for many historical novels and plays. His *Moralia* presented examples of the Greek essay. Lucian (2d century A.D.), in his *Dialogues of the Dead* and *Dialogues of the Gods*, furnished models in skepticism and satire that modern satirists in the Renaissance and afterward used with profit. Longinus (3d century A.D.) is primarily remembered for a single work, *On the Sublime*, in which he established the comparative method followed so often since in literary criticism. Mention should also be made of the anthologies of poetry that appeared in the early part of the Christian Era and the Greek romances that anticipated the modern novel.

Greek literature did not die, however, with the decay of pagan culture. It was revived and transformed by the introduction of Christianity. This era of Greek literature, called the Byzantine period, extended from 527 to the fall of the Eastern Roman Empire in 1453. The culture of the Eastern Empire was of an extremely mixed character, including Roman, Greek, African, and Asiatic elements. Greek was the language in which Byzantine literature was written, but a large proportion of the authors came from Asia and Africa. Oriental influence was therefore strong. The whole literature, indeed the whole intellectual life of the period, was dominated by ecclesiastical interests. Theology took first rank in Byzantine letters, the work of the Greek fathers taking the lead in quantity and quality. Among these Greek fathers, Eusebius of Caesarea, Gregory of Nyssa, St. John Chrysostom, and John of Damascus deserve particular mention. In hagiography, the accounts of the lives of saints and martyrs, a voluminous literature arose. Sacred poetry appeared in considerable quantity, the highest excellence being reached, perhaps, in the hymns of Romanus (6th century). Church history was a chief concern of the fathers. Other literature embraced philosophy—Neo-Pythagoreanism and Neoplatonism—history, rhetoric, the sciences, prose, fiction, drama, and poetry. The importance of Byzantine culture and literature cannot be overestimated. For a thousand years the Christians of the Eastern Roman Empire preserved the culture of antiquity while the Western Empire was being overrun by barbarians. They carried the pagan and Christian heritage to neighboring peoples: Russians, Bulgarians, Armenians, Copts, Syrians, and Arabians.

GREEK MYTHOLOGY is the name given to the fables, legends, and tales told and written by the ancient Greeks. Greek mythology is sometimes divided into three classes. The first of these is called the myth proper. The legends in this group try to explain problems that the Greeks, who did not have modern scientific knowledge, could not explain in any other way. Among these problems are the origin of the universe, the origin of man and the animals, and the growth of religion and customs.

The second mythological group includes historical tales about wars and heroes. These stories are usually based on an actual event. The poet Homer's tales about the Trojan War are an example of this type of mythology. (See HOMER.) The third group consists of adventure stories told for amusement only, such as the tale of Atalanta and the golden apples.

The explanatory myths deal mainly with the gods and other superhuman beings. The Greeks believed that actions of the gods caused the events of nature. For example, many thought that the creation of the world was caused by Gaea (Mother Earth) rising from a shadowy area called Chaos. Gaea gave birth to Uranus, or Heaven, while she slept. Then Uranus showered down rain on Gaea. The Greeks believed that this rain led to the creation of the first grass, flowers, trees, animals, rivers, and oceans. Another myth explained lightning and thunder as the actions of Zeus hurling his thunderbolts in anger.

The most important of the Greek

gods and goddesses (with their Roman counterparts) were Zeus (Jupiter), Hera (Juno), Poseidon (Neptune), Athena (Minerva), Apollo, Artemis (Diana), Aphrodite (Venus), Hades (Pluto), Ares (Mars), Hephaestus (Vulcan), Hestia (Vesta), Demeter (Ceres), and Hermes (Mercury). Separate articles about each of these gods and goddesses appear in this encyclopedia under their Roman names, as given in parentheses. The Greeks were the first people to believe that gods and goddesses had the forms of men and women. The gods of earlier peoples, such as the Egyptians and Babylonians, did not resemble human beings.

The ancient Greeks borrowed much of their mythology from other peoples of the ancient world. Such countries and civilizations as Egypt, Crete, Babylonia, and Palestine contributed to the Greek myths. The Greeks in turn passed down much of their mythology to the Romans. See ROMAN MYTHOLOGY.

GREEK ORTHODOX CHURCH. See EASTERN ORTHODOX CHURCH.

GREEK SCULPTURE consisted of decorative relief in stone and of statues that represented homage to the gods, or celebrated a victory, or honored a public figure. The first lifelike figures in stone, which were statues of the gods, began to appear in the 7th century B.C. They were massive, rigid figures that conformed to a definite geometrical design. The cylindrical trunk of the body strongly suggested the four sides of the original stone block. Standing figures were shown with the left foot slightly forward; seated figures were rigid and erect. Both types of statues were meant to be viewed directly in front. Shoulders, according to the convention, were made broad and square. The sculpture of anatomical details was also stylized. Hair was indicated in flat, wavy lines; eyes were large and staring; the mouth was usually shown smiling. Ridges on the surface marked lines between the limbs and suggested muscular tension. Parallel lines cut into the stone represented folds in the garment. These early statues were painted in bright colors in harmony with a particular setting.

Thus in the early period of Greek sculpture the human form was conceived as a composition of geometrical forms. Realism was limited not only by this conception but also by the prevailing attitude toward the

These figures are part of the famous Porch of the Caryatids, on the Acropolis, Athens.

material used. Bronze and stone were meant to impose solidity and massiveness on the figures carved; surfaces were intentionally left unfinished. Of course, the design of a statue was based on the appearance of the human body and could not help being somewhat realistic. In the later archaic statues especially, the very placement of bodily parts suggested tension and energetic movement.

Sculpture in relief was also stylized. Figures were placed in groups along a pediment or a horizontal bar, assuming attitudes that would fit in a given space. Though these poses were sometimes forced, they expressed force and vitality. Early sculptors also managed to give an illusion of depth to a flat surface. By the time the Temple of Zeus at Olympia was built, sculpture in pediments had become particularly effective. In the "Battle of Centaurs and Lapiths" the figures were arranged in related groups, so that

This relief once decorated the Parthenon.

In Greek mythology Ares is the god of war.
Brown Brothers

even the crouching fighters in the corners played an integral part in the total design.

As sculpture approached the classical period, it became more realistic. Though a fundamental design still dominated the figure, organic motions now affected every bodily part, and statues could thus be viewed from more than one angle. Gods and men alike were rendered as types, rather than as individuals, combining beauty of form and moral excellence. The great sculptor Phidias carved a statue of Zeus in gold and ivory, reputedly so magnificent that it could make a man forget his sorrows. Statues of athletes were greatly admired for their sheer physical beauty. Classical sculptors maintained a balance between forms dictated by design and visual appearance. And they were able to reconcile this same realism with the various properties of bronze, marble, gold, or ivory. A work such as Myron's "Discus Thrower" shows intense physical concentration of forces; the facial expression is relaxed, as though personal emotion were irrelevant to the total effect of energy and physical grace. As was customary, statues were painted. Different colors were used to distinguish between hair and flesh and garments.

As sculpture became increasingly realistic, it attempted to imitate other textures. Deeper cuts in the stone reproduced folds in the garments and revealed the limbs underneath. Praxiteles made the marble surface of his "Hermes" smooth and subtly undulating to suggest warm flesh. The heads done by Scopas showed emotional intensity in the turn of the head, the set of the eyes, and the formation of the brow. In Lysippus' time the new idea of the human body was one of slenderness and suppleness. There was also an insistence on three-dimensional carving, so that movement became restless, and the body could be viewed from a number of angles. Curves and folds in the garments became more complicated. In the "Winged Victory of Samothrace," the drapery is done so realistically that it almost detracts from the figure itself. Reliefs on the "Altar of Zeus" at Pergamum and the figure of Laocoön show violent movement and agonized facial expressions. Subjects for statues became more various, and emotion was more immediate and personal. Technical skill did not decline, but the general excellence of earlier works was lost.

GREELEY, HORACE (1811-1872), a famous American editor and writer, was born at Amherst, N.H. He learned to read when two years old, and before he was ten he had borrowed books from miles around. He worked as a journeyman printer in newspaper offices until 1833. The next year he began a weekly paper called the *New Yorker*, which was in 1841 combined with another paper to form the New York *Tribune*. The *Tribune* was the best and most influential newspaper of its time. It had on its staff 18 foreign correspondents. Its circulation was, except for the South, nationwide. Through the newspaper and through his frequent and highly popular public lectures, Greeley opposed both slavery in the South and the low wages and working conditions of workers in the North. During the Civil War Greeley, who had helped found the Republican party, favored immediate emancipation of Negroes. After the war he supported Reconstruction. He urged the release of Jefferson Davis from his postwar imprisonment. This stand cost Greeley a sharp drop in the circulation of the *Tribune* and in the sale of his books. Greeley was a candidate for the presidency in 1872 but was defeated by Grant. His health was broken by his hard work during the election, and he died when 61 years old.

Greeley is often remembered for his saying, "Go west, young man." He urged that the federal government make land on the frontier available cheaply so that eastern workers could escape poverty by migrating west.

Horace Greeley set a standard of vigor and good taste in American journalism.
Chicago Hist. Soc.

GREENBACK-LABOR PARTY, a political party in the United States during the 1870's. It combined the interests of both farmers and workingmen. Both groups suffered from the lowering of prices after the Civil War and from a severe economic depression that occurred in 1873.

The Greenback party, a forerunner of the Greenback-Labor party, was organized in 1874 and in 1876 ran a presidential candidate, Peter Cooper, who received less than 1 percent of the total vote cast. The greenback was a type of paper money first issued during the Civil War. The party demanded that it be given the same status and value as metal money. This measure was proposed in order to relieve many farmers who were in debt because of post-Civil War economic conditions, which the party attributed to the influence of financiers. In 1878 the Greenback party fused with the National Labor Reform party, thus forming the Greenback-Labor party. At its convention at Toledo, Ohio, that year this party adopted in its platform resolutions calling for the limitation of working hours by law, the establishment of state and national bureaus of labor statistics, and the prohibition of the importation of cheap Chinese labor. In 1880 the party also favored women's suffrage, federal income tax, government regulation of interstate commerce, and social-welfare legislation.

The party's greatest success occurred between 1878 and 1880, when it actually controlled a bloc of 14 representatives in the House of Representatives. However, in 1879 the return of prosperity and the resumption of the redemption of greenbacks in gold resulted in the virtual disappearance of the party after 1880. Some of its members became leaders in the Populist movement and the Knights of Labor.

GREENE, NATHANAEL (1742-1786), an American Revolutionary War general, born in Potowomut (now Warwick), R.I. From his childhood Nathanael had to work hard, but he was fond of study, and by reading whenever he could, he got a fair education. He took great delight in studying about the art of war and was turned out of the Society of Friends, or Quakers, for attending a military parade. In 1775 he was made brigadier general and was given command of the Rhode Island troops in the army at Boston. Greene, who took part in battles around New York in 1776 and New Jersey in 1777, became the trusted

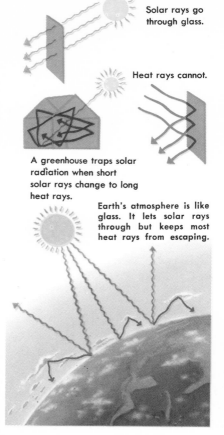

Solar rays go through glass.

Heat rays cannot.

A greenhouse traps solar radiation when short solar rays change to long heat rays.

Earth's atmosphere is like glass. It lets solar rays through but keeps most heat rays from escaping.

As shown above, the earth's atmosphere operates like the glass of a greenhouse.

aide of George Washington. Greene's greatest talent lay in finding and providing army supplies, for lack of which the army had suffered during the long winter at Valley Forge. In 1778, after misconduct of the quartermaster's department came to light, Greene was appointed its head and did a fine job of reorganization. However, the interference of Congress, which had been egged on by Greene's jealous predecessor, caused Greene to resign in 1780. In December of the same year he was put in command of the army in the Carolinas. For that army he raised troops, provided medical and engineering corps, and ordered the building of transport barges. Because he had these barges, Greene was able to cross the Dan River quickly to overtake Cornwallis and to defeat him at the Battle of Guilford Courthouse near Greensboro, N.C. Greene drove the British from the Carolinas with the aid of such famous guerrilla fighters as Francis Marion, Thomas Sumter, and Andrew Pickens.

GREENHOUSE EFFECT is the increase in the earth's temperature resulting from part of the sun's radiation being trapped as heat by gases in the atmosphere, just as the glass in a greenhouse traps much of the radiant heat inside the greenhouse. Light and other radiation from the sun pass easily through the atmosphere and are converted largely to heat (infrared) radiation when they strike the earth. The heat radiation released by the earth would escape into space were it not part of it trapped by carbon dioxide, water vapor, and ozone in the atmosphere. The reason the sun's rays are so penetrating is that the wavelength of its radiation is short, while the waves given off by objects in the greenhouse are long and much less penetrating.

Since the beginning of the 20th century, there has been a marked increase in the concentration of carbon dioxide in the atmosphere as a result of the increased burning of fuels, which form carbon dioxide, and the removal of forests, which use up carbon dioxide. This period has also shown the marked disappearance of glacial ice. It has been suggested that an increased greenhouse effect, owing to the increase in carbon dioxide in the air, may be at least partially responsible. Should a continual increase in the greenhouse effect cause a sufficient continuous rise in the earth's temperature to melt all glacial ice, including that covering the arctic and antarctic regions, the level of all oceans would rise about 100 feet. Many coastal cities would be flooded.

GREENLAND is the largest island in the world (if Australia is identified as a continent). In 1953 it became an integral part of the kingdom of Denmark as a department. Greenland has self-government, and it has representation in the Danish Parliament.

Greenland is situated off the northeast coast of North America. It has an area of 840,000 square miles, four times the size of France. It measures about 1,660 miles in length and has a maximum width of 750 miles. Cape Morris Jesup, 440 miles from the North Pole, is the world's northernmost point of land. The population is about 27,000.

Greenland's high interior is uninhabitable. About five-sixths of the island's surface is covered with a thick icecap. The inhabitants, many of whom are Eskimos, are largely dependent on hunting and fishing. The land animals are the Eskimo dog, the reindeer, the polar bear, the arctic fox (blue and white), the ermine, the arctic hare, and the musk ox. The walrus and seal are common, and the seas abound in fish and whales. Seafowl are plentiful in summer. The chief mineral is cryolite, mined at Ivigtut.

Greenland was discovered in 982 by a viking, Eric the Red. The coasts were charted by numerous explorers and whalers from the 16th to the 19th centuries. The island was a Danish colony from 1721 to 1953. Noted explorations have taken place in the 19th and 20th centuries. In 1933 the Hague Tribunal disallowed Norwegian claims to the eastern coast.

Most of Greenland, as this photograph indicates, is covered by an icecap about 7,000 feet thick. Glaciers move from the icecap into the fiords along the coast, where they produce icebergs by a process called calving. The island was shrewdly named Greenland by its discoverer, Eric the Red, who wanted to attract settlers from Iceland.

Rutherford Platt

U.S.S.R. | Arctic Ocean | Iceland
GREENLAND
Alaska | Davis Strait
Pacific Ocean | Hudson Bay | Atlantic Ocean
Canada
United States
0 — 1000
Miles

GREEN MOUNTAIN BOYS, heroes of the Revolutionary War. This armed band was formed at least four years before the war by settlers from New Hampshire. Its purpose was to drive New York settlers from the lands west of the Green Mountains in what is now Vermont. This organization was the New Hampshire settlers' answer to King George's 1770 decision that New York rather than New Hampshire should have control of this territory. The Green Mountain Boys were led by Ethan Allen. Allen and his men made a spectacular capture of Ticonderoga at the opening of the Revolutionary War. In 1777 the Green Mountain Boys declared themselves the independent republic of Vermont. Because of New York's opposition, Vermont was not admitted to the Union until 1791.

GRENADE, an explosive military weapon designed to be thrown by hand or to be propelled from a rifle. Simple grenades originated in the 16th century and were particularly effective against field fortifications. Grenades fell into general disuse in the late 18th century and were not revived until World War I. The standard U.S. Army type is about the size of a large lemon. The case is of serrated cast iron, and the hollow interior is filled with high explosive. When the grenade is exploded, the iron fragments are hurled violently in all directions. The detonating mechanism is screwed into the top of the case. It consists of a safety pin, a safety lever, a striker, a primer, a fuse, and a detonator charge of fulminate of mercury. Approximately five seconds elapse between the time the safety lever is removed and the time the grenade explodes. The grenade can be thrown about 35 yards and can be propelled from a rifle using a blank cartridge for about 250 yards. It has a killing radius of from 5 to 10 yards and is dangerous up to 50 yards. Smoke grenades are also used.

GRENFELL, SIR WILFRED (1865-1940), English medical missionary, was born near Chester and was educated at Oxford and London Hospital. Always a skillful sailor, Grenfell became interested in the welfare of mariners and fishermen. He joined the medical service of the Royal National Mission to Deep Sea Fishermen in 1889 and fitted out a hospital ship, the first such vessel to be used in the North Sea area. In 1892 Grenfell accepted a mis-

Brown Brothers

Sir Wilfred Grenfell's career was dedicated to the welfare of the mariners and fishermen who sailed the North Atlantic Ocean.

sionary post in Labrador, where he established hospitals, nursing stations, and orphanages and promoted children's welfare. In 1897 he became chief surgeon in charge of the hospital ship *Strathcona II*, which subsequently made annual cruises along the coasts of Labrador and Newfoundland. In 1912 Grenfell founded the King George V Seamen's Institute in St. John's, Newfoundland. Grenfell was the recipient of several honorary degrees and was a member of both the Royal College of Surgeons and the American College of Surgeons. He was knighted in 1927 in recognition of his many years of service. His many written works include *Vikings of Today* (1895), *Tales of the Labrador* (1916), and *Forty Years for Labrador* (1932).

GRIEG, EDVARD (1843-1907), a Norwegian composer, born in Bergen. He studied music at Leipzig, in Germany, but afterward returned to Norway where he determined to develop the Norwegian folksongs by making them the basis of compositions for piano and orchestra. When he was 31 years old, the Norwegian government granted him a life pension, which relieved him of the necessity of teaching. He then devoted himself entirely to composition, with occasional concert tours. The best known of his compositions are his beautiful lyrics of the northland. Of his orchestral works the *Peer Gynt* suites are the most popular.

GRIMM, JACOB (1785-1863) and **WILHELM** (1786-1859), German philologists and writers, born in Hanau, Hesse-Kassel. They collected and published in three volumes old German folk and fairy tales, generally known as *Grimm's Fairy Tales*. Among the famous stories in the collection are "Hansel and Gretel," "The Elves and the Shoemaker," and "Snow White." They were educated at the German city of Marburg and served as librarians at Kassel and as professors at Göttingen (1830-1837). Jacob was one of the seven professors dismissed from his post for signing a protest against the action taken by the new king of Hanover that abolished the constitution. Both were invited in 1841 to Berlin, where they became members of the Prussian Academy of Sciences. The brothers were inseparable even after Wilhelm married and had a family. Jacob did the most original philological work, but Wilhelm was the better writer. Wilhelm put the fairy tales into their final form. In *Deutsche Mythologie*, Jacob Grimm laid a scientific foundation for the study of folklore. Together they also published songs from the *Elder Edda*, *Deutsche Sagen*, and a German dictionary. Jacob's most important independent work was the *Deutsche Grammatik* (from 1819), which remains a fundamental work in German philology. It laid the foundation for the historical investigation of language. In it he began the formulation of what was later named Grimm's Law, which traces the consonant changes in the Indo-European languages that evolved into the Teutonic language group.

GROTTO, a natural underground vault or an artificial recess made to resemble a cave. Pagan worshipers of southern Italy appeared before the famous prophetess, or sibyl, in the grotto at Cumae and trembled to hear her portents of the future. Later, her grotto became a Christian tomb, and now it is merely a tourist attraction. The Blue Grotto at Capri, Italy, was also used at one time by pagan worshipers in their religious rites. A statue of the Virgin Mary now stands in the grotto at Lourdes, France, where St. Bernadette claimed to have her visions of Our Lady.

Artificial grottoes were a feature of Chinese and European gardening. They were fanciful rather than practical constructions, which appealed to a taste for exotic and picturesque retreats. By the 17th century both

Italian and French villas had splendid grottoes with elaborate mechanical devices for reproducing sounds of birds and running water and the echoing of the wind and for shooting out sprays of water. In 18th-century England grottoes were constructed on the grounds of estates to decorate the landscape. Inside, they were lined with shells, spar, crystals, or bright coal. The rooms contained stone or marble figures of the god Neptune surrounded by sea nymphs and dolphins. The more elaborate apartments were furnished with baths and seats of marble; the floors were carpeted with moss. Water trickled down from crevices in the ceiling, which was ornamented with shells, coral, pieces of driftwood, and sometimes bones of whales. One could sit and brood in this atmosphere of romantic melancholy or look at the owner's collections of fossils, shells, and rocks. Such grottoes went with the house, much as swimming pools go with houses today.

Later in the century fantastic grottoes decorated in Indian and Japanese styles were fitted inside with make-believe opium dens, bazaars, and cafés. By the end of the 19th century various types of grotto designs were being used in city oyster bars, teashops, and cabarets.

One of the most beautiful of all grottoes is Blue Grotto, on the island of Capri, Italy.

GROUND HOG, a popular name for the woodchuck, a burrowing rodent that inhabits open farms and the edges of woods. Ground hogs spend much of their time on the ground searching for grass, clover, and grain to eat. They live in underground burrows, beside which they often stand erect and motionless on their hindlegs while scanning the nearby countryside. Occasionally they climb a short distance up the trunks of trees. Despite their small size ground hogs fight when cornered.

During autumn ground hogs eat much and acquire fat on which they

A ground hog is surveying his small domain.

live during their long winter's hibernation, or sleep.

According to an old legend, the ground hog comes out of his burrow on February 2. If the sun is shining, he sees his shadow and is frightened back into his burrow; winter will then continue for a long time. If, however, the sun is not shining, the ground hog will not see a shadow; as a result, spring will arrive earlier. This is only a legend; the ground hog does not interrupt his hibernation to forecast the weather on February 2 or any other date.

GROUND SQUIRREL, a ground-dwelling, burrowing rodent of the same family as tree squirrels. Ground squirrels, which are of several kinds, are native to central and western North America, Europe, Asia, and parts of Africa. They are often confused with gophers.

A common North American ground squirrel has internal cheek pouches, while those of the gopher open on the outside beside the mouth. This ground squirrel is about 10 inches long, including its 4-inch tail. Its general color is reddish brown above, with six or eight light stripes alternating with lines of dots, making about 13 streaks in all. The animal lives chiefly on seeds, berries, and roots, but it also eats birds' eggs. It is native to the prairies from Texas to Michigan and northwestward.

The ground squirrel is a social animal, living in colonies and digging honeycomb-like burrows in open plains. It often digs in newly seeded cornfields, where it runs along the furrows and digs up and eats the grains in hill after hill. It is thus sometimes a great nuisance, and farmers have to use every means to get rid of it. It hibernates and stores food for winter use.

GROUND WATER is the water that saturates sediments and rocks beneath the earth's surface. The source of ground water is rain and water from melting snow.

Rain or snow water seeps into the earth's soil and percolates slowly downward because of the action of gravity. At first the water passes through an unsaturated zone called the zone of aeration. Eventually the water reaches the local water table, the top surface of the zone of saturation. In the zone of saturation every crack and every pore space between mineral grains is filled with ground water. See WATER TABLE.

Ground water is an important natural resource. The water supplies of many cities, manufacturing areas, farmlands, and grazing lands are dependent on ground water obtained from wells. The availability of ground water is different in different areas. The amount of water that can be pumped from a well depends on the size of the well, the character of the rock or sediment in which the well is drilled, and how quickly new ground water replaces the water pumped out of the rock. Rocks or sediments in which a high percentage of the total volume is pore space or other openings have a high porosity. The permeability of a rock or sediment is the ease with which water moves through it. A rock with larger openings and pore spaces is more permeable than a rock with smaller openings. Rocks that are quite permeable and that have a sufficient porosity can supply a well with much water. As soon as water is pumped out of a well in such a rock, ground water from the surrounding rock flows into the well. Rocks or sediments that can yield water rapidly to wells are called aquifers. See AQUIFER; ARTESIAN WELL.

Ground water is never stationary. It is constantly moving from higher

The ground squirrel never climbs trees.

Ground water occurs in spaces in the rock under the earth's surface. The well at the far right had to be sunk below the less porous shale to the more porous limestone. The well at the left obtains water from porous sandstone. The well between these two no longer reaches the water table. Lakes, springs, rivers, and swamps form where the water table reaches the earth's surface.

places to lower places. Ground water usually moves from under hills toward valleys. Where the water table intersects the land surface, ground water appears as springs. If a stream in the valley intersects the water table, ground water may flow into the stream. A stream receiving ground water is called an effluent stream. Some streams in arid regions are slightly higher than the local water table, and water leaks from the streams to become part of the ground-water supply. Such streams are influent streams. The movement of ground water is usually quite slow. The velocity depends on the permeability of the material through which the water is moving and on the local hydraulic gradient (the slope of the water table). The greater the permeability and the steeper the slope, the greater the velocity. Ground water, like the water in rivers, eventually discharges into an ocean or sea.

GROUP DISCUSSION. See DIS-CUSSION.

GROUSE, PTARMIGANS, PRAIRIE CHICKENS. These ground-dwelling, fowl-like game birds constitute a family of 18 species, sometimes known collectively as grouse. They inhabit primarily the northern parts of the Northern Hemisphere. In general they are larger than quails, sometimes the size of turkeys; males are always larger than females. All have feathered tarsi; some have feathers on the feet to serve as snowshoes. Many have on the neck two colorful, unfeathered air sacs, which are distended at mating time. Two types of breeding behavior occur in this family: The monogamous species are paired for a season, and the male helps care for the

young; the polygamous species are marked by a sort of changing harem attracted to a communal display ground by competing males, who assume no responsibility for the nest or the young.

Grouse in North America include five species—the ruffed, blue, spruce, sharp-tailed, and sage grouse. The ruffed grouse, rich brown with fan-shaped tail, wears a crest and a conspicuous neck ruff. The blue grouse, found at high altitudes, includes the dusky grouse of the Rocky Mountain ranges and the sooty grouse of the coastal ranges. In northern coniferous regions is the spruce grouse, so curious and trusting that it is easily killed for food by northern campers. It has a black throat and breast. The sharp-tailed grouse, a fine game bird of the brushy prairies, seems doomed to extinction. The largest American grouse, the sage grouse, lives largely on the nutritious sagebrush of arid western regions.

Ptarmigans of North America include three species, all monogamous —the white-tailed, the rock, and the willow. The white-tailed is found in the mountains of Alaska and Canada and in the U.S. Rocky Mountains. Its tail always remains white. The rock ptarmigan is unique in having three plumage changes: It is brown when the ground is exposed, gray when the autumn foliage is dry and grayish, and white when snow covers the ground. In winter rock ptarmigans often dig little burrows in the snow as shelters. The willow ptarmigan of the arctic tundra is brown in summer; in winter, white with a black tail.

The prairie chicken, an almost extinct game bird, was once plentiful in the American Midwest and eastward to New England. The last eastern prairie chicken, known as a heath hen, died in 1932 on Martha's Vineyard, an island off the coast of Massachusetts. Prairie chickens no longer exist east of Indiana. Male prairie chickens attract the females to their communal display areas, the so-called booming grounds, by resounding pumping noises.

The male spruce grouse, left, has black under parts; his mate, right, is a brownish bird.

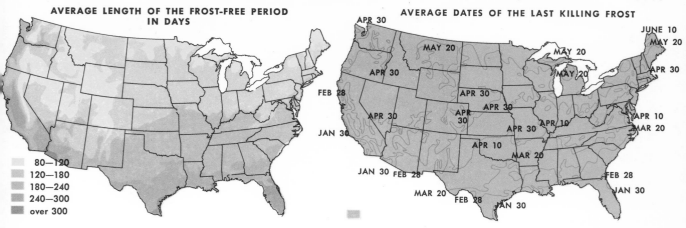

AVERAGE LENGTH OF THE FROST-FREE PERIOD IN DAYS

- 80—120
- 120—180
- 180—240
- 240—300
- over 300

AVERAGE DATES OF THE LAST KILLING FROST

GROWING SEASON, the period of the year during which it is warm enough for the growth of plants. The growing season is defined meteorologically as the number of days between the last killing frost of spring and the first killing frost of autumn. The criterion of a killing frost is a temperature of 32° F. or lower. A few exceptionally hardy plants like the crocus can endure near-freezing temperatures and frost that would kill other plants. In most regions the length of the growing season varies considerably from year to year.

The growing season extends throughout the entire year in those tropical regions that are not mountainous, such as northern South America, Central America, southern India, Indonesia, and the northern margin of Australia. The average growing season in southern England, Ireland, central France, and northern Germany is between 180 and 240 days. In northern England, Scotland, southern Germany, Austria, and Hungary the average growing season is between 120 and 180 days. In most of Italy it is more than 240 days. In most of central U.S.S.R. and central China it is between 120 and 180 days. In southeastern China and in most of central Australia it extends throughout most of the year but is interrupted by occasional winter frosts. Southeastern Brazil, Uruguay, and northeastern Argentina also have an almost yearlong growing season that is interrupted only by occasional winter frosts. In central Argentina the growing season is decreased to approximately 240 days.

In the United States only the region of the Florida Keys never has near-freezing temperatures and consequently has a yearlong growing season. In the rest of Florida, in the regions bordering the Gulf of Mexico, and in certain parts of southern California and Arizona the average growing season is longer than 260 days. In the northern part of the Cotton Belt it is about 200 days. In the northern part of the Corn Belt it varies from 140 to 150 days. In northern Maine and northern Minnesota it is only about 100 days. At higher altitudes in the western states it is about 90 days. In southwestern Alaska it is between 90 and 120 days. In much of central and western Canada it is between 60 and 90 days. The tundra regions of North America, Scandinavia, and Siberia have a growing season of less than 60 days.

GROWTH is an increase in size or a developmental increase of any sort. Human growth has two aspects: the physical and the mental and emotional.

Physical growth is primarily influenced by diet and glandular activity, although the weather, sunlight, and exercise are recognized secondary factors. In the diet the intake of proteins (amino acids) and of vitamins are the main growth determinants. The amino-acid requirements for building the new tissue inherent in the growth process are more specific than those required for maintenance through repair; some amino acids essential in childhood can be dispensed with in adult life. Proteins of animal origin are most suitable for growth. Vitamin B_1 and other factors in the B complex also affect growth. Glandular influences are primarily those of the growth hormone of the anterior pituitary, which stimulates growth of tissues generally, and of estrogens and androgens, which influence the rate of skeletal growth during the period of adolescence.

Emotional growth covers highly complex integrations in personality and character development, leading to mature relationships and emancipation from the family.

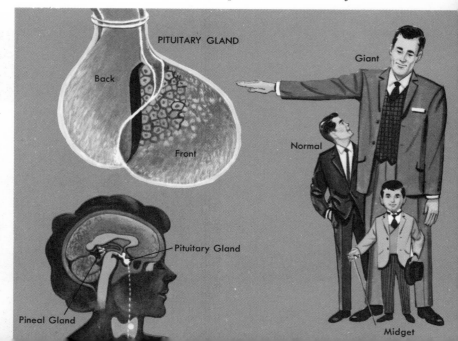

PITUITARY GLAND

Back

Front

Pituitary Gland

Pineal Gland

Giant

Normal

Midget

GUAM is the largest and most populous of the Marianas Islands in the western Pacific. It is an unincorporated territory of the United States. The island has an area of 216 square miles; it had a 1960 population of 66,910. The natives, called Chamorros, are of a mixed Malay origin. The small export trade is chiefly in copra. Rice, coffee, coconuts, cacao, and tobacco are raised on the island. Guam was discovered in 1521 by Magellan.

GUATEMALA is the northernmost republic of Central America. More than half of its people are pure-blooded Indians, descendants of the Mayas, who developed one of the great Indian civilizations of the Americas. Guatemala has the highest percentage of Indians in all Latin America. Indian customs have changed little since the Spanish conquest. The rest of the people are mainly of mixed Indian and Spanish blood; these persons are called Ladinos in Guatemala. Only a small part of the population is of unmixed Spanish ancestry. Although Spanish is the official language, Indian languages are widely spoken. Roman Catholicism is the chief religion. Guatemala covers 42,000 square miles and has about 3,500,000 people.

The republic is largely mountainous. The mountains that run through Central America cross Guatemala along the narrow Pacific coastal plain and cover most of south-central Guatemala. Many of the high volcanoes found here are still active. Earthquakes occur frequently. Tajumulco, the highest peak in Central America, rises to more than 13,800 feet in southwestern Guatemala. Most of the population lives in the valleys and plateaus of the highlands in the southern part of the country. The northern third of the republic consists of tropical lowlands covered with thick forests. Here are ruins of ancient Maya cities, including Tikal, one of the greatest of the Maya Empire.

The rivers of Guatemala are not generally used as waterways. Those flowing down the Pacific side of the mountains are short, swift, and shallow. Longer rivers, flowing northward, include the Motagua, which enters the Caribbean Sea, and the Usumacinta, which enters the Gulf of Mexico. Of chief commercial importance is the short Río Dulce, through which Lake Izabal drains into the Caribbean. Lake Izabal is Guatemala's largest lake.

Climate varies with the altitude. It ranges from hot and humid in the lowlands to cool in the mountains. The year is divided into a rainy and a dry season, except in the Caribbean lowlands, where there is rain throughout the year.

Guatemala's economy is agricultural. Coffee and bananas are the principal money crops and make up most of the country's exports. Cotton, chicle (used in making chewing gum), and citronella and lemon-

The blue-and-white flag of Guatemala carries the nation's coat of arms in its center.

grass oils (used in perfumes) are also exported. Foreign trade is mainly with the United States. Corn, sugarcane, rice, beans, and wheat are grown for domestic use. Livestock raising is also important.

Forests cover about 60 percent of the country's area. Chicle is gathered in the tropical forests of

Guatemala's Lake Atitlán, surrounded by volcanoes, is shown at lower left. The picture directly below is of the famous Indian market at Chichicastenango. At the right a Guatemalan schoolteacher is shown with his class of young boys.
John Strohm

David Forbert—Alpha

Tom Hollyman—Photo Researchers

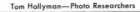

northern Guatemala. Mahogany and other fine woods enter into the export trade. Mining is relatively unimportant. Manufacturing is concentrated largely on processing agricultural products.

Long before the coming of the Spaniards Guatemala was inhabited by the Mayas. (See MAYA.) What is today Guatemala was settled by Spaniards from Mexico under Pedro de Alvarado, a lieutenant of Cortes. The captaincy general of Guatemala, a part of the Vice-royalty of New Spain (Mexico), included the present-day republic of Guatemala and also El Salvador, Honduras, Nicaragua, and Costa Rica.

Independence from Spain was achieved in 1821 through a bloodless revolution. After a short period as part of Mexico, the provinces of the former captaincy general became the independent United Provinces of Central America in 1823. But differences of interest caused civil war, and the federation began to break up in 1838. Guatemala, El Salvador, Honduras, Nicaragua, and Costa Rica became separate republics. Many unsuccessful attempts have been made to revive a Central American federation. For detailed map, see MEXICO.

GUATEMALA

Area: 42,000 sq. mi.
Population: 3,500,000
Capital: Guatemala City
Largest cities: Guatemala City, Quezaltenango, Puerto Barrios
Highest mountain peak: Tajumulco (13,816 feet)
Chief rivers: Motagua, Dulce
Chief lakes: Izabal, Atitlán, Amatitlán, Petén
Climate: Hot and humid in lowlands, cool in mountains—rainfall seasonal
National flag: Three vertical stripes of blue, white, blue—coat of arms in center
National anthem: *Guatemala feliz!* (Happy Guatemala)
Form of government: Republic
Unit of currency: Quetzal
Languages: Spanish, Maya Indian languages
Chief religion: Roman Catholic
Chief economic activity: Agriculture
Chief crops: Coffee, bananas, corn, beans, wheat, sugarcane, rice, cotton
Chief minerals: Lead, zinc
Chief exports: Coffee, bananas
Chief imports: Machinery and vehicles, textiles, petroleum products, foodstuffs, iron and steel manufactures, clothing

GUERRILLA, a fighter who engages in irregular warfare behind enemy lines. Guerrilla warfare is often part of peasant revolts, struggles for national independence, or struggles by peoples whose land has been invaded. The weaker side in an armed conflict often resorts to guerrilla warfare, or such warfare may form part of the plan of an organized army. The minutemen of the beginning of the American Revolutionary War were guerrillas. They were armed citizens who had agreed to leave for battle at a minute's notice. However, some of them (in Massachusetts, for instance) were enrolled in the regular militia.

Napoleonic Wars were marked by guerrilla fighting, some of the most famous of which was conducted in Spain from 1808 to 1812. But it also existed elsewhere. When Napoleon advanced to Moscow, Davidov organized bands of guerrillas behind the French lines. They cut lines of communications, ambushed French foraging parties, and forced small groups of French soldiers to huddle within their barracks. Davidov later wrote a classic textbook on guerrilla warfare.

During the 19th century before the states of Greece, Bulgaria, and Rumania broke away from the Ottoman Empire, they fought as guerrillas against the Turks almost continuously. In the American Civil War John Mosby's famous Rangers harassed Union supply lines. The struggles of Emiliano Zapata and Pancho Villa in Mexico were examples of guerrilla warfare. Villa, in fact, began his career as a brigand, which is not untypical of guerrilla fighters. World War II witnessed guerrilla activity in almost all the nations invaded by Germany—the *maquis* in France and the partisans of Josip Broz (Marshal Tito) in Yugoslavia, for example.

The Hague Conference of 1899 formulated rules regarding guerrillas. They provided that guerrillas be treated as soldiers so long as they wore distinguishing emblems and recognized the international laws of war. However, unless guerrillas have been attached to regular army units, the Hague rules have seldom been adhered to. The main object of guerrilla war, therefore, has been its propaganda value in cases of struggle for national independence. The Riffs under Abd-el-Krim, for example, fought a long, hopeless struggle against France and Spain in Morocco, but they succeeded in arousing the Moslems in other occupied countries.

GUIANAS, THE, three European possessions in northeastern South America. Some of the world's largest bauxite (aluminum ore) deposits occur in British Guiana and Surinam, which is also known as Dutch Guiana. Devil's Island, one of the small islands off the coast of French Guiana, was formerly a notorious French prison colony. British Guiana covers an area of 83,000 square miles and has a population of about 550,000. Its capital and chief seaport is Georgetown. Surinam's area is 55,000 square miles, and its population numbers about 240,000. Paramaribo is its capital and main port. The area of French Guiana is 35,000 square miles, and it has about 30,000 inhabitants. Its capital and principal port is Cayenne.

Along the coast of the Guianas is a narrow belt of lowland, where most of the people live and where all the towns are located. Here also is all the farmland. From this coastal plain rises a vast plateau covered with dense tropical forests. This is where the region's mineral resources lie. In the south are forested mountains, extending eastward from Venezuela, with occasional stretches of grassland. The highest point in the Guianas is Mt. Roraima, a tabletop mountain that rises to

British Guiana and Surinam bauxite is shipped to North American aluminum refineries.

Fritz Henle—Photo Researchers

Davis Pratt—Rapho Guillumette

Devil's Island, a rocky, forested islet off the French Guiana coast, was until 1945 a notorious French penal colony. Alfred Dreyfus was confined here.

9,000 feet at the place where the borders of Venezuela, Brazil, and British Guiana meet. The Tumuc-Humac Mountains on Brazil's border with Surinam and French Guiana are only about 3,000 feet high.

From the mountains a great number of rivers flow northward to the coast. The principal rivers include the Essequibo, Courantyne, Maroni, and Oyapock. Although interrupted by many spectacular waterfalls, the rivers are the chief transportation routes into the interior. The famous Kaieteur Falls, more than 700 feet high, are on the Potaro River in British Guiana.

The climate of the region is hot and humid, but the northeast trade winds lessen the heat along the coast. Rainfall is heavy. The year is divided into rainy and dry seasons, but some rain falls throughout the year.

Farming is carried on only in the coastal belt. Much of this area is marshy, and drained areas must be protected from the sea by dikes. Sugarcane is the chief money crop in British Guiana. In Surinam it is rice. Besides sugarcane and rice, the fertile coastal plain produces sweet potatoes, citrus fruits, cacao, coffee, coconuts, and other food crops.

Great deposits of bauxite constitute the leading mineral resource. Gold and diamonds have been mined for hundreds of years. Manganese, quartz, and other minerals also exist. Forests cover more than four-fifths of the Guianas. Some lumber is cut and exported, but lack of transportation facilities prevents fuller exploitation.

The people of British Guiana and Surinam are largely of East Indian ancestry. The East Indians were brought to the Guianas as plantation laborers after the abolition of slavery. Negroes, descendants of former slaves, are the next largest group. Persons of European extraction are few. Bush Negroes, whose ancestors were escaped slaves, and native Indians live in the interior forests. The official languages of British Guiana, Surinam, and French Guiana are English, Dutch, and French, respectively.

The Guiana coast was sighted by Columbus in 1498. Although the Spaniards explored the area for gold, the vast forests and sparse Indian population had no attraction for them. The Dutch made the first settlements about 1600. The British and French followed. Until 1815 the settlements changed hands among the Dutch, British, and French many times. In agreements after the Napoleonic Wars, the present ownerships were established. For detailed map, see SOUTH AMERICA.

GUIDED MISSILE, a self-propelling unmanned vehicle that travels through space and is controlled or controls itself during flight. A guided missile is made up of an airframe (body, wings, tail, steering devices), a warhead (usually of nuclear explosives), guidance and control mechanisms, and a thermal-jet or rocket engine. A guided missile is put into flight from an appropriate launching device. See MISSILE.

The airframe design of a guided missile depends upon whether the missile is to travel through the earth's atmosphere or outside the atmosphere. Missiles that travel through the atmosphere have airframes designed much like those of airplanes. Missiles that travel outside the atmosphere cannot steer themselves by the resistance of air against their body parts. They steer themselves by the reactive forces of rockets.

Guided missiles that travel through the atmosphere use thermal-jet engines to propel them-

Long-range guided missiles now fly above the atmosphere, where the stars are always visible. These missiles carry automatic star-tracking telescopes and celestial-navigation equipment, enabling the missiles to navigate without outside guidance.

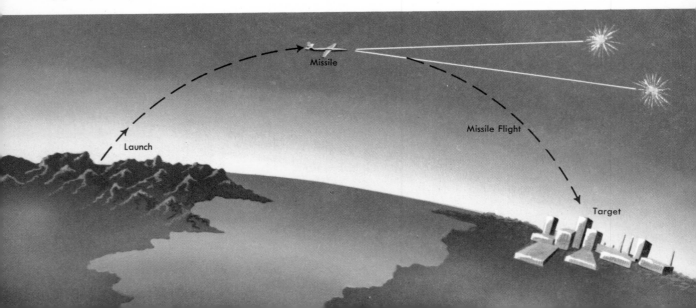

Launch

Missile

Missile Flight

Target

The Atlas guided missile carried the first United States earth satellite into space.

U.S. Army Photograph

The U.S. Army Hawk is a surface-to-air guided missile. It is designed to intercept aircraft flying at a low level to avoid radar detection. The Hawk finds its target with its own radar. It is seen here being launched from a mobile-type launcher. A Hawk installation such as this one can be transported from one location to another by a single helicopter. The Hawk became operational in 1959.

The Nike short-range guided missile is able to intercept and destroy enemy airplanes.

selves. (See JET PROPULSION.) Thermal-jet engines use air. Ramjet and turbojet engines are used in missiles. Missiles that are launched through the atmosphere but travel outside the atmosphere must use rocket engines, which do not need air. (See ROCKET.) Booster rockets may be used in launching missiles that need extra power to reach flight speed. After the missile reaches full flight speed, the booster rockets are dropped from the missile.

The guidance-and-control system of a guided missile is complex. It must include devices to perceive the target, to measure the position of the missile with respect to the target, to control the flight of the missile, and to change the missile's flight course when necessary.

Some of the devices that help to guide a missile may be located on the ground or in airplanes. Command guidance uses ground radar stations and a ground radio-sending station. Radar stations determine the location of the target. When the missile is launched, other radar stations track the missile in flight. Radio signals are sent to equipment in the missile to guide the missile's flight to the target. A weakness of command-guidance systems is that at long distances from the launching place the radio waves may become

distorted. As a result, the guidance information the missile receives may be inaccurate.

A beam-riding system may be used to guide missiles against aircraft. This system uses two beams: A radar beam tracks the target, and a radio beam guides the missile. Information from the tracking beam is fed into a ground computer. The ground computer directs the guidance beam so the missile will fly a course that will intersect the tracking beam at the target.

Passive homing guidance systems use a radar-sending station located on the ground or in an airplane. The sending radar station bounces radar signals off the target. Radar receiving equipment in the missile perceives the radar signals that reflect from the target. The missile's guidance equipment interprets the reflected signals and aims the missile at the target. In active homing guidance systems, a missile has its own radar sending and receiving equipment.

Heat-homing guidance systems for missiles depend on the fact that radiations are given off from bodies at intensities that differ from those of their surroundings. These radiations, or infrared rays, are detected by a device in a missile that trans-

lates the variations of radiation into voltage changes. The voltages are amplified into steering directions for the missile. Missiles guided by homing systems may follow one of several types of flight paths. If a missile constantly changes its course so that it is always aimed at the target, it follows a pure pursuit path. Pure pursuit was used in early guided missiles but is now obsolete. A missile that sets its flight path on a collision course with a moving target uses proportional navigation. Proportional navigation is the commonest homing system flight path.

Guidance systems that depend on radio and radar signals have disadvantages. The signals can be detected and may be used to determine the position of the missile-launching site. The signals also may be rendered ineffective by countersignals. Countersignals may even be used to seize control of the missile during flight. Radar signals are only effective in a straight line. Radar signals cannot follow a missile for great distances because of the curvature of the earth.

A long-range surface-to-surface missile may use an inertial guidance system. In this system the missile has gyroscopes that maintain the same axis of spin in space regardless of the path of the missile. (See GYROSCOPE.) The missile also has equipment to determine the direction of the force of gravity. By comparing the direction of the force of gravity and the direction of the axis of gyroscope spin, the missile can determine its own location with respect to the target. Another type of long-range guidance is guidance by stars (celestial navigation). The missile has instruments to observe star positions and to determine the direction of the force of gravity. The missile compares the two types of information to determine its own position.

much political power and in some cases even governed their boroughs and evolved courts of justice of their own. They were so rich that they could buy, or force, privileges from their rulers, and they never yielded a point once it was gained. Craft guilds developed in England by the 13th century and on the Continent at about the same time.

The craft guilds had three classes of members. Boys entered the guilds as apprentices and paid a fee to a master craftsman to learn the trade. The apprentices lived in the master's home. They were sometimes given an elementary education, and the master was also responsible for the development of their characters. After about seven years the apprentice became a journeyman, able to hire himself out and to keep his

GUILLOTINE, an apparatus for inflicting capital punishment by beheading. Some authorities ascribe its invention to the Persians. It was in use in parts of Scotland, England, Germany, France, and Italy during the Middle Ages, long before it attained notoriety under its present name. In 1789 Joseph Ignace Guillotin proposed to the National Assembly that such a machine be adopted for capital punishment in France. His proposal was based on the argument that decapitation, formerly restricted to the nobility, should be made available to all, in true revolutionary spirit. Eventually adopted, the machine was known at first as the *Louison*, or *Louisette*, after the man who directed its construction; but the public fancy soon reverted to the name of the man who had first proposed its use.

The guillotine decapitates by means of a weighted steel blade that slides up and down between two upright posts grooved on their inner sides. The victim's neck is confined in a circular opening between two boards, the upper one of which slides up and down. The knife is fixed to the cap, or lintel, atop the posts, by a claw. The claw is released by a lever, which is operated by a cord.

The same name is given to a machine for cutting paper, straw, and like material by means of a knife descending between grooved posts.

GUINEA is a republic on the west coast of Africa. Formerly one of the territories of French West Africa, it became an independent nation by voting to reject the new French constitution in 1958. Conakry is the capital and chief seaport. Extend-

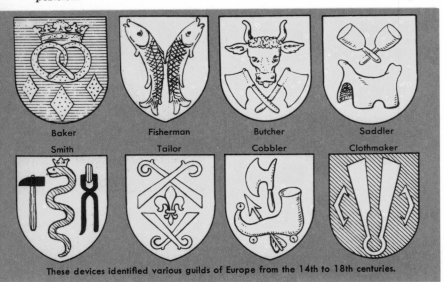

Baker   Fisherman   Butcher   Saddler

Smith   Tailor   Cobbler   Clothmaker

These devices identified various guilds of Europe from the 14th to 18th centuries.

GUILD, an association of the members of one profession, trade, or craft, formed in the towns of Europe in the Middle Ages for the protection and development of commerce and for mutual benefit. The first guilds known were in England before the Norman Conquest (1066). They were both social and semireligious in character and helped support the church by paying tithes. Some were made up of merchants, who worked to maintain the privileges of their special class and to establish proper conditions of work, wages, and prices. By the end of the 12th century these guilds were general throughout the cities of Europe. The Drapers' Company of Hamburg, Germany, dates from 1153, and that of the Shoemakers of Magdeburg, Germany, from 1157. The merchant guilds came to have

wages. The journeyman generally remained in the master's house, however. If he saved his money diligently and passed an examination in his craft, the journeyman could set himself up as a master in his own shop. The masters had full voting rights in their guilds. The strict discipline of the guild system was described by Carl Schurz in 1839, in which year he stayed in a master locksmith's home at Cologne, Germany. Schurz told in his diary of how only the eldest journeyman could speak at the dinner table. The rest of the journeymen were not permitted to speak unless they were spoken to by the master.

The rise of the factory system during the Industrial Revolution destroyed most of the guilds. Some of the functions of the guilds, however, were taken over by the trade unions.

This is the three-colored official flag of Guinea. The coat of arms appears below.

ing inland a considerable distance, Guinea covers an area of about 95,000 square miles. Its population numbers about 2,500,000.

Guinea's coastal lowland is indented and fringed by reefs. Inland lies the Fouta Djallon, a rolling mountain mass about 3,000 feet high, with some peaks reaching 6,000 feet. The Gambia, Niger, and Senegal rivers rise in these mountains. Temperatures along the coast are high, but in the Fouta Djallon the climate is more moderate. Guinea has a monsoon-type climate, with the heaviest rainfall along the coast. The dry season is from November to April.

The country possesses rich deposits of bauxite (aluminum ore), considerable low-grade iron ore, and some gold and diamonds. Bauxite-mining operations are being developed, but the economy remains basically agricultural, and most of the population is occupied in either growing or processing agricultural products. Bananas, rice, palm nuts, and coffee are among the chief crops. Coffee is grown in the interior highlands, which are also used extensively for cattle grazing. Guinea's chief exports are bananas, coffee, palm kernels, and minerals. Formerly, trade was mainly with France, but the Soviet-block countries now have a considerable share.

Guinea's largest tribes are the Fulah and the Malinke. Most of the people are Moslems or pagans. Comparatively few persons of European origin live in the country.

In the late 1880's the French claimed the area now constituting Guinea and made it a dependency of Senegal. It became the separate colony of French Guinea in the 1890's. The struggle with the native chiefs continued into the next decade. Included in French West Africa when it was organized in 1895, Guinea remained under French control until 1958, when voters elected to become an independent republic. For detailed map, see ALGERIA.

GUINEA PIG, a common South American rodent whose name conveys two errors, for it is not from Guinea and it is not a pig. *Guinea* is perhaps a corruption of *Guiana*, from where the animal is said to have been brought by the Dutch in the 16th century, and the name *pig* is probably derived from the grunting noise it makes when it is hungry. The common guinea pig is about 10 inches long and weighs about 1 pound. Its fur is coarse, rather long, and usually uniformly grayish brown, though often white. In its native lands the guinea pig lives generally in groups of 6 to 15, preferring marshy places covered with aquatic plants or sand, in which it digs burrows. It makes regular beaten paths near its haunts and seldom wanders far from home.

The domestic guinea pig is supposed to be derived from a smaller species, called Cutler's cavy, which was domesticated by the Incas of Peru and is still kept and bred by Peruvian natives. Domestication has brought about many variations in color, and the animals are now usually pure white or marked with yellow and black. Unlike the wild guinea pig, the domesticated one is very prolific, having several litters of 4 to 12 each in a year. Though clean in their habits, guinea pigs have a somewhat unpleasant odor, but as they never bite and are gentle, they make pleasing pets for children.

GUITAR, a stringed musical instrument, used chiefly to accompany the voice in singing. It has a flat, violin-shaped soundbox, or body, with a long, thin neck, on which the fingering is done and from the end of which the head bends back at an angle. There are six strings, three of gut and three of silver wire. They stretch from the pegs in the head and across the well, or round opening, in the body and are attached to a small ebony bridge at some distance from the foot of the body.

When it is played, the guitar is held across the body, the strings being plucked by the thumb and fingers of the right hand, while the stopping, or fingering, is done by the fingers of the left hand on little raised wood or metal strips on the neck, called frets. The compass of the guitar is about three and one-half octaves, and its music is particularly suited for accompanying the human voice.

Types of guitars include the classical (left) and the electric, or jazz (right), guitar.

Guinea pigs are the subjects of many medical, genetic, and psychological experiments.

The guitar is one of the oldest of stringed instruments and has existed in one form or another for nearly 4,000 years. The cithara, which was very similar to the guitar, was used by the Egyptians in at least 1500 B.C.

In its modern form it comes from Spain, where since the early Middle Ages it has been played by all classes of society. It has also enjoyed great popularity in France, Italy, and England.

The ukulele is the miniature four-stringed Hawaiian guitar, which, though not of native origin, has become the musical instrument of Hawaii. See UKULELE.

GULF, a wide and deep indentation in a coastline. It is usually larger than a bay and smaller than a sea. Gulfs are caused by a depression in the earth's crust or by the overflow of the sea into a low area of a continental landmass. Some examples are the Gulf of California, Gulf of Alaska, and, in Europe, the Gulf of Bothnia between Sweden and Finland.

GULF OF MEXICO, a basin of the Atlantic Ocean, lying on the southeast coast of North America. It is bounded on the southwest by Mexico and on the north by the United States. The gulf has an area of about 700,000 square miles, or about one-fifth the area of the United States. The average depth is 4,700 feet, and the greatest depth is 12,480 feet. It is connected with the Atlantic by the Straits of Florida between Cuba and Florida. The Yucatan Channel between Cuba and Yucatan connects it with the Caribbean Sea. The Mississippi, Rio Grande, and other rivers flow into it. Principal ports include Galveston, Tex., Houston, Tex., New Orleans, La., Havana, Cuba, and Veracruz, Mexico.

GULF STREAM. See ATLANTIC OCEAN.

GULLIVER'S TRAVELS (full title *Travels into Several Remote Nations of the World by Lemuel Gulliver*), a satire by the Anglo-Irish author Jonathan Swift, was published in 1726. It is a social and political satire in prose, written as if it were a travel book. In it Swift bitterly attacks many of the follies of mankind, and by the end of the book has proclaimed a thorough hatred of the whole human race. Yet Gulliver's fantastic adventures are described in such vivid detail that the intent of Swift's satire is often overlooked, with the result that the book has become something of a children's classic.

Gulliver's Travels is divided into four books, each of which is a narration by one Lemuel Gulliver of a voyage to a previously unknown land. On the first and third voyages he encounters peoples whose exaggerated follies and shortcomings emphasize similar faults in humanity. Among them are the Lilliputians, a race of people only 6 inches high,

whose country is torn by petty politics and intrigue; the Laputans, a nation of supposedly wise men who are so involved in thinking out weighty problems that they are incapable of solving the smallest problems of everyday life; and the professors of Ladago, who waste their hours in such fruitless projects as attempting to extract sunbeams from cucumbers.

In the second and fourth books Gulliver encounters races who are far superior to humanity. One is a race of horses, the Houyhnhnms, who are endowed with reason far superior to that of people. They are the masters of a race of disgusting beasts, the Yahoos, who look very much like people. The other land is inhabited by the giant Brobdingnagians. In each country Gulliver's attempts to justify his own country's way of life prove to all concerned that people are little better than Yahoos; or, in the words of the king of Brobdingnag, that men are "the most pernicious race of little odious vermin that nature ever suffered to crawl upon the surface of the earth."

GULLS AND TERNS are graceful, long-winged water birds, usually white or gray and white, often with black markings, such as caps, head spots, or wingtips. These two types of birds, members of the same family, are so similar that one is often mistaken for the other. Size is not of much help in separating them. But there are differences that aid in identifying them. Terns are whitish and often have dark caps. Adult gulls are usually white with gray upper parts; young gulls are brownish. The tern is slenderer than the gull and has narrower, more pointed wings. The tern's bill is pointed and slender; the bill of the gull is slightly hooked. In flight the tern holds its bill downward, while the gull points its bill forward. The tern's tail is usually forked, while the gull's is usually slightly rounded. The tern dives headfirst into the water for live prey; the gull alights on water or land and often feeds on carrion.

Worldwide there are 43 species of gulls, about 20 of them appearing regularly or occasionally in North America. Principally they are along the oceanic coasts. However, one gull, the kittiwake, spends most of its time far out over the ocean. Other species are found on lake shores, and Franklin's gulls swarm over the western fields to feed on

From left to right, below, the gulls shown are the black-headed gull (on the crossbar) the California gull, Heermann's gull, great black-backed gull, and the laughing gull.

grasshoppers. The sea gull was named Utah's state bird because of its help when an enormous flock of gulls freed the fields from devastating grasshoppers. The early Mormons, thus saved from starvation, in gratitude erected Sea Gull Monument in Salt Lake City.

Gulls usually build their nests of seaweed or grass on rocks or on the ground. Two or three brown eggs are laid. The young are cared for by both parents for a month or two. Some gulls take eggs and young from other nests, even from those of their own species.

The 39 species of terns include about 14 in North America. Two species breed within the Arctic Circle, and four breed in Antarctica. Most terns live over water, and they commonly feed on fish and crustaceans. The most famous is probably the arctic tern, which is said to spend more time in daylight than any other bird. It breeds in summer in the very long days of the Arctic Regions. Then it migrates to Antarctica, where it again spends its days in almost continuous light.

Terns are vigorous in protecting their nests. Some species attack predators, even man, by dive-bombing. A number of terns may collaborate in the attack until the intruders are driven away.

COMPARATIVE SIZES OF NORTH AMERICAN GULLS AND TERNS

GULLS	Length in Inches
Little Gull	10-12
Bonaparte's Gull	12-14
Ross's Gull	13-14
Sabine's Gull	13-14
Franklin's Gull	14-15
Black-Headed Gull	14-15
Laughing Gull	16-17
Ivory Gull	16-17
Common Gull	16-17
Kittiwake	16-17
Ring-Billed Gull	18-20
Heermann's Gull	18-21
California Gull	20-23
Lesser Black-Backed Gull	21-24
Iceland Gull	23-26
Herring Gull	23-26
Glaucous Gull	26-32
Great Black-Backed Gull	28-31

TERNS	
Least Tern	9-10
Black Tern	9-10
Gull-Billed Tern	13-14
Bridled Tern	14-15
Forster's Tern	14-15
Common Tern	14-16
Sandwich Tern	14-16
Arctic Tern	14-17
Roseate Tern	14-17
Noddy Tern	15-16
Sooty Tern	15-17
Royal Tern	18-21
Caspian Tern	19-23

GUM, the vegetable secretion sometimes occurring in intercellular spaces. It is formed by the disintegration of cellulose by the action of enzymes. The term *gum* is also used loosely to include the thick, sticky, liquid secretion of many trees and shrubs. Some gums are soluble in water; others are insoluble. A typical water-soluble gum is gum arabic, which is obtained from a tree that grows abundantly in Africa and India. Gum arabic occurs in transparent white tears, which are often colored yellow or brown by impurities. It cracks on exposure to the air, is brittle and inodorous, and has a bland, mucilaginous taste. It is used widely in the making of confections, medicines, inks, and adhesives.

Chewing gum is the name given to a popular confection. The principal ingredient of chewing gum is chicle, a milky juice, or latex, obtained from the bark of the sapota tree; it is not a true gum. See CHEWING GUM.

GUN, a weapon consisting essentially of a metal tube that discharges a projectile by means of an explosive or, occasionally, by compressed air or a spring. Particularly, the term is applied to firearms, including revolver, rifle, and machine-gun, and to artillery pieces such as mortars and howitzers. The term, as it applies to weapons carried in the hand and fired from the shoulder, refers to the sporting gun, which discharges small shot. The first handguns were invented in China in the 14th century.

In military usage the term *gun* usually refers to cannon with a long barrel, low angle of fire, and high muzzle velocity. Guns and firearms in military organizations are elements of the organization's firepower, its ability to attack and defend against an enemy. Guns are also carried by policemen in order to protect themselves and others against criminals who may also carry a deadly weapon. Guns also provide sport, such as hunting, target shooting, and trapshooting.

Since guns are dangerous weapons, it is necessary that all persons who use them abide by rules of safety. Guns not in use should be unloaded and carried in cases to hunting or target areas. Guns should

Above is a Model 70, bolt-action, high-power Winchester repeater in closed position.

Winchester Repeating Arms Co.

Above is a Model 77 .22 rimfire autoloader Winchester repeater feeding ammunition.

be kept clean. They must never be pointed at anything except an intended target. Bullets must not be fired at water or flat, hard surfaces. See RIFLE; TRAPSHOOTING.

GUNCOTTON, a highly explosive mixture, made by treating cotton with nitric acid in a process that uses sulfuric acid as a catalyst. Actually any cellulose material is used, but since cotton is almost pure cellulose, it is oftenest used.

Guncotton is manufactured in long strings, which can be cut to any desired length. It is frequently used in connection with other explosives as well as by itself. Many types of artillery shells, for example, have double base powder for their explosive propellant. Double base powder is guncotton and nitroglycerin. The shell itself may contain such explosives as TNT or Composition B to explode on the target. Guncotton, which does not produce the great amount of smoke that gunpowder does, goes by the chemical name nitrocellulose.

GUNPOWDER, the explosive used in blasting and formerly in guns to give the propelling force to projectiles. Smokeless powders, including nitrocellulose, have largely taken the place of gunpowder in guns. Gunpowder, or black powder, is a mixture of carbon in the form of charcoal, potassium nitrate, and sulfur. The Chinese employed gunpowder in fireworks as early as the 9th century. Roger Bacon mentioned a method for making it in the 13th century. And a German monk, Berthold Schwarz, has been cited for the discovery of gunpowder. During the 16th century it came into wide military use. See GUNCOTTON.

These chanting monks are on a fresco in the famous Caves of Ajanta in India. Much of the splendid Buddhist artwork in these caves was done during the Gupta Dynasty.

GUPPY, a small tropical fish native to Barbados, Trinidad, and Venezuela. It has been introduced into many countries as an aquarium fish. The males have black, yellow, and red coloring, the color patterns being highly variable. The females are plain and when mature average 1¼ inches, being larger than the males. The males average about an inch in length. The guppy is well known as a viviparous species; that is, the young are born alive. Upward of 20 young are born each month. They mature within 12 weeks and then may have young.

GUPTA DYNASTY, one of India's greatest historical periods, lasted from about A.D. 320 to 535. The Gupta Dynasty embraced northern India. It gave that country two centuries of economic prosperity and a renaissance of art and religion.

The dynasty was founded by Chandragupta I, who ruled from 320 to 330. His successor, Samudragupta, who ruled from 330 to 375, extended the empire until it united almost as much territory as the empire of the great Asoka, who had ruled from 273 to 232 B.C. Samudragupta was a patron of poetry and music. Chandragupta II, who ruled from about 375 to 413, pushed the empire to the Arabian Sea. The acquisition of ports on this sea allowed a thriving trade with the Roman Empire. The introduction of gold and silver coins made trade much

easier. The Chinese pilgrim Fa-Hsien described the administration of Chandragupta II and was impressed with India's peace and prosperity. Kumaragupta I, who ruled from 413 to 455, may have founded the Buddhist monastery at Nalanda, which was the center of Buddhist culture until 988. Skandagupta, who ruled from 455 to 467, fought and defeated the Ephthalites (White Huns) pressing India's borders, but they persisted in their attack and eventually caused the downfall of the empire. Kumaragupta II was the last Gupta prince of the imperial line.

During the Gupta Dynasty both Hinduism and Buddhism enjoyed a revival. The social and administrative structure was defined by Brahman writers on law. The period is

known as the classical age of Sanskrit. Kalidasa (400-455) wrote great dramas, lyric poems, and epic poems. The art of the era was restrained, dignified, and refined. Important progress was made in the fields of astronomy and mathematics. Aryabhata taught the rotation of the earth and the correct value of *pi* (π). Brahmagupta organized the principles of arithmetic, geometry, and algebra. Steps were made toward a decimal system and the concept of zero in that system.

GUSTAVUS ADOLPHUS (1594-1632), the Swedish king known as the Lion of the North, was born at Stockholm. He became king in 1611. His reign was marked by a continual series of wars, the first of which were waged to settle his claim to the Swedish throne and to gain territory. Between 1611 and 1613 he fought against Denmark; between 1614 and 1617, against Russia; and from 1617 to 1629, against Poland.

In 1630, with the aid of France and Cardinal Richelieu, he entered the Thirty Years' War as a defender of German Protestantism. He first fought in Pomerania and was in the beginning opposed by German princes who favored the Holy Roman Empire. The neutrality of the elector of Brandenburg (who would not allow Adolphus to cross his territory) allowed Catholic forces to sack the city of Magdeburg in 1631. Later, Adolphus invaded Brandenburg, and the elector joined him. He fought and defeated Tilly at Leipzig in 1631. In 1632 occurred the great Battle of Lützen. He defeated the Bohemian general Wallenstein, but he himself was killed.

During the Polish campaign Gustavus Adolphus was so disabled that he could never again wear armor. Despite this, he continued to lead his troops into battle.

Brown Brothers

This monument to Johann Gutenberg (left) stands in Mainz, Germany, the printer's birthplace. Also in Mainz is the Gutenberg Museum, which has in its collection several books and manuscripts believed to have been printed by Gutenberg himself. The page reproduced below is from the priceless original Gutenberg Bible, now in the Henry E. Huntington Library and Gallery, San Marino, Calif.

Huntington Library

German Tourist Inf. Off.

Johann Gutenberg sets a page of type. At the left is his press. Printed sheets hang drying along the line at the upper right.

GYMNASTICS, a term interpreted differently in various countries. In ancient Greece young athletes and gymnasts met in the palaestra to talk with, listen to, and learn from the various great men of the day. Music was considered an essential part of education and always accompanied gymnastics.

In Germany J. F. Guts Muths wrote a famous book, *Gymnastics for Young People*, in 1793. Many of his exercises were derived from those of ancient Greece, although he added carrying exercises, balance, lifting, and climbing. However, it is to another German, F. L. Jahn, that the gymnastics of our day owes so much. He devised *Turnen*, and in 1811 he opened the first exercising area, called a *Turnplatz*, near Berlin. The gymnasts who exercised there were called turners, a term used even now. They exercised on parallel bars, horizontal bars, ropes, ladders, and rings.

In Sweden P. H. Ling devised another type of gymnastics. He said, "The aim of gymnastics is to develop the human body in the right way by means of suitable exercises." He designed different types of gymnastic equipment—wall bars, box horse, beams, and the window ladder. He also developed what he called medical gymnastics.

Franz Nachtegall of Denmark opened an outdoor gymnasium in Copenhagen in 1799, and in 1814 gymnastics became a part of the curriculum in all boys schools. Gymnastics in this case included exercises on horizontal and parallel bars

GUTENBERG, JOHANN (1400?-1468?), one of the most important developers of movable type. He was born in the German city of Mainz about 1400. He was of noble birth and held a good position in his native city until, in 1420, he was obliged to leave because of political troubles. He went to Strasbourg and is supposed to have worked at printing, though we know of no books printed by him there. In 1448 he returned to Mainz, and two years later he set up a printing office in partnership with Johann Fust, a rich goldsmith, who furnished the money. They printed a book with letters cut out of wood. Soon after, they made letters out of copper or tin and printed a Latin Bible. He and Fust separated after working together for five years, and Fust carried on the business at the same place with his son-in-law Peter Shöffer. Gutenberg set up another printing office and worked there until 1465, when he gave it up and entered the service of the Elector Adolphus of Nassau.

GUTTA-PERCHA is a tough, rubber-like gum extracted from the boles and leaves of certain wild and cultivated trees in the East Indies. It is a harder and better electrical insulator than rubber, absorbs very little water, but is not as elastic nor as strong as rubber. However, if properly protected, gutta-percha is quite stable at cool temperatures.

Gutta-percha is sold in the refined state and also in many mixtures with other and generally inferior gutta saps.

Gutta-percha is used in temporary dental fillings, golf balls, and insulation for deep-sea cables, where its imperviousness to water and its high insulating power are highly valued. However, gutta-percha is now being replaced by balata, a South American rubber-like material of similar chemical composition, and by polyethylene in the manufacture of cable insulation.

Only the finest gymnasts take part in international competition. This gymnast is displaying his skill on the side horse.

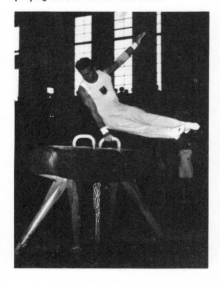

Rear Vault   Front Vault   Squat Vault   Flank Vault

SIDE HORSE

Swing from Shoulders

PARALLEL BARS

TUMBLING

Straight-Arm Handspring

Skip

as well as tumbling on mats. Later, in Denmark, Niels Bukh introduced his own system of primary gymnastics specifically to aid round-shouldered youth who worked on the farms in that agricultural nation.

Today Japan, the U.S.S.R., Germany, Czechoslovakia, Finland, Poland, and the United States rate high in gymnastics. In the United States the first national tournament for men took place in 1897, and women had their first national competition in 1931. The U.S. men's team at the 1960 Olympics performed creditably, taking fifth place; the women's team also did well. At present, gymnastics as a sport is practiced in a few schools, in more gymnastics clubs, and in a greater number of colleges and universities.

Meets are contested between two or more teams, usually in the following events: long horse, parallel bars, horizontal bar, still (sometimes swinging) rings, side horse (pommel horse), free exercises, trampolin, and tumbling. Participation by individual athletes of each team in each event is stressed; thus a high standard of fitness is both demanded and achieved. The sport for girls develops poise, grace, and a well-formed body; for boys, strength and agility without bulky muscles.

GYMNOSPERM, a seed plant whose seeds are not enclosed by an ovary during their development. The gymnosperms constitute the class Gymnospermae, which is one of the two large classes of the division Spermatophyta (the seed plants). The angiosperms, or flowering plants, which constitute the other large spermatophyte class, have their developing seeds enclosed by an ovary. Present-day gymnosperms include the pine, spruce, fir, hemlock, cypress, redwood, and other coniferous trees, also yew, cycads, and the ginkgo tree.

The ovules of gymnosperms do not develop within flowers and are not enclosed by ovaries. Gymnosperms do not grow any type of flower. The word *gymnosperm* is derived from two Greek words that mean "naked" and "seed." The naked ovules of coniferous gymnosperms grow upon the upper surface of the scales of their ovulate cones. The ovules develop into seeds after they have been fertilized by pollen, which is borne by the wind from staminate cones.

The gymnosperms evolved before the angiosperms did and are lower in the evolutionary scale than the angiosperms. The gymnosperms flourished and were most numerous during the remote geologic past. Certain gymnosperms that lived about 250 million years ago formed part of the coal that is burned today. Three entire orders and many species of these ancient gymnosperms are now extinct but are represented by fossils.

Most gymnosperms of the North Temperate Zone are coniferous trees and shrubs, the leaves of which are in the form of needles or scales. Most of these conifers are evergreen; they retain most of their needles during winter and shed them a few at a time throughout the entire year. The large forests of northern and northwestern North America consist largely of pine, spruce, fir, and other coniferous trees. See ANGIOSPERM.

The twigs, needles, and cones of several coniferous gymnosperms are shown below. Needles of conifers are actually modified leaves. All conifers bear two types of cones: ovulate and staminate. Ovulate cones produce ovules, which, when fertilized, will develop into seeds. Staminate cones produce pollen grains that fertilize the ovules. In all coniferous species ovulate cones are larger than staminate cones.

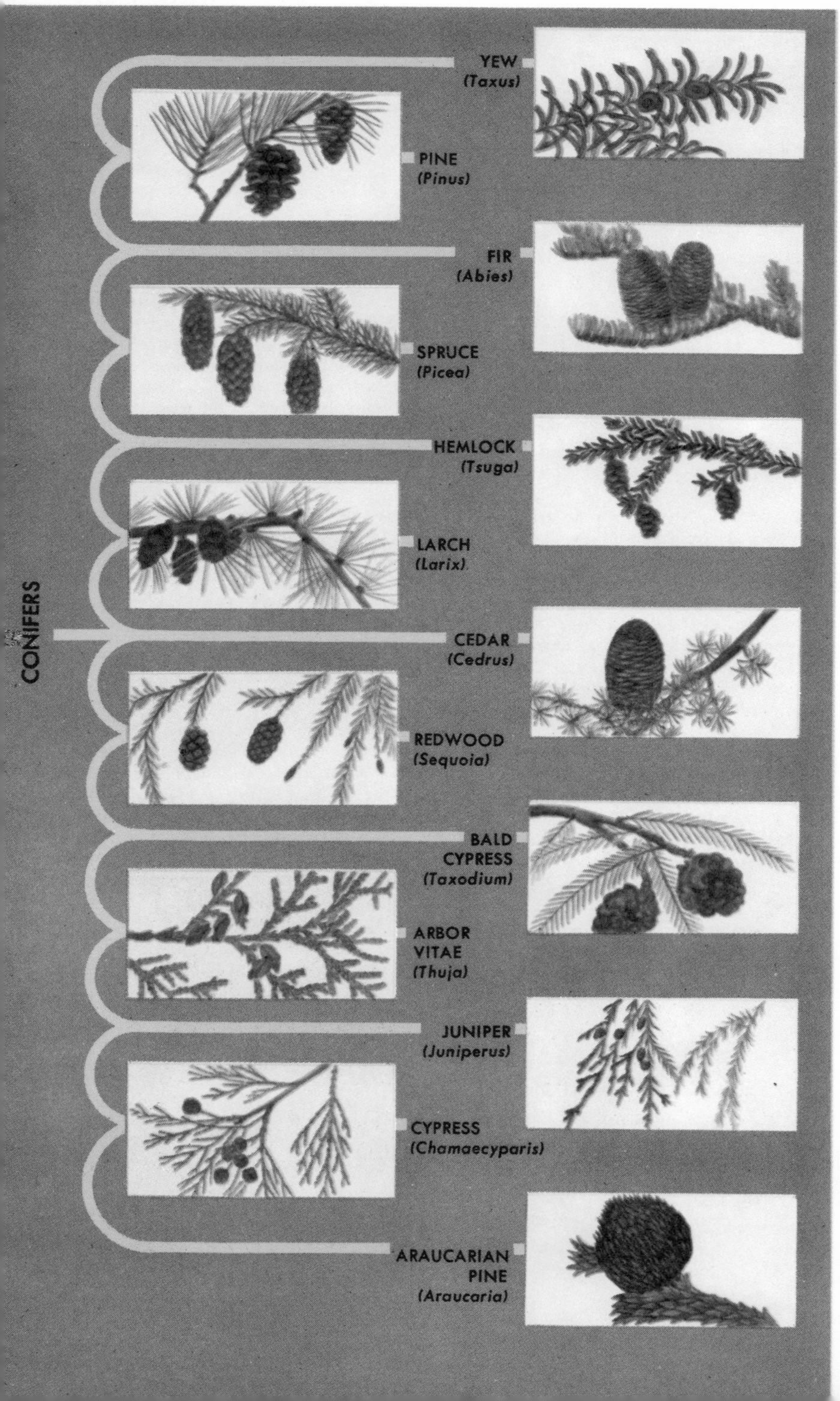

CONIFERS

YEW
(Taxus)

PINE
(Pinus)

FIR
(Abies)

SPRUCE
(Picea)

HEMLOCK
(Tsuga)

LARCH
(Larix)

CEDAR
(Cedrus)

REDWOOD
(Sequoia)

BALD
CYPRESS
(Taxodium)

ARBOR
VITAE
(Thuja)

JUNIPER
(Juniperus)

CYPRESS
(Chamaecyparis)

ARAUCARIAN
PINE
(Araucaria)

GYPSIES. One day about 500 years ago the residents of Lüneburg, Germany, crowded to the city walls to see a strange group of people who wanted admittance into the city. These wayfarers were short, dark, and well proportioned, with jet black hair and eyes. Some of the men were very handsome, and the women, beautiful. Children were very numerous. They had traveled on carts drawn by donkeys and horses. The spokesmen, who were called the Count and the Duke, told a romantic tale of a flight from exotic Egypt to escape the Saracens. The people of Lüneburg were moved by the tale and allowed the "Egyptians" to encamp in the city. A day later the wanderers disappeared, and the inhabitants of Lüneburg were somewhat poorer in eggs, poultry, silver, and purses.

These were the Gypsies, and they did not really come from Egypt as their name suggests. They probably came from the Indus River valley and were first heard of in Persia in about 900. They entered Europe in the 14th century and since then have spread throughout the world. Real Gypsies are Romany, a distinct Oriental people. They have their own language (the word *Dad* was originally from Romany), their own customs, and even their own laws.

The Gypsies are noted musicians. They may even have introduced the violin into Europe, a splendid gift to bring with them if this is so. The Gypsies excel in handicrafts: basketmaking, copperwork, and the mending of chinaware. The women are often good herbalists, and the men are sometimes capable animal doctors. Most of the women also engage in fortune telling, a practice that they pursue with a great deal of pomp and ceremony. Sometimes their predictions prove to be surprisingly accurate.

Unfortunately the Gypsies are not noted for their respect for property rights. This fact, plus the natural suspicions aroused by any strange, wandering people, gave rise to stories about poisoning, child stealing, and witchcraft. The fact that major crimes were rare among the Gypsies did not prevent the persecution of them throughout Europe.

A number of Gypsies have become quite famous. Sir Richard Burton, who was half Gypsy, became a great English explorer, and in all probability John Bunyan, the author of *Pilgrim's Progress*, was a pureblooded Gypsy.

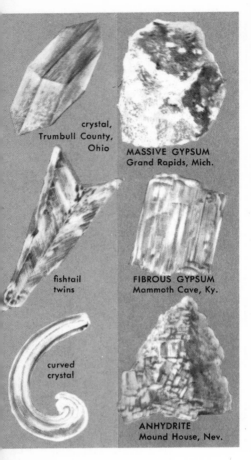

crystal, Trumbull County, Ohio

MASSIVE GYPSUM
Grand Rapids, Mich.

fishtail twins

FIBROUS GYPSUM
Mammoth Cave, Ky.

curved crystal

ANHYDRITE
Mound House, Nev.

Gypsum appears naturally in many forms. Its commonest occurrence is in thick sedimentary beds. Gypsum may also be deposited from the fumes of a volcano, from hot mineral springs, or from sulfate solutions seeping through veins of rock. Gypsum is sometimes lightly tinted with impurities of different colors.

GYPSUM, a colorless or white mineral when pure, found in many parts of the world and widely used in plaster, plasterboard, and other building materials. Gypsum is also a chemically precipitated sedimentary rock. It is precipitated from sea water and is commonly found near limestones and salt deposits. (See SEDIMENTARY ROCK.) When dried and ground into white powder, it is called plaster of paris, as it was first made in the Montmartre district of Paris. Each year over 8,000,000 tons of gypsum are mined in the United States, most of it in New York, Ohio, Michigan, South Dakota, Kansas, Texas, and California. Large quantities of gypsum are also produced in Canada, the United Kingdom, Austria, Germany, France, the Union of Soviet Socialist Republics, and Mexico.

GYROSCOPE. A gyroscope is a heavy wheel or disk that can be made to rotate rapidly about an axle. The disk and axle are usually mounted in a ring. This ring is mounted on delicate bearings inside other rings, called gimbal rings. The outer rings can be moved or turned without applying force to the axle of the gyroscope disk.

When a heavy wheel or disk spins rapidly about an axis, it has a large angular momentum. It not only tends to continue spinning, but it tends to maintain its axis of spin in a constant direction. If a coin is placed on its edge while it is stationary, the coin falls on its side. If the coin is rolling, however, it will stay on its edge for some time. When the coin rolls, it tends to maintain its horizontal axis of rotation.

When a force is applied to a spinning disk, or the axle of a spinning disk, to make the axis change orientation, the disk responds with a distinctive motion called precession. The spinning disk tends to move so that its axis of rotation is at right angles to the plane in which the force is applied. The motion of precession can be observed in a simple hoop. When a hoop is rolling, its axis of rotation is horizontal. To make a hoop turn a corner, press sideways against the top of the rolling hoop with a stick as if you wanted the hoop to fall on its side. You are trying to change the axis of rotation to a vertical axis in the same plane in which the force is applied. The hoop will refuse to have its axis of rotation shifted in this manner. It will promptly turn its horizontal axis in a new horizontal direction so that the hoop goes rolling off in a new path.

Because the gyroscope can furnish a reference axis that is unaffected by such disturbing forces as gravity and acceleration, it has been utilized in devices used in many fields, especially in navigation. Applications of the gyroscope in navigation, both marine and air, include the gyrocompass, which provides a constant true-north direction despite rolling, pitching, and yawing movements of a vessel. The turn indicator, one of the basic flight instruments, is an aircraft instrument that utilizes gyroscopic precession to register the rate of turn.

The automatic pilot uses gyroscopes to keep an aircraft on a straight and level course. Any movement causes a change in relative position of the gyro cases (fastened to the airplane) and the gyro wheels (which remain rigid in space). The amount of change is transmitted hydraulically or electrically to move the ailerons, elevators, and rudder, the total amount being that necessary to correct the aircraft's position. The automatic pilot thus relieves the regular pilot from the necessity of making the countless movements of the controls needed to keep the aircraft on course. (See AUTOMATIC PILOT.) Ships may also be equipped with automatic steering devices that are connected with the gyrocompass.

Gyroscopes are used in inertial guidance systems in guided missiles. See GUIDED MISSILE.

The gyroscope resists any tilting force applied to its axis. A ship's gyrocompass is a gyroscope mounted horizontally and oriented toward the north. As the ship turns and moves about over the earth, the gyrocompass moves in its fixed mounting to indicate true north. The gyrocompass is not affected by magnetism and so can be used to navigate in the polar regions, where the magnetic compass is unreliable because of magnetic deviation.

Sperry Gyroscope Co.

H is the eighth letter of the English alphabet and most cognate alphabets. In classical Greek the symbol appears as *eta*, representing the long, open e sound. In music H is the German name for B natural, B being reserved for B-flat. In chemistry H is the symbol for the element hydrogen. Lowercase italic H (*h*) stands for Planck's constant in physics.

HABEAS CORPUS, a legal order, or writ, compelling an authority holding a person prisoner to present the prisoner and the evidence against him before the court or the judge issuing the writ. The writ must be issued on request. Its purpose is to decide whether the detention of the prisoner (usually one accused of a criminal offense) is legal. The writ is dismissed if detention is legal. It is sustained if the prisoner is held illegally, in which case he is released. Habeas corpus is the most famous of the legal writs and has been called the writ of liberty.

The writ of habeas corpus came into use after the Magna Charta in 1215. Its use was common by the reign of Henry VI of England. At first it was used to relieve private restraints, but during the reign of Henry VII it was also used against the crown. Gradually, habeas corpus came to be regarded as a constitutional remedy. The Habeas Corpus Act of 1679 imposed heavy penalties on judges refusing without adequate reason to entertain the writ and on authorities ignoring it. The English colonists held habeas corpus in high regard. Its use is provided for by the Constitution, although it may be suspended "when in Cases of Rebellion or Invasion the public Safety may require it." In 1863 President Abraham Lincoln was authorized to suspend the writ partially, and the Confederacy also suspended it. The right of habeas corpus does not exist in most European countries, where provisions of the criminal code are used instead to protect individuals against illegal imprisonment. A number of Latin American nations have adopted the writ.

In England the writ of habeas corpus may be issued by a divisional court of the Queen's Bench Division or by a judge of the High Court. State courts or federal courts, in cases of federal jurisdiction, may issue the writ in the United States.

It may be issued when an individual is held on a criminal charge or for a number of miscellaneous cases, such as when a test is made of the jurisdiction of a court in committing a person for contempt or when the legality of the detention of a person held under quarantine or health regulations is in question.

HABIT, a tendency or disposition to perform, in a given manner, certain actions, acquired by frequent repetition. Both mental and bodily habits come about as the result of the repetition of a specific act. The phrase "practice makes perfect" refers to this repetition. Each movement of the body involves reactions in the nervous system; brain, spinal cord, and nerves branching from the nerve cells are under the law of habit. The body gradually comes to be a complex nerve-muscle machine responding to stimuli in certain definite ways because such responses have been made before. In physical acts, such as swimming or riding a bicycle or any act requiring skill, one must continually repeat a performance before it becomes a habit. Repetition eliminates unnecessary movements, coordinates those needed, and permits attention to be withdrawn from the process. A boy riding a bicycle for the first time has many movement habits but none that fits this situation. He cannot gain balance at first; he makes too many movements and expends too much energy, characteristics of the beginning of

every habit. The boy finally establishes his balance and rides the bicycle for a few feet before losing balance, but his memory recalls the successful performance and aids him in repeating it. Unnecessary movements are eliminated, and in a comparatively short time he is riding without paying close attention to the manner in which he is succeeding. Bad or undesirable habits are acquired in the same manner as beneficial habits and become so thoroughly automatic that they can be thrown off only with the greatest difficulty.

HABITAT, the type of natural environment to which an animal or plant is best adapted and in which it normally lives. Examples of different animal and plant habitats are a tropical rain forest, a temperate forest, a desert, a prairie, the arctic tundra, a fresh-water lake, and a fresh-water stream. In biological terminology the habitat of an animal or plant species is not the same as its range. The term *habitat* designates the particular type of natural environment to which a species is best adapted, whereas the term *range* designates the actual geographical distribution of the species.

The major and most comprehensive habitats are the ocean, fresh water, and dry land. Each of these major habitats, however, is divisible into many minor habitats, each of which differs considerably from the others.

Different types of land habitats have produced the fast running antelope and the aquatic beaver. The sea urchin and the starfish flourish in a tidewater habitat.

The minor habitats of the ocean, for example, are the littoral zone, the pelagic zone, and the abyssal zone. The littoral zone extends from the high tide line of the shore to a depth of 300 feet. Fauna of the littoral zone include clams, barnacles, mussels, snails, and starfish. Littoral flora include kelp and algae. The pelagic zone is the open sea from its surface to the maximum depth of light penetration. Most familiar ocean fish inhabit this zone. The abyssal zone, which lies beneath the maximum depth of light penetration, is a region of absolute darkness and tremendous pressure, where the temperature remains constantly near the freezing point. Although plants do not live in the abyssal zone, animals such as fish, starfish, clams, sponges, and crustaceans inhabit even the deepest parts of it. Abyssal fish either have very large eyes or no eyes whatsoever. They have long, extremely sensitive tactile antennae. Many are luminescent.

HACIENDA, an enormous landholding found throughout Latin America. For many years after the Spanish conquest much of the land of Latin America was divided into haciendas. The hacienda system meant that only a few wealthy people owned land. The majority of the people lived on the haciendas and worked for the landowners at such low wages that they were never able to buy their own land. The discontent of these landless people, the peons as they are called in Mexico, was one of the causes of the Mexican revolutions lasting from 1911 to 1920. In some Latin American countries the land is still chiefly in the hands of the hacienda owners.

HADES. See PLUTO.

HAGEN, JOHN (1908-　　　), an American astronomer, was born in Amherst, Nova Scotia. He completed his education at Yale, where he received a Ph.D. in 1933. He was subsequently engaged in astronomical research and was a member of various expeditions to study eclipses. In the 1950's he was appointed project director for the U. S. earth satellite project and later became head of the U. S. Navy Vanguard project for space exploration.

HAGUE, THE, the seat of government of The Netherlands, on the coast of the North Sea. It has a population of about 600,000. The Hague is principally a royal city and a city of upper-middle-class residences, with many large parks and tree-lined streets. Among the fine old buildings of the city are the royal palace; the royal library; the Gothic church of St. James, dating from the 15th century; the Mauritshuis Gallery, housing works of the famous Dutch painters; and the Peace Palace, a gift from Andrew Carnegie.

Before 1250 the counts of Holland had a hunting lodge here. In 1250 William II, emperor of the Holy Roman Empire, built a castle on the spot, around which a town grew. Count Albert moved the Court of Justice of Holland and Zeeland to the castle at the end of the 14th century. The Hague became the seat of government in 1618 when Prince Maurice took residence here. The city has often been the center of international conferences. Meetings of the European governments were held here in 1899 and 1907 to discuss ways of preventing war, and in 1922 the Permanent Court of International Justice was established at The Hague. In 1946 the name was changed to International Court of Justice. This court continues to meet in the Peace Palace. During World War II the city suffered damage from the German occupation and from Allied bombing but was quickly rebuilt.

HAGUE TRIBUNAL. See PERMANENT COURT OF ARBITRATION.

HAIL. It used to be supposed that hail was merely rain frozen on its passage to earth by passing through a very cold layer of air. But now, on more careful examination with better instruments, we know that hail formation is not so simple.

Frozen rain does fall, but it is called sleet, and there is also a form of globular or granular snow, like fine shot, which often precedes an ordinary snowfall, but this is not true hail. (See SLEET.) True hail falls only in hot weather, at the beginning of a thunderstorm. It is more plentiful, and often the hailstones are larger, in tropical climates than in temperate ones. It never falls in the arctic regions.

When examined, hailstones are found to be lumps of ice with a nucleus, or kernel, sometimes of snow, sometimes of clear ice. Around this nucleus are layers of ice that are clear, opaque, or mixed. Sometimes they have a radial, or wheel-spoke, structure. In shape they may be spherical, drop shaped, conical pyramidal, or even flat, like lenses. They vary greatly in size but are

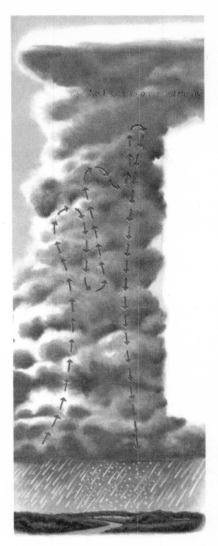

The arrows in this picture trace the path of a hailstone in a thundercloud.

At right is a giant hailstone. Below, a cross section of a hailstone.

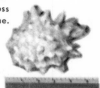

usually from $\frac{1}{10}$ to $\frac{1}{4}$ inch in diameter. Many instances have been recorded of larger hailstones, sometimes as much as 3 or 4 inches in diameter, falling and, of course, doing enormous damage. In July, 1928, a hailstone weighing $1\frac{1}{2}$ pounds fell at Potter, Neb. It was $5\frac{1}{2}$ inches in diameter. Hailstorms very rarely last more than a few minutes, but a five-minute fall will often wreck the crops of a whole neighborhood.

Fritz Henle—Photo Researchers

Haitian men and women transport their wares either on their heads or on small burros. The Negroes lead a primitive life.

HAIR, one of numerous filaments growing from the skin of most mammals. In structure a single human hair is a shaft projecting from a pit, or depression, in the skin. The projecting part of the hair is dead. The root, concealed at the base in the pit, expands into a club-shaped bulb, which derives nourishment from the living cells below. Directly beneath the bulb is tissue that has blood vessels and nerves that supply the hair root.

Hair varies in length, thickness, and color on different parts of the body and in different races of mankind. Straight hairs are stronger than curly hairs and present a cylindrical or oval outline. Curly hairs, on the other hand, are flattened.

Gray hair is hair that has lost its natural pigment. Hair may become gray at any age and in either sex. People frequently have gray hair in their twenties, but in most people the first signs of grayness appear in the forties. Severe illnesses and sudden shocking experiences may hasten the process of graying. Also, gray hair has been known to regain its original coloring with no apparent cause. The reason that pigment fails to form in the hair with increasing age is unknown.

The hair of animals may be used in the manufacture of fabrics and other materials, such as bristles and stuffing. See FUR.

HAITI, a republic that forms the western third of the island of Hispaniola in the West Indies. It is the only Negro nation in the Western Hemisphere. Haiti is famous for its voodoo ceremonies, but stories of these have been greatly exaggerated. The capital is Port-au-Prince; other chief cities are Les Cayes, Gonaïves, Jérémie, Jacmel, and Cap-Haïtien. The country is 10,714 square miles in area, or a little larger than Vermont. It has a population of a little more than 3,500,000.

Haiti is almost entirely mountainous and is shaped roughly like a horseshoe with the two arms pointing westward and the Gulf of Gonaïves between them. There are five plains on which most of the people live. The only large river is the Artibonite, which flows across the country and into the Gulf of Gonaïves. The climate is pleasantly warm all year except for a few spots, notably Port-au-Prince, which has the highest average temperature of any large city in the Caribbean area. Haiti is rich in timber and minerals, but these are undeveloped. Most of the people work in agriculture. They grow coffee, bananas, sugarcane, sisal, cotton, cacao, and castor beans. Most of the trade is with the United States, Italy, France, and Belgium, with the United States receiving the largest part. There are very few industrial plants.

Ninety-five percent of the people are Negro; the rest are mulatto. Haiti is one of the most thickly settled countries in the Western Hemisphere, with 291 people per square mile as compared with 50 per square mile in the United States. The people have a very low standard of living and have kept some of their African customs. Only 15 percent of the people can read and write. The official language is French, but most of the uneducated people speak a dialect known as Creole.

The two outstanding sights of the country lie in the Cap-Haïtien region in the north; they are the mountaintop citadel of La Ferrière and the palace of Sans Souci. The citadel, built as a fortress by order of the Negro king Henri Christophe (1811-1820), is one of the most imposing ruins in the Western Hemisphere. The palace, also built by the king, suggests one of the splendid residences of an 18th-century European monarch.

The island was discovered by Christopher Columbus on his first voyage in 1492 and was settled by the Spaniards. The native Arawak Indians were put to work on the sugar plantations, and soon the entire native population died out. Negro slaves were imported from Africa to replace them. About 1630 some Frenchmen settled on the west coast, and by the Treaty of Ryswick, in 1697, Haiti was given to

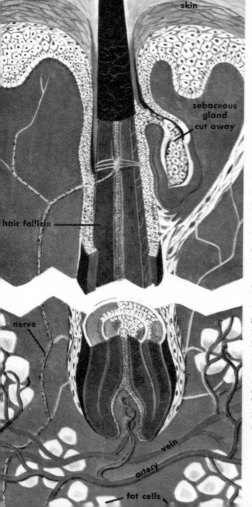

The root of a human hair is set in a special shaft called a follicle. A cutaway drawing of a hair and hair follicle is presented below. Veins and arteries supply the growing hair through living tissue that extends into the bulb, or lower part, of the root. The sebaceous gland produces an oily secretion that helps keep the skin supple.

skin

sebaceous gland cut away

hair follicle

nerve

vein

artery

fat cells

Florida

Atlantic Ocean

Bahama Islands

Cuba

HAITI

Dominican Republic

Puerto Rico

Caribbean Sea

0   200

Miles

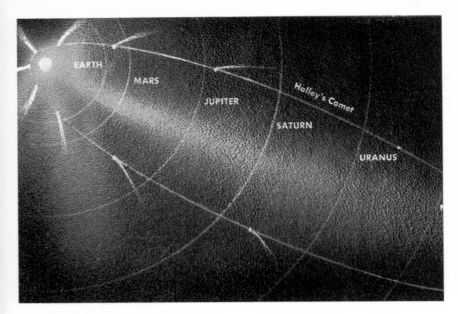

Halley's comet travels in a very eccentric orbit that extends beyond the orbit of Neptune. The comet requires about 75 years to complete one revolution.

In 1910 the tail of Halley's comet stretched for 37 million miles halfway across our sky. On May 21 of that year the earth passed through the tail, but no effects at all could be detected.

HALL OF FAME, a memorial, on the Bronx campus of New York University, to great men and women of the United States. Every five years up to seven new people are chosen by a majority vote of the electors. The names of those chosen and their likenesses in bronze are in the colonnade of the Hall of Fame.

Since 1922 only people who have been dead for 25 years are eligible. Before that, people who had been dead for ten years could be represented in the memorial.

The people who elect the members of the Hall of Fame are prominent men and women from all 50 states and from various fields. The electors are chosen by the director of the Hall of Fame and serve for life. The nominations come from citizens of the United States.

HALLOWEEN, also known as Allhallows Eve, is a celebration held every year on the evening and night of October 31. The name is a shortened form of "Hallows Evening," the evening before Allhallows, or All Saints' Day, when all saints are honored.

Since the 9th century All Saints' Day has been a Roman Catholic feast, and its eve has been a time of vigil and fasting. However, in some countries, particularly in the United States, the night of October 31 has become chiefly one of merrymaking.

Jack-o'-lanterns carved from pumpkins, cardboard skeletons, witches on broomsticks, and ghost costumes are popular as symbols of the day. Boys and girls attend "spooky" Halloween parties and go from house to house demanding "trick or treat." If they do not get the treat, usually candy or cookies, they are likely to perform such pranks as soaping the windows of the house. The trick-or-treat custom probably originated in Ireland during the 1600's. At that time peasants went from door to door asking for money to buy food for a feast.

The ancient Druids in Britain are thought to have started the customs of Halloween hundreds of years before the birth of Christ. They believed that on October 31 the lord of death gathered together all the souls of the dead who had been condemned to enter the bodies of animals. He then decided which animals the dead souls would enter the next year.

During the Middle Ages people believed that Halloween was the night when witches and ghosts were most likely to wander across the earth. The Scots are thought to have originated the belief that witches rode broomsticks through the sky to meet the devil.

HALLUCINATION, a false perception or group of perceptions usually produced by a disordered nervous system. Hallucinations usually occur during a tense emotional state and may be related to any of the sense organs. The most common are hallucinations of hearing, in which case the sounds may seem to come from any part of the body. The dan-

ger in such situations is that the voices may compel abnormal activities. Hallucinations of sight are frequently related to the emotion of fear and produce a greater distortion of reality. They may be associated with the form of alcoholic poisoning known as delirium tremens. The strength of hallucinations varies, and the person experiencing them may be unsure of their reality. Hallucinations are symptoms, and their basis may be mental disease, various forms of poisoning, or organic diseases of the body.

HALO, a colored or whitish ring that sometimes surrounds the sun or the moon. Halos are formed in high cirrostratus clouds. When the light from the heavenly bodies strikes the tiny needles of ice that make up these clouds, it is refracted as it passes through them. The refraction breaks the light into the colors that compose it. A large ring, with red on the inside and blue on the outside, is formed. These colors are in opposite order to those in a corona, which is formed differently. The whitish halo is formed when the light is reflected from the surface of the ice particles but does not pass through them.

The halo may be a sign of bad weather coming. This is because cirrostratus clouds are often followed by lower, rain-bearing clouds.

The halo came to be identified with the idea of perfection. That is the reason halos, or glories, are shown in religious paintings of saints. See CORONA.

This halo is caused by the refraction of moonlight by ice crystals in the sky.

HALOGEN. The elements fluorine, chlorine, bromine, and iodine are similar in many of their chemical and physical properties. They are classed together as a family and are called halogens. They combine with sodium to form substances much like common salt. This family includes the most chemically active of the nonmetallic elements. Because of their strong tendency to remove electrons from other substances, they are powerful oxidizing agents. The halogens form salts by electron transfer and nonpolar compounds by electron sharing. See IONIZATION.

Courtesy of The Art Institute of Chicago

This oil painting entitled "The Rommelpot Player" is by the Dutch artist Frans Hals.

HALS, FRANS (1580?-1666), was a Dutch painter. He is famous for his portraits and his scenes from everyday life. One of his most outstanding characteristics was his ability to portray the facial expressions of his subjects.

Hals was born in Antwerp, but he went to Haarlem as a youth and remained there for the rest of his life. He headed the painter's guild in Haarlem and painted many works for groups in the city, but he never became wealthy, and during his last years he lived on a pension granted to him by the city.

Hals's works include eight group portraits of organizations and officials in Haarlem. He is considered one of the leaders in the development of group portraiture. His outstanding single paintings include "The Laughing Cavalier," "The Merry Drinker," "The Rommelpot Player," "The Merry Lute Player," and the "Fisher Boy."

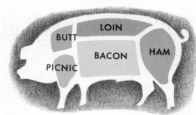

Courtesy of Ford Motor Company

The illustration above shows the location of ham in relation to other pork cuts. The ham may be divided into the shank half, the butt half, ham roast, center slice, or boneless ham roll. Each hog has two hams, which make up about 19 percent of the hog's pork.

HAM, the thigh of the hog. It is usually cured rather than sold as fresh pork. Curing is done by injecting the fresh meat with a sweet pickle solution of salt, sugar, and other materials, which give a characteristic flavor, texture, and appearance. Smoking follows, which also adds flavor and heats the meat to a temperature of 137° F. or more.

The two main types of ham on the market are the cook-before-eating ham, which is heated to 140 degrees or more and requires further cooking, and the fully cooked ham, which has the flavor, texture, and color of a cooked product and may be used cold or heated to serving temperature. Country-style cured hams, with less moisture and sharper flavor, are rarely found on the market; if so, they belong in the category of gourmet foods. Ham may be purchased in many styles and forms—shankless and skinless, or with the bone and skin partially or completely removed, and whole, half, or sliced and canned.

HAMBURG is a free city in Germany and, at the same time, a small state divided into seven administrative districts. It is located on the north German lowland, along the Elbe River, about 55 miles from the North Sea. It is the largest port and the second largest city in Germany. Canals from the Elbe intersect the eastern and lower parts of the city in all directions. By 1954 the harbor damage of World War II had been repaired so that about 200 large ships could be accommodated at one time. By 1960 the city had about 1,800,000 inhabitants. In addition to being a port and a shipbuilding city, Hamburg is an important financial center and also manufactures rubber, tobacco, food products, textiles, and machinery.

There are few old buildings left in Hamburg; a disastrous fire gutted the city in 1842, and 50 percent of

the city was destroyed in World War II. Broad boulevards and new buildings erected in the course of reconstruction have also taken a large toll of the city's historic sites. Many modern buildings have been constructed since 1945.

Hamburg was founded by Charlemagne in the early 9th century. In the 13th century, with Lübeck, it set up the Hanseatic League. In 1871 Hamburg joined the German Empire as a free port. After World War II it was occupied by the British. The British moved out in 1948. The city constitution of 1952 vested the supreme power in the city in a house of burgesses of 120 members.

HAMBURGER, finely ground beef, was originally eaten raw. Today it is usually broiled, fried, or baked in any of a variety of dishes. The term is also applied to a sandwich, usually a bun containing a broiled or fried cake of hamburger.

Hamburger is named for the city of Hamburg, Germany. The early traders of Hamburg brought back from the Baltic provinces of Russia a taste for red meat, shredded with a dull knife and eaten raw. Thus the original Hamburg steak was raw meat, shredded and seasoned. Recipes for this dish, called steak tartare, still appear in cookbooks.

One of the most adaptable of the less expensive meats, hamburger may be served in hamburger steaks, meat loaf, hash, meatballs, chili con carne, and many other dishes. Like the ice-cream cone, the popular sandwich was supposedly introduced at the Louisiana Purchase Exposition of 1904.

Although Hamburg, Germany, was bombed in World War II, it again is a great seaport.
Inter Nationes

HAMILTON, ALEXANDER (1755-1804), a famous American statesman, was born on the island of Nevis, West Indies. His father having failed in business, young Hamilton was cared for by relatives, who sent him to New York, where he entered King's College (now Columbia). When the Revolutionary War broke out, Hamilton sided with the Americans and made speeches and wrote against the English. Although only 17 years old, he became famous in the city. He joined a company of soldiers. He took part in several battles and soon attracted the attention of Washington, who made him his secretary. He later resigned this post to participate in active fighting and distinguished himself at the Battle of Yorktown. When the war ended, he became a lawyer in New York City and was soon very successful. He took great interest in politics and devoted much effort to strengthening the federal government. He was largely responsible for the calling of the convention that drew up the Constitution. He persuaded the New York legislature to ratify the Constitution. As author of most of *The Federalist*, a group of essays that are political classics, he did much to win acceptance of the Constitution in other states.

When Washington became president, he chose Hamilton to be the first secretary of the treasury. Hamilton placed the new government on a firm financial basis by his policies, which included payment of the national debt in full, assumption of the state debts, increased excise duties, and the establishment of a national bank. He believed also in a strong central government and developed the doctrine of implied

Secretary of the Treasury Alexander Hamilton (right) speaks to President Washington.

Independence National Historical Park Collection; Courtesy of TIME

The American statesman Alexander Hamilton was the author of most of *The Federalist*.

powers. He distrusted the common people, whom he believed incapable of self-government, and he thought the safety of the nation lay in keeping power in the hands of the intelligent, educated, and propertied classes. Hamilton's policies made him a leader of the Federalists and brought him into constant conflict with Thomas Jefferson, who favored a weak central government. In 1795 Hamilton resigned to reenter private law practice.

In 1800 his influence defeated Aaron Burr, who was Jefferson's chief rival for the presidency. In 1804 Hamilton again used his influence to defeat Burr, this time when he was seeking the governorship of New York. Burr became angry with him and challenged him to fight a duel. The duel took place at Weehawken, N. J., opposite New York. Hamilton received a wound of which he died the next day.

HAMILTON, EMMA. See NELSON, HORATIO.

HAMLET (full title *The Tragedy of Hamlet, Prince of Denmark*), a tragedy by William Shakespeare, was first performed at the Globe Theatre in London in 1600 or 1601. Since then it has probably been played more often than any other tragedy, and it is considered by many to be the greatest tragedy ever written.

The drama is set in a castle in Elsinore, Denmark. Hamlet, a prince, returns home from his studies in Germany to find that his

father, the king, has died and that Claudius, the dead king's brother, not only has made himself king but also has married the dead king's widow, Hamlet's mother, Gertrude. The ghost of Hamlet's father informs Hamlet that he had been murdered by Claudius and extracts from Hamlet a promise of revenge. Hamlet seems fully determined to fulfill this vow and to murder Claudius, but he is plagued by a desire to justify in every detail any action he may take. His resulting hesitation proves to be his undoing.

In order to hide his intention to kill Claudius, Hamlet pretends to be insane. He gives the impression that Ophelia, daughter of the court official Polonius, is the cause of his distress. In order to test the ghost's story, Hamlet has a group of traveling players re-enact the murder. The king's reaction convinces Hamlet of his guilt, but Hamlet almost immediately forgoes an excellent opportunity to kill the king and instead violently reproaches his mother for her relations with Claudius. During his tirade Hamlet realizes that someone is eavesdropping behind a tapestry and, thinking it to be Claudius, stabs him, only to discover that he has killed Polonius.

Claudius is now fully aware of Hamlet's intentions and so sends him to England with orders that he be killed. Hamlet escapes and returns to Denmark to discover that Ophelia, driven mad by his rejection of her and by his killing of her father, has drowned. Laertes, Polonius' son and Ophelia's brother, has meanwhile returned from Paris to avenge his father's death. Claudius and Laertes conceive a plot against Hamlet: Hamlet and Laertes will engage in a supposedly friendly fencing match, but Laertes will use a poisoned foil, a scratch from which will prove fatal. To insure success, a poisoned drink will be given Hamlet. In the course of the fencing match both Hamlet and Laertes are wounded by the poisoned foil, Gertrude mistakenly drinks some of the poison, and Hamlet, now on the verge of death, finally kills Claudius. All four are dead when the curtain falls.

Hamlet is among the most complex characters ever created, and many theories have been put forward to explain the behavior of the "melancholy Dane." Perhaps the commonest is that Hamlet is a victim of introspection—that is, he thinks too much about himself and his planned course of action to the extent that his ability to act force-the Renaissance, unconsciously realizes are outdated. There has also been much discussion about the nature of Hamlet's madness. Many accept it at its face value as a pretense, but others maintain that Hamlet is genuinely mad or that he is a madman pretending to be even more insane than he really is. Freudian psychologists attribute Hamlet's problems to a neurotic attachment to his mother. Whichever theories are correct—and there is probably some truth in all of them—what is most important is that *Hamlet* remains among the most moving and thought-provoking creations of the human mind.

In 1953 Swedish statesman Dag Hammarskjöld became secretary general of the UN.
UPI

The Rank Organisation

This is a scene from a popular film version of Shakespeare's great play *Hamlet*, starring Sir Laurence Olivier, Jean Simmons, Basil Sydney, and Eileen Herlie.

fully is dissipated by his moral scruples. Other scholars explain his difficulties by pointing out that murdering a king is a rather difficult task; others, that Hamlet, being a very intelligent man, realizes that revenge will accomplish nothing good and is therefore unable to work up the passionate fury necessary to commit murder; still others, that he is being asked to act according to medieval ideals that he, a man of

Excellent productions of Shakespeare's plays are given annually at the Stratford Festival, Ontario, Canada. Below, Christopher Plummer and others in a scene from *Hamlet*.

Photo, Peter Smith, Stratford Shak. Festival

HAMMARSKJÖLD, DAG (1905-   ), secretary general of the United Nations since 1953, was born in Jonkoping, Sweden. His family has furnished many statesmen and military men to Sweden. Trained at Uppsala University in law and political economy, Hammarskjöld soon entered government service. Some of his positions have been secretary of the Bank of Sweden (1935-1936), under secretary of the Swedish department of finance (1936-1945), chairman of the board of governors of the Bank of Sweden (1941-1948), vice-chairman of the Organization for European Economic Cooperation (1948-1949), deputy foreign minister of Sweden and Cabinet member (1951-1952), vice-chairman of the Swedish delegation to the UN General Assembly in 1952, and chairman of the Swedish delegation in 1953.

As secretary general, Hammarskjöld has been noted for his ability to work around the clock in times of crisis and for his quiet and continuous diplomatic negotiations with leaders in all parts of the world. The latter have included his 1955 talks with leaders in Communist China, talks that eventually resulted in the release of U.S. and other airmen taken captive in the Korean War, and discussions with leaders in the Middle East on the various difficulties contributing to the friction between the Arab countries and Israel and on other middle-eastern problems.

Hammarskjöld's actions during the Suez and Congo crises significantly increased the strength and authority of the United Nations. Under the authorization of the UN General Assembly he planned and supervised the formation of the United Nations Emergency Force sent to enforce the cease fire after the Suez crisis. Its patrolling of the Gaza Strip has largely prevented the type of border raids and incidents that resulted in Israel's invasion of the Sinai Peninsula. Hammarskjöld also laid the groundwork for, and directed the formation of, the larger UN force sent to the Congo. The UN under his direction also sent to the Congo food, fuel, and medical and technical aid. Hammarskjöld and members of his staff have observed and reported on the situation in the Congo and have negotiated with local leaders. In the course of the Congo crisis Hammarskjöld was twice attacked severely by the Soviet Union, which claimed that the secretary general was too powerful and was furthering the interests of the Western powers in the Congo and suggested that the secretary general be replaced by a three-man presidium. After the first attack the General Assembly gave Hammarskjöld a vote of confidence. After his reply to the second attack, which had been made by Soviet Premier Khrushchev himself, the Assembly gave Hammarskjöld a standing ovation.

Hammarskjöld was less successful in coping with the third major event of his administration, the Hungarian Revolt of 1956, because Hungary refused to permit entry to the committee appointed by Hammarskjöld to investigate the situation. At his suggestion the General Assembly appointed another committee to collect evidence, from outside Hungary, of Soviet military intervention. This committee condemned Soviet military interference and the activities of the Hungarian Communist political police.

HAMMER, a tool used for applying the force of impact to beat malleable materials into a required form or to drive nails or wedges. The common hand hammer consists of an iron head, usually faced with steel, fixed crosswise on a wooden handle. When one side of the head is thinned out to a wedge form or to a point, this is called the peen of the hammer. The face is the flat disk that strikes the work. Carpenters' and joiners' hammers have a bent peen with a V-shaped notch, which is used as a bent lever for drawing nails. The peen is sometimes sharpened to form an adz or chisel. There are many other modifications in the form of hammers. Power hammers are much used in industry.

When using a hammer to drive a nail, you should follow a few simple rules to avoid smashing fingers and damaging wood. First, hold the hammer near the end of its handle. This gives you greater leverage and reduces your chances of bending the nail.

As you start to hammer, guide the nail into the wood with thumb and forefinger. Tap gently at first, because a heavy blow may smash fingers or send the nail flying. Always keep your eye on the nail, not the hammer.

After the nail is started into the wood, hit it firmly and squarely on its head. To avoid denting the wood, drive the head only to the surface of the wood. Then use a nail set to drive the head below the surface so that it will not show.

HAMMERSTEIN, OSCAR, 2d (1895-1960), songwriter and musical-comedy writer, was born in New York. He was graduated from Columbia University in 1916. After his success in helping to write the musicals *Rose Marie, Sunny,* and *The Desert Song,* he adapted *Show Boat* from the Edna Ferber novel of the same name. In 1943 *Oklahoma* set a new fashion in musical plays. For the first time Hammerstein's lyrics and libretto were considered to be as important as the music by his partner, Richard Rodgers. Together they wrote *Carousel, Allegro, South Pacific,* and *The King and I.* They also wrote the TV production of *Cinderella* in 1957. A few of the many hit songs for which Hammerstein wrote the words were "Ol' Man River," "Lover Come Back to Me," "The Last Time I Saw Paris," and "Younger than Springtime."

HAMMOCK. The hanging bed or couch that is so familiar on verandas and under trees in the summer is an American invention. It was first seen by Europeans when Columbus arrived in the West Indies at the end of his first voyage. It is made of netted cords, woven fiber or grass, or light canvas strung on cords at the ends and often very fancifully decorated. It has wooden or metal spreaders that prevent a person lying in it from sinking uncomfortably deep. It forms an ideal summer couch, being light and cool and easily rocked.

Sailors aboard ship sometimes sleep in hammocks. These are slung between decks and are taken down and rolled up during the day. They are neither as ornamental nor as comfortable as the hammocks for lawns. They are of heavy canvas, 3 by 6 feet, slung by ropes at each end to hooks in the deck beams. In earlier days a sailor who died at sea was always wrapped in his hammock and lowered into the water.

Some of Oscar Hammerstein's finest lyrics were written for *The King and I.*

Photo from THE KING & I in Grandeur 70, Courtesy of Twentieth Century-Fox

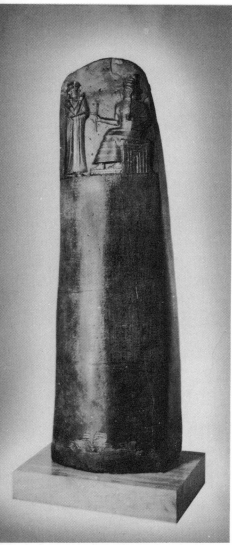

Courtesy of the Oriental Institute, University of Chicago

This 8-foot diorite column, bearing the most complete known inscription of the 4,000-year-old Code of Hammurabi, is considered one of the greatest of all archaeological finds. In addition to 248 laws of the code, the column also bears a prologue and an epilogue. The bas-relief at the top represents King Hammurabi (left) receiving the laws from Shamash, the Babylonian sun god (right).

HAMMURABI (flourished 2100 B.C.), Babylonian king, is noted for his formulation of the most enlightened of the ancient law codes. It was found on a diorite column in cuneiform at Susa, Persia. In spite of its adherence to the retributive policy of an "eye for an eye," many humanitarian principles are found in it. During the reign of Hammurabi Babylon flourished as a great cultural and industrial center.

HAMPTON ROADS CONFERENCE, an informal consultation held on the *River Queen* at Hampton Roads, Virginia, Feb. 3, 1865, with regard to the conclusion of peace between the federal government and the Confederacy. The representatives of the United States were President Abraham Lincoln and William Henry Seward, secretary of state. Representing the Confederacy were Vice President Alexander Hamilton Stephens, John Archibald Campbell, assistant secretary of war, and Senator Robert M. T. Hunter. Since Lincoln refused all terms that did not provide for full reestablishment of the Union—and apparently insisted upon emancipation—and the Confederate representatives were instructed to hold out for recognition of Southern independence, no basis of agreement was secured.

HAMSTER, a fur-bearing rodent that inhabits eastern Europe, many parts of Asia, and South Africa. Hamsters are not native to the New World.

The European hamster, which is about a foot long, has thick, soft fur that is light brown on the back and black on the underside. Its legs are short, and the soles of its feet are padded with hair, which makes its nocturnal scampering inaudible. In the sandy soil of farms the European hamster digs a burrow consisting of several tunnels leading to a central nesting chamber and storehouse. At night during summer this hamster forages for potatoes and grain kernels, carrying the former home between its teeth and the latter in its large cheek pouches. These foods are stored in large quantities in the underground storehouse for winter, during which the animal remains partially dormant in its burrow.

Hamsters multiply rapidly. The European one annually bears four or five litters with from five to twelve young in each. In two weeks

The hamster is a docile laboratory rodent.

the young are mature enough to leave their mother and dig burrows of their own. Although it will flee from pursuers whenever possible, the hamster when cornered will lunge at an attacking dog or man and perhaps injure him.

The warm fur pelts of hamsters are used to line coats. Many hamsters are used in laboratory experiments, especially in those studying nutrition and disease. Because of their gentleness and docility, hamsters are popular as pets.

Chicago Hist. Soc.

John Hancock

HANCOCK, JOHN (1737-1793), a noted American statesman, was born in Quincy, in Massachusetts. He was graduated from Harvard College in 1754 and became a merchant and heir to a large fortune. He took part in the protest against the Stamp Act, as a result of which his ship, the *Liberty*, was seized by the British. Later he was the head of the Boston Town Committee. In 1774 he became president of the Provincial Congress, which met at Concord, Mass., to prepare to fight if necessary for the rights of the colonies. The British called him an arch rebel and made many unsuccessful attempts to take him prisoner. In 1775 he was made president of the Continental Congress, which met in Philadelphia and by which Washington was elected commander in chief of the American army. Hancock was the first signer of the Declaration of Independence, July 4, 1774. In 1780 he became the first elected governor of Massachusetts, and he was reelected eight times to this office.

HAND. A human hand is the most highly developed and flexible grasping organ in the animal kingdom. True hands are found only among the animal order of Primates, which includes monkeys, apes, and man. In a human hand, the arrangement of bones and muscles makes possible the shaping of tools, something no animal but man is capable of doing. The human hand consists of five bones (the metacarpals) with the finger bones (the phalanges) joining the wrist bones (the carpals). The thumb is so placed that it can be opposed to any of the four fingers.

The human hand contains 27 bones. The finger bones, or phalanges, are classified as first-row phalanges, **A**; second-row phalanges, **B**; and third-row phalanges, **C**. There are 14 phalanges in all—3 in each finger and 2 in the thumb. The first row phalanges connect with the 5 bones of the palm, or metacarpals, **D**. The metacarpals connect, in turn, with the 8 wrist bones, or carpals, **E**.

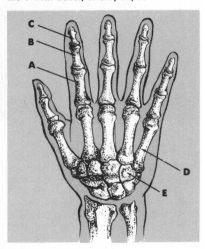

HANDBAG. The word *pocket* originally meant "little bag," and the word *poke* meant "big bag." These were the first purses or handbags. In the Middle Ages men carried bags attached to their waists to hold money and other objects. They were usually made of leather.

Handbags, in some form, probably date from prehistoric time. Ancient Egyptians carried bags of cotton or leather, as did the Assyrians. The Greeks and Romans carried little leather purses for money. In the 14th century Geoffrey Chaucer described the leather purse worn by the Wife of Bath. Such purses were hung at the waist by leather thongs. They were fairly large and were used for carrying money and other objects that might be used during the day. In the 15th and 16th centuries men and women wore embroidered handbags. Usually they were flat bags closed with tasseled strings. In the 17th century, with the appearance of coats and waistcoats, men began to wear pockets sewn into their clothing. Small silk purses were often carried inside the pockets. Women wore little pockets rather than handbags. In the 18th century women's clothes became too flimsy for pockets. Some women wore drawstring bags, or reticules, attached to the petticoat with tape tied around the waist. Others carried small, elegant reticules. Skirts became ample, and handbags were less frequently used, until 1909. With hobble skirts it was impossible to wear any kind of pocket. Large handbags came into use, sometimes with long chains or strings. In the 1920's handbags became almost a necessity.

HANDBALL is a fast and exciting competitive sport. It is played in many parts of the world but is especially popular in Great Britain, Ireland, and the United States. Most authorities believe the game was first played in Ireland during the 11th century. Irish immigrants brought the game to the United States in the 1880's. It is popular in large cities because relatively small space is required for playing.

The ball used is made of black rubber, has a diameter of $1\frac{7}{8}$ inches, and weighs $2\frac{3}{10}$ ounces. Originally handball players used a solid ball somewhat like a baseball, but this type was gradually replaced during the early 1900's by the rubber ball. A player may wear gloves of soft leather or of cloth on either or both hands; the gloves must not be webbed.

There are two types of handball courts. The four-wall court is enclosed by four walls, a floor, and a ceiling. This court is 23 feet wide and 46 feet long; the front wall is 23 feet high; the rear wall is at least 10 feet high. A line, called the short line, is drawn 23 feet behind the front wall and parallel to it. The service line is 5 feet in front of the short line and parallel to it.

The one-wall court is 34 feet long and 20 feet wide; the wall is 16 feet high. The short line is drawn parallel to the front wall, 16 feet behind it, and the service line is 9 feet behind the short line. One-wall courts are often outdoors.

RULES

Handball may be played as a contest between two persons or two teams. A team consists of two players. The game begins with the serve. The server stands between the short line and the service line. If he is playing with a partner, the partner stands in a service box during the serve. The service box lies between the short line and the service line and can be no more than 18 inches from a sidewall.

To begin play the server bounces the ball, then hits it with his hand. The ball should hit the front wall before it bounces anywhere else. The ball must then bounce back beyond the short line before hitting the floor. If the server fails to serve properly, a second attempt is given. If he again fails, his opponent serves. After a successful serve the receiving player hits the ball back, at

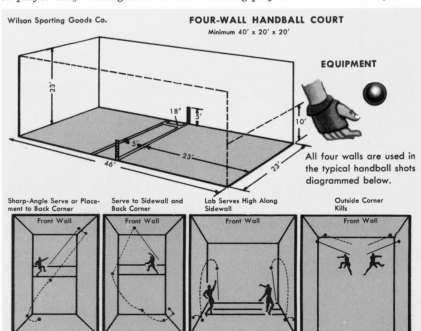

Wilson Sporting Goods Co.

FOUR-WALL HANDBALL COURT
Minimum 40' x 20' x 20'

EQUIPMENT

All four walls are used in the typical handball shots diagrammed below.

Sharp-Angle Serve or Placement to Back Corner — Front Wall

Serve to Sidewall and Back Corner — Front Wall

Lob Serves High Along Sidewall — Front Wall

Outside Corner Kills — Front Wall

the front wall. He may hit the ball either before it has bounced or after it has bounced once. On a return the ball may be hit against the ceiling or against any sidewall, but it must hit the front wall before eventually bouncing on the floor.

The opponents alternate in hitting the ball until one fails to return it properly. Subsequent to the serve that starts the game, the server loses the right to serve if he fails. If the receiver fails, the server scores one point. Only the server or the serving side scores. The first side or individual to score 21 points wins the game.

German-born composer Handel scored most of his artistic triumphs in England.

HANDEL, GEORGE FREDERICK

(1685-1759), a German musician, born in Halle. His father wanted him to be a lawyer and forbade him to play any instrument, but the boy secretly taught himself to play on an old spinet in the garret. Finally, his father was persuaded by the duke of Saxe-Weissenfels to let George Frederick study music. In 1710 he became chapelmaster to the elector of Hanover, afterward George I of England, and this took him to London where most of his later life was spent. He became one of the most famous musicians that ever lived and wrote a large number of works. Among them were more than 50 operas, but he is best known for his oratorios, the most famous of which are *The Messiah, Israel in Egypt, Judas Maccabaeus,* and *Samson.* He died in London when he was 74 years old and was buried in Westminster Abbey.

HANDICAPPED, AID FOR THE.

Tens of millions of people in the world are handicapped as the result of accidents, wars, diseases, and deficiencies at birth. Their handicaps include deafness and blindness, loss or incapacitation of arms and legs, nervous disorders, and psychological and mental maladjustment. Many nations are increasingly adopting programs of total rehabilitation that enable handicapped persons to do useful work.

The prevalence of diseases causing lifelong disability is a major health problem in many countries. In industrially underdeveloped countries especially, the economic and social burden of a large, unproductive segment of the population contributes to the general poverty and backwardness. But even in highly industrialized countries such waste of productiveness is a matter of great concern. The highly industrialized nations have developed a concept that isolated services are not sufficient—that total rehabilitation of the individual is necessary. Underdeveloped nations are also beginning to adopt this concept.

Total rehabilitation involves an integrated program of medical, educational, psychological, social, and vocational services. These services include diagnosis and necessary treatment (including surgery), artificial limbs and other such aids, counseling, training, and placement in a job suited to the individual's abilities.

The cost of a total rehabilitation program is very great. In the United States this cost is shared by the federal government and the governments of the separate states. The actual services to the handicapped are provided by state vocational re-

habilitation agencies. Through the office of Vocational Rehabilitation in the Department of Health, Education, and Welfare the federal government encourages the extension and improvement of state services by means of financial aid and coordinating, advisory, and research functions. Federal financial aid is also available to nonprofit voluntary organizations for work consistent with the state-federal program.

Many other industrialized nations, including the United Kingdom, Sweden, Finland, Canada, Australia, the Soviet Union, and Poland, have programs similar in scope to that of the United States but differing in the pattern of administration. In no country do the existing programs meet the demand for aid to the handicapped.

In the less-developed nations services are generally not adequate to meet even the minimum needs. However, in recent years some of these nations have adopted social security, medical care, and other programs designed to meet the great need. Since 1947 the United Nations has carried on a technical-assistance program in rehabilitation. Some of the major industrialized nations have established their own technical-assistance progams as well.

Vocational rehabilitation of the handicapped has primarily a human and social objective—that of restoring persons to useful and active lives. But rehabilitation can also be advocated from a purely economic standpoint. For instance, a careful evaluation of results in the United States has shown that the federal income taxes alone paid by a person rehabilitated into gainful employment are likely to amount to several times the cost of rehabilitation.

Physically handicapped children can be helped through proper medical treatment and special programs of education. This child is hard of hearing, and she is receiving speech therapy through play from a specialist in the speech clinic of a large university.

Chamber of Com., Cincinnati, Ohio

HANDKERCHIEF, a small square piece of cloth, usually cotton or linen, used for wiping the face or nose. The more elaborate kinds, edged with lace or decorated with embroidery, are carried for display.

Just before the 16th century in England, when such cloths were first called handkerchiefs, only the upper classes used them. Many were made of costly materials—fine silks and cloth with gold threads—and were elaborately decorated. Lovers sometimes exchanged them as tokens of their affection. In the 17th century lace handkerchiefs were fashionable. Members of the lower classes, who could not afford display, had handkerchiefs made of coarser cloth, such as calico.

By the 18th century a handkerchief had become a symbol of good breeding, and by the 19th century its use had spread throughout the populace.

Since World War I men have used handkerchiefs as an accessory to their clothing. They insert a folded handkerchief in their breast pockets, sometimes in a color that matches the tie, but more often in white to set off the dark color of their suits. Women still use lace and embroidered handkerchiefs for display, but for ordinary use most people prefer plain cotton or linen handkerchiefs or the soft paper tissues that are inexpensive and disposable after use.

HAND SIGNAL, a gesture made with the hand that serves to tell something. Its meaning is agreed on in advance by the people who use it. A hand signal is sometimes like a code in that each signal stands for a certain message. See CODE.

Hand signals usually serve to warn, direct, or command. Sometimes they serve as a language among people who speak different languages. See GESTURE.

Roman Script

Chinese Script

Uncial Script

Penmanship Sample by P. Frank (1600?)

Down-strokes   Up-strokes

PALMER SCRIPT

Swing   Space   Downstroke   Curve   Upstroke

HANDWRITING, script written by hand. Usually, tablets such as those of wax, and papyrus, parchment, and paper have been used by persons for handwriting.

In ancient Greece and Egypt handwriting was developed before the Christian Era. Papyrus was the material on which a large number of documents were preserved.

Vellum was widely used in Greece by the 4th century. This material offered a wider possibility of styles than the softer papyrus. A round, strong hand, with contrasts of fine lines and heavy downstrokes, evolved. The codex Vaticanus is written in this fashion. There are no large capital letters.

Until the introduction of printing, writing was in two main styles, the cursive and the book hand. The book hand was even and regular. This type of writing disappeared before the printing press was used. The cursive continued, and each country developed its own style. English writing was influenced by the round Italian letters of the 16th century.

Individuals develop their own style within the national style. For this reason, there are students of handwriting who analyze character traits by the way people write.

HAN DYNASTY, a Chinese dynasty lasting from about 206 B.C. to A.D. 220. The short-lived Hsin Dynasty (A.D. 9-23), founded by Wang Mang, divided the Han Dynasty into the Earlier Han Dynasty and the Later Han Dynasty.

The Han Dynasty followed the Ch'in Dynasty, which had broken down into anarchy. The first Han emperor, Liu Pang (later called Han Kao-tsu), was faced with serious problems. With only a handful of loyal followers Liu had to suppress groups of marauding soldiers, attacks by hordes from north of the Great Wall, and desertions to the Ch'in military overlord. Liu was not a prince; he was a rude warrior. But he was clever, and he maintained

Hand signals used by football referees include: 1, illegal procedure; 2, illegal motion; 3, illegal shift; 4, illegal return; 5, ineligible receiver downfield; 6, delay of game; 7, illegal use of hands and arms; 8, ball illegally touched, kicked, or batted; 9, start the clock; 10, unsportsmanlike conduct; 11, personal foul; 12, interference with fair catch or forward pass; 13, offside; 14, incomplete forward pass, penalty declined, or no score; 15, illegal forward pass; 16, clipping; 17, roughing the kicker; 18, first down; 19, ball ready for play; 20, ball dead; 21, touchdown or field goal; 22, safety; 23, time out; 24, crawling, pushing, or helping runner; 25, intentional grounding.

the strong government measures of Shih Huang Ti, the first emperor of the Ch'in Dynasty. Liu, however, was too weak to hold back the barbaric Huns, who swept over the Great Wall and trapped the emperor in a fort. Liu had to come to humiliating terms with the Huns. Wu Ti, who ruled from 140 to 87 B.C., was in a better position to defend the empire. While one of his generals pressed the Huns on the border, a 22-year-old cavalry officer penetrated into the area north of the Great Wall and captured many Hun chieftains. As a result, the Chinese firmly established themselves behind the Great Wall. Wu Ti expanded his territory into Korea as far as Seoul, thus developing the bridge that spread Chinese culture into Japan. His forces recaptured the kingdom to the south, with Canton as its capital. In 36 B.C., Chinese troops confronted the Roman legions for the first and last time in Transoxiana. By A.D. 2 Chinese traders exchanged silk and gold for the wares of the areas beyond the Indian Ocean.

These exploits, however, cost much money. Taxes were very high, and government monopolies and inflation were resorted to. Eventually, however, the tribute from foreign sources began to pay for the maintenance of the empire. Camels, mules, and donkeys were said to have entered China in an unending line. Furs, precious stones, carpets, and other treasures made the Han Dynasty a time of prosperity. Court intrigue resulted in the establishment of the Hsin Dynasty in A.D. 9.

Following the death of Wang Mang, founder of the Hsin Dynasty, several persons struggled to gain the

This is a gilt bronze bear that dates from the Han Dynasty. Decoration and outline in Han art tended to be severe. An attempt was made to portray realistically the forms of men and animals. There is a charming naturalness in this simple sculpture of a bear.
Courtesy of City Art Museum of St. Louis

vacant throne. Kuang Wu-ti, a distant relative of the last ruler of the Earlier Han Dynasty, triumphed and established the Later Han Dynasty in A.D. 25. It took ten years for the new emperor to subdue the country. A rebellion in the south led to an expedition that conquered much of what is modern Vietnam. The area comprising modern Yunnan was reconquered in 69. The troublesome Huns were held at bay by the Chinese, and the small states in Turkestan were forced into submission. One Chinese general pushed all the way to the Persian Gulf in 97. Toward the end of the 1st century, however, misrule created an agricultural crisis that eventually caused a major rebellion. Thereafter, Hsien Ti, the last ruler of the Later Han Dynasty, was controlled by the ruthless warlord Tung Cho. Tung razed China's magnificent capital, an act that caused other warlords to rebel. Tung was slain in 192, and Ts'ao Ts'ao took over the government. The death of Hsien Ti in 220 ended the Later Han Dynasty.

Commerce was active during the Later Han Dynasty. Merchants from India, Persia, and even the Roman Empire gathered in Cochin China and even traveled to China. With the subjugation of Turkestan, silks could be carried overland to the Roman Empire. Japan was in contact with China after about 57.

Buddhism was introduced by missionaries into China. Religious Taoism, quite different from the philosophy of Lao-tzu, was introduced by Chang Tao-ling and his son. Science was advanced in the Later Han Dynasty by Chang Heng, who invented a seismograph (earthquake detector), and Wang Chung, who tried to foster a scientific attitude toward natural events. A history of the Former Han Dynasty was written by Pan Ku, and a wordbook of old script was prepared by Hsu Shen in 100. A very remarkable invention, paper, was presented to the emperor by Ts'ai Lun in 105.

HANGING GARDENS AT BABYLON. See SEVEN WONDERS OF THE ANCIENT WORLD.

HANNEFORD is the name of a family of circus performers. Edwin Hanneford and his wife, Elizabeth, performed as bareback riders, tightrope walkers, and knife throwers in British circuses during the 1880's and 1890's. They organized their own circus in 1903 in Ireland and performed there and also in England

and Scotland until 1915. During this time, two of the Hanneford children, Edwin, Jr., and Elizabeth, joined the family bareback-riding act. A second son, George, later became a performer. Edwin Hanneford, Sr., died in 1913. Two years later, the Hannefords moved to the United States, where they joined the Barnum and Bailey Circus. After the children grew up and were married, they formed their own bareback-riding acts, but the family continued to perform together occasionally. The Hannefords appeared in such well-known circuses as Ringling Brothers, Cole Brothers, and Sells-Floto.

HANNIBAL (244?-183?B.C.) a Carthaginian general, was one of the greatest military geniuses the world has ever known. For nearly 15 years he commanded an army within the territory of his enemies, the Romans. He inflicted many defeats on the numerically superior Roman legions while never losing a battle in Italy. Hannibal's exploits were written down about 50 years after his death by the historian Polybius.

Rome and Carthage fought three wars, called the Punic Wars (264-241 B.C.; 218-201 B.C.; 149-146 B.C.), for the control of the western Mediterranean. In the First Punic War the Romans annihilated the Carthaginian fleet, but Carthage continued to flourish and even occupied the peninsula that is now Spain and Portugal. Hannibal's father, Hamilcar Barca, was the Carthaginian leader there, and he is said to have made his son swear to revenge the defeat in the First Punic War. Hannibal took over the command in Spain when he was 25 years old and soon destroyed the fortress of Saguntum near modern Valencia. Rome was jealous of the Carthaginian power in Spain and demanded the surrender of Hannibal. When the Carthaginian government supported Hannibal, Rome declared war.

Carthage had no fleet that could have carried an army into Italy, but Hannibal conceived an audacious plan and, using elephants, led 100,000 men across the Pyrenees, east through southern France, and finally, the greatest feat of all, through the Alps to Italy. He lost about one-fourth of his army on the way, and his elephants died also. In 218 he defeated a Roman army near the Ticino River and gained control of the Po Valley. The next spring he was joined by Gaulish tribes and with them cut to pieces another

Hannibal's army crossed one of the headstreams of the Rhine River in the Alps.

Roman army at Lake Trasimeno. Hannibal could have occupied Rome, but instead he marched to the south and wintered in Apulia. The Roman consul Quintus Fabius Maximus cleverly avoided Hannibal's army, but another Roman general, the rash Varro, accepted battle at Cannae in 216. Hannibal's brilliant strategy of encirclement won the victory and cost the lives of 40,000 Romans. Hannibal's fame spread, and King Philip V of Macedon joined him against the Romans. But a Roman army occupied Spain, and Carthage was unable to send reinforcements to Hannibal. In 203 he was recalled to Carthage, and the next year he was defeated by Scipio Africanus at Zama in North Africa. In 195 Hannibal had to flee from Carthage, and he sought refuge with Antiochus III, king of Syria, and later with Prusias, king of Bythina. However, these kings were ready to extradite him to Rome for money. To avoid being taken captive by the Romans, Hannibal committed suicide.

HANSEATIC LEAGUE, an economic and political confederation of German commercial towns that guaranteed to its members the trading privileges obtained by it. The organization was not definitely formed as a league of cities until about 1360. Until then the term *hanse* was commonly applied to an association of merchants.

By the early 13th century Lübeck, Danzig, and other towns favorably situated in northern Germany grew into prosperous trading centers. Their merchants founded colonies, known as factories, in such foreign cities of commercial importance as London, England, and Novgorod, Russia. To provide for the protection of their merchants abroad and their merchandise on sea, the German Hanse towns regulated the

sharing of losses from shipwreck and piracy and provided uniform rules for wages of sailors and for joint ownership in foreign factories.

At the time of its greatest extension the league included some 80 or 90 towns, but the membership varied. The league had its own fleet and was considered an independent state. Periodically the delegates of the cities gathered in the guildhall at Lübeck to decide on matters of common importance, to settle disputes, and to secure new trading privileges from foreign governments. The Hanseatic fleet exchanged the products of northern Europe (grain, salt, fish, fur, lumber, potash, and beer) for the goods of southern Europe and the Orient.

The zenith of the league's power was reached after 1370, when the united Hanse towns defeated Waldemar IV Atterdag, king of Denmark. The league acquired virtual monopoly of the Baltic trade and substantial political influence in the affairs of northern Europe. Its foreign factories, like the steelyard in London, enjoyed extensive privileges and self-government under the protection of the kings, princes, and cities. The Hanseatic League declined in importance during the 15th century because of rivalry among the towns, the emergence of new trading centers elsewhere, and

the hostility of powerful Hohenzollern princes.

The existence of such independent bodies as the Hanseatic League contributed to the weakness of the Holy Roman Empire, whose boundaries encompassed the Hanseatic cities.

HANSEN'S DISEASE. See LEPROSY.

HANUKKAH is the name of a Jewish religious festival. It is sometimes called the Feast of Lights because of the practice of lighting candles. Using the Jewish calendar, Hanukkah begins on the 25th day of the month of Kislev. This day may occur on any day between November 27 and December 27, depending on the year. The festival lasts eight days.

Jews throughout the world observe Hanukkah by placing candles in special candelabra. One candle is lit at the beginning of the festival. At dusk on each of the next seven days one more candle is lit. In recent times Hanukkah has become a children's holiday, and many Jewish families give their children a gift on each of the eight days.

The word *hanukkah* is Hebrew for "dedication." Hanukkah is celebrated to mark the rededication of the Temple in Jerusalem after it had been defiled by the Syrians. A Jewish family named the Maccabees led the Jews in their victory over the Syrians from 168 to 165 B.C.

HAPSBURG, the name of a ruling family that played an important role in European history for over six centuries.

The name Hapsburg was derived from *Habichsburg* (hawk's castle), the name of the original family castle in what is now Aargue canton, Switzerland. The title "count of Hapsburg" was first assumed by Werner I, who died in 1096. In 1273 Rudolf I of Hapsburg, a descendant, was elected king of Germany and Holy Roman emperor. Even as early

Once the Hapsburgs' favorite palace, the Hofburg, in Vienna, now houses several museums.
Robert J. Bezucha

as the 13th century the Hapsburgs had acquired substantial land holdings in Alsace and in Switzerland. To these Rudolf added the duchy of Austria. "Archduke of Austria" became a hereditary family title in 1453.

The Hapsburgs' rise to great power began in the latter part of the 15th century with the reign of Maximilian I, Holy Roman emperor and king of Germany. Maximilian was sole heir to the Hapsburg possessions. By his marriage in 1490 to Mary of Burgundy he acquired Burgundy and The Netherlands. The Spanish Hapsburg line was established when Maximilian's son, Philip, married the daughter of the Spanish monarchs Ferdinand and Isabella. Philip's son Charles, who ruled as both Charles V of the Holy Roman Empire and Charles I of Spain, was one of the most powerful rulers of the 16th century. His immense domain consisted principally of the Spanish Empire (with holdings in the New World and Italy); the Burgundian inheritance; and the traditional strongholds of Hapsburg power—Austria, Germany and Switzerland. Hapsburg power was even further extended when Charles's brother, Ferdinand, married Anne of Bohemia and Hungary.

The gradual disintegration of the Hapsburg Empire began in the latter half of the 17th century. By the end of that century most of the Burgundian inheritance had been lost. In 1714 Spain fell to the French Bourbons as a result of the War of the Spanish Succession. The Hapsburg male line became extinct in 1740 with the death of Charles VI, Holy Roman emperor and king of Hungary. However, by virtue of the Pragmatic Sanction, first issued in 1713, Charles's daughter, Maria Theresa, inherited the holdings of the Austrian Hapsburgs. After her marriage to Francis Stephen (later, Francis I, Holy Roman emperor), a member of the French ducal family of Lorraine, the line was renamed Hapsburg-Lorraine. The title of "Holy Roman Emperor" became meaningless when Napoleon dissolved the Holy Roman Empire in 1806.

Although the Hapsburg-Lorraine line managed to regain some of its territories at the Congress of Vienna in 1815, the next hundred years witnessed a decline in power. The House of Hapsburg-Lorraine continued to rule in Hungary and Austria until the last of the line to wear a royal crown, Charles I of Austria, abdicated in 1918.

Artha Hornbostel

Nearly 50,000 vessels—ocean-going ships, launches, junks—use Hong Kong harbor every year.

Artha Hornbostel

Sydney's harbor is the principal port of the Commonwealth of Australia.

HARBOR, an inlet of a body of water, either landlocked or artificially protected, affording shelter for ships. Harbors may be roughly classified as harbors of refuge and harbors of refuge and commerce. All good harbors should possess the following characteristics: a deep, broad entrance channel, which can be entered by ships of all kinds in all sorts of weather, and an ample anchorage, free from rocks and shoals, with good holding ground, and protected from winds and waves. In addition commercial harbors should be supplied with adequate shore constructions and appliances for loading and discharging vessels. The question of appropriate depths for a harbor is a complex one. It is governed somewhat by the tidal range, as a large rise in the tide may increase the depth. The requirements for the width of a channel vary greatly according to the density of traffic and the presence of rocks and shoals.

One large port may have many channels, and it must be determined which ones are appropriate for the large vessels and which ones for the light-draft vessels. The methods used to improve channels in harbors are dredging, the construction of jetties to preserve suitable depth at the entrances from the sea or other open water, and the construction of breakwaters to afford protected anchorage and terminal areas. Breakwaters are constructed to provide safe anchorage areas for vessels seeking refuge from storms and to protect port facilities from wind and wave action. Breakwaters are especially necessary at harbor entrances on exposed coastlines. Some of the best known natural harbors are those of Rio de Janeiro, Manila, Havana, New York, San Francisco, and Boston.

HARDING, WARREN GAMALIEL

(1865-1923), the 29th president of the United States, was born near Caledonia, Ohio, Nov. 2, 1865. He bought and edited the Marion (Ohio) *Star* in 1884. His oratory and personal charm, coupled with a certain amount of natural leadership, soon made him prominent in local affairs. He began his political career as a Republican state senator. After a term as lieutenant governor he was chosen to nominate William Howard Taft in the 1912 Republican Convention, and in 1914 he won the Republican nomination to the United States Senate. He was nominated in 1920 for the presidency and was elected by a large majority.

The outstanding accomplishment of the Harding administration was the Washington conference for the limitation of armament, held in 1921-1922. Other notable achievements were the conclusion of treaties with Germany and Austria establishing peace after World War I and the passage of an act restricting immigration.

The record of Harding's administration was blackened by corruption scandals, especially the Teapot Dome scandal involving his secretary of the interior, Albert B. Fall. A congressional investigating committee found that Fall had leased rich government-owned oil reserves at Teapot Dome in Washington to oil operator Harry F. Sinclair and had received from Sinclair a so-called loan of $25,000. He also leased oil lands in California to Edward L. Doheny in return for a $100,000 loan without interest or collateral. Fall was convicted of accepting a bribe and was sentenced to one year in prison and a fine of $100,000. The leases were canceled. Harding died in San Francisco while returning from a vacation in Alaska.

Warren G. Harding

HARDWOOD. Broad-leaved angiosperm trees are known as hardwoods. In contrast, the gymnosperm trees, which usually have scalelike or needle-like leaves, are classed as softwoods. The term *hardwood* does not refer to the actual hardness of the wood, although the wood of such hardwoods as ash, beech, hickory, and oak is usually close grained, dense, and heavy. Balsa wood, which is lighter than cork, is a hardwood, however.

Hardwoods usually require better soils than softwoods. Hardwoods need plenty of water, and if the soil is of a type that absorbs water readily, so the tree roots can get it without difficulty, a hardwood plantation is usually successful. Hardwoods grow best in a deep, loose, crumbly type of soil, where the roots have plenty of room to develop and where the subsoil is of the type that permits good root development.

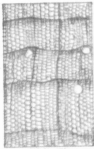

White Pine

This is a magnified view of the wood of the white pine, a softwood tree. White-pine wood, soft and light of weight, is made into shingles, telegraph poles, and railroad ties.

Red Oak

This is a magnified view of the wood of the red oak, a hardwood tree. Red-oak wood, which is hard, tough, close grained, and reddish brown, is made into furniture and flooring.

Hardwoods find a wide variety of uses. Some are particularly admired by cabinetmakers because of the beauty of the wood. Others are used for railroad ties, fenceposts, flooring, cutting blocks, barrels and boxes, tool handles, baseball bats, and all types of furniture.

Mahogany is the world's foremost hardwood for cabinetmaking, and it is the most valuable timber tree in tropical America. In the United States it is planted only in Florida, as an ornamental and shade tree. The wood takes a fine polish, has beautiful coloring, is almost as easy to work as pine, and stays glued better than any other kind of wood. See MAHOGANY.

The wood of deciduous hardwood trees (below) is usually harder, heavier, stronger, and more closely grained than that of evergreen softwood trees (right).

HARDY, THOMAS (1840-1928), English novelist and poet, was born near Egdon Heath in Dorsetshire, the son of a builder. He was educated in Dorchester and at the age of 16 was apprenticed to an architect. In 1863 he won a national competition with an architectural essay he wrote.

Hardy's first novel, *The Poor Man and the Lady*, was rejected. Hardy consequently destroyed it. From this period on, Hardy wrote a good deal of poetry, none of which was published until 1898, when he had achieved fame as a novelist. Hardy's second novel, *Desperate Remedies*, was published anonymously, and the author contributed to the cost of publication. In 1869 appeared *Under the Greenwood Tree*, followed by *A Pair of Blue Eyes*. In 1874 *Far from the Madding Crowd* was serialized in the *Cornhill Magazine*. From 1878 to 1891 Hardy published his great novels *The Return of the Native*, *The Mayor of Casterbridge*, and *Tess of the D'Urbervilles*. In 1896 appeared *Jude the Obscure*. This novel was ill received, and Hardy wrote no more fiction. Instead he turned to the drama and published the three parts of *The Dynasts*. Hardy was buried in the Poets' Corner of Westminster Abbey.

HARE, THE (constellation). See LEPUS.

HARGREAVES, JAMES (1720?-1778), an English inventor, was born near Blackburn, Lancashire, and at an early age began training as a weaver and carpenter. About 1764 Hargreaves invented a machine that had eight spindles in a row and enabled one person to spin several threads at once. The machine was called the spinning jenny. In 1768 the spinners in his neighborhood, fearing that the new invention would endanger their jobs, broke into Hargreaves' house and destroyed his machine. He moved to another location and in 1770 took out a patent. The spinning jenny soon became widely used. He continued to carry on the business of yarn manufacture until his death at Nottingham.

HARLEQUIN, a comic character of the early Italian theater. Later the character was taken over by the theater of other countries, principally in pantomime shows. In the Italian *Commedia dell'arte, Arlecchino* was a nimble, simple-minded, but witty figure with a shaven head, a masked face, and a particolored suit. He had a light wooden sword to carry with him on his misadventures. He was either in love or in trouble, easily cast down but quickly recovering.

In French pantomime of the 17th and 18th centuries Harlequin was sometimes a simple, good-natured hero but more often was a shrewd sort of bumpkin, both blundering and clever. He wore the familiar tight-fitting, diamond-checked costume. The German Hanswurst, a caricature of Harlequin, was a fat and clumsy buffoon.

The English Harlequin of the 18th century was a gallant type of comic figure in pantomime shows. He was portrayed as the invincible rival of his master, Pantaloon, and the clown for the affections of the maid Columbine. Later, Harlequin became a character in fairytales and appeared in children's shows. See COMMEDIA DELL'ARTE.

HARMONICA, a name applied to two different musical instruments. The first, invented by Benjamin Franklin, is the same thing as the "musical glasses." It consists of a number of thin glass bells rotated on a stand and played by holding moistened fingers on the glasses. Different notes are produced by different sizes of glass. Many attempts to play these musical glasses mechanically were made, but none of the devices was successful.

The Bettmann Archive

Inventor James Hargreaves' spinning jenny helped bring on the Industrial Revolution.

The later harmonica is also known as the mouth organ. It consists of a set of small metal reeds mounted in a wooden or metal case with breath holes in a row along one edge. It is played by blowing and inhaling through the holes, the two processes producing different tones from the same reeds.

HARNESS, a term formerly applied to the complete equipment carried by a soldier, including the equipment for his horse. It is now used only in connection with the gear worn by draft animals and the trappings put on riding, harness, or carriage horses. A collar harness is used on draft animals when heavy work is intended. When horses are used for lighter purposes, such as riding and trotting, a breast harness is ordinarily worn. In both instances the complete harness consists of a head harness, including the bridle, reins, and browband; the breast harness, including the breastband (or collar), the hames with straps, and the traces, the last being connected to the whiffletree; and the body harness, including, in the case of a riding horse, the saddle, bellybands, and other attachments. The harness worn by a horse varies with the use to which the animal is put.

HARNESS RACING is a sport in which horses race against each other while pulling drivers in small two-wheeled carriages called sulkies. Harness races are divided into two general types. In a trotting race the horses move by thrusting forward their front right and back left legs at the same time and then their front left and back right legs. The horses in a pacing race move both right legs forward at the same time and then both left legs.

A special type of horse, called the Standardbred, is used in harness racing. Many of the Standardbred horses in the United States are descended from Hambletonian, a stallion of the middle 1800's.

Horses in harness races must pull a sulky, a light two-wheeled carriage that usually weighs between 29 and 37 pounds. Sulkies have small, wire-spoked, rubber-tired wheels. A driver sits in the sulky and holds a whip, which he uses to control the horse.

Harness races are usually run on oval-shaped dirt tracks ½ mile in length. The length of the races varies, but is usually 1 mile. The number of horses in a race is limited by the length and width of the track.

Harness racing is popular throughout the United States and in Europe. One of the most famous races in the United States is the Hambletonian. This is a 1-mile race for three-year-old trotters, and it has taken place each summer since 1926. It is held now at DuQuoin, Ill. Many harness races are attended by thousands of spectators, who often bet money on the horses that they believe will place either first, second, or third.

No one knows exactly when harness racing began. It is known that the ancient Romans owned pacing horses and probably raced them. The first trotting horse probably did not appear until the middle 1700's. Harness racing in the United States began in the early 1800's.

Harness racehorse Titan Hanover pulls the sulky in a fast heat around the dirt track. Leg action indicates the horse is a pacer.

Photo, H. G. Strong

James," popularly called "The Heathen Chinee."

In 1871 Harte moved to Boston, where he wrote several stories for the *Atlantic Monthly* magazine. He moved to New York in 1872 and for the next six years continued to write many works. These included a novel, *Gabriel Conroy;* two plays, *Two Men of Sandy Bar* and *Ah, Sin;* and such collections of poems and short stories as *Mrs. Skaggs's Husbands* and *Tales of the Argonauts.* But Harte never again achieved the popularity or praise that he had won in California. He left the United States in 1878 to become United States consul at Krefeld, Prussia. From 1880 to 1885 he served as U.S. consul at Glasgow, Scotland. In 1885 he left government service and moved to London, where he lived until his death.

HARTFORD, the capital and largest city of Connecticut, seat of Hartford County, on the Connecticut River, 34 miles northeast of New Haven. Its population in 1960 was 162,178.

Hartford has been a major insurance center since 1794. Its factories produce firearms, typewriters, airplane parts, electrical equipment, tools, and brushes. Hillyer College, Trinity College, some schools and colleges of the University of Connecticut, and Hartford Seminary Foundation are located here. The city was founded in 1635 by settlers from Cambridge, Mass., on the site of a Dutch trading post built in 1633. It was given its present name in 1637. The town served jointly with New Haven as the state capital until 1875. One of the oldest U.S. newspapers, the Hartford *Courant,* was founded here in 1764. Many famous Americans lived or were born in Hartford, among them Noah Webster, Harriet Beecher Stowe, John Fiske, Samuel Clemens, and Charles Dudley Warner.

HARTFORD CONVENTION, an assembly of 26 leading New England Federalists who met at Hartford, Conn., in December, 1814. These men were opposed to the policies of Jeffersonian Republicanism and the war (1812-1814) with England and aimed to advance the sectional interests of New England, for the war had done severe damage to New England's shipping and overseas trade. They met to discuss the possibility of calling a convention to make major revisions in the Constitution of the United States. See WAR OF 1812.

The convention adopted resolutions calling for cooperation among states in repelling British attacks, using federal funds in state defense, and protecting civilians from unconstitutional military acts. It also urged constitutional amendments that would limit the political power of the Southern States and the government's ability to declare war, admit new states, and impose trade restrictions.

Massachusetts and Connecticut sent commissioners to Washington, D.C., to attempt to secure adoption of the measures recommended in the report, but the war had ended and the commissioners abandoned their mission. Because of its secrecy and bad timing (the peace was signed at Ghent while the convention was in session), the convention was widely ridiculed. The doctrines of states rights that were advocated by the convention also lost prestige temporarily.

HARUN AI-RASHID (763?-809), the fifth Abbasside caliph, born at Rhagae (now Rai, near Teheran, in Iran). When only 22 years old Harun succeeded his father to the caliphate. At that time the Abbasside family ruled over most of the Arab world, an enormous territory stretching from the Indus River to Morocco. Young Harun needed the support of his secretary, and later grand vizier, Yahya to obtain the throne. Yahya belonged to the Barmecides family, which wielded great power in the caliphate for over 50 years. In the latter part of his reign, however, Harun became suspicious of Yahya and had him executed.

Harun was neither an exceptional administrator nor an outstanding military leader. Though he fought a successful war against the Byzantine emperor in Asia Minor (now Turkey), he lost some territories to the east. He was chiefly remembered by his people as a generous ruler. He liked to steal out of his palace in the evenings and mingle incognito with the people on the streets. Harun's capital, the city of Baghdad, was one of the richest and the gayest in the world at that time. His court was filled with philosophers, poets, musicians, and lawyers from all parts of the caliphate. Harun himself was a poet of some ability. Stories and tales about him spread, and some of these found their way into the *The Arabian Nights' Entertainment.* His fame reached the ear of Charlemagne, and they not only exchanged gifts but also set up embassies.

Harun practiced his Moslem faith very seriously and is said to have traveled to Mecca, the holy city of Islam, nine or ten times in his life. He died while on the way to Khurasan to crush a revolt.

HARVESTING MACHINERY, farm equipment used for processing a ripened crop into a conveniently transportable form. The equipment falls roughly into five categories: grain and seed-crop machines, hay and silage machines, root-crop machines, row-crop machines, and tree-crop machines.

The Romans had perhaps the first harvesting machine. It was a simple bar with projecting teeth that pulled off the heads of small grains (wheat, oats, and so forth) as the machine was being drawn by oxen. A noteworthy development came in 1732 when Michael Menzies in Scotland attached beaters to a water wheel in order to loosen grain kernels from the stems. Later sieves and a fanner were added to the machine to separate the loosened kernels from weed seeds and the straw.

A major advance in harvesting machinery occurred in the early 1800's, when all the major types of grain harvesters came into being. In 1831 Cyrus McCormick first demonstrated a reaper for cutting the grain plants. In 1837 John Pitts patented a threshing machine for loosening the grain kernels and separating them from the straw and other foreign matter. In 1836 the Moore-Hascall combine appeared; this was the machine that combined the reaper and thresher into one unit.

The combine was invented before a practical engine existed to power all its operations. Steam-powered combines with wheels as much as 10 feet wide could be used only on the large, flat, labor-deficient farms such as those of the western United States. Reapers and binders (binders were reapers that also tied the grain plants into bundles) harvested grain in the eastern and midwestern United States until the early 1900's, when the gasoline engine permitted smaller, one-man combines to take over the harvesting.

Harvesting machines, other than for grains, came into use in the latter half of the 19th century. The hay mower, similar to the reaper in operation, was in general use by 1865. The cotton stripper, a type of cotton picker, was patented in 1871 but did not come into practical use until cotton gins (mills) could separate the cotton from the trash. The cornpicker appeared in 1893 as a

This Kansas wheatfield is being harvested by combines. Emptied stalks are left in rows.

binder, cutting and tying the cornstalks for shocking. Its later development paralleled that of the combine. The use of hay balers and sugar-beet harvesters started in the 1930's; potato diggers, in the 1940's. The tree-crop and row-crop machines are essentially products of the 1950's.

GRAIN AND SEED MACHINES

Grain and seed machines harvest small grains (wheat, oats, and so forth), dry beans, peas, soybeans, many types of seeds, and corn. These machines are the reaper, binder, thresher, combine, and cornpicker. The reapers and binders, formerly in wide use, cut the standing small grain. Between the two wheels of the reaper was a long bar that moved rapidly back and forth as the wheels turned. The grain stems were cut by a series of knives attached to the rapidly vibrating bar. The binder, in addition to cutting the small grain, carried it on a canvas conveyer to a needle and metal

fingers, where it was bunched and tied in small bundles.

The threshing machine, in conjunction with cutting machines, was used to harvest small grain and also for threshing such crops as dry beans and peas. The threshing machine was a stationary or semistationary unit with a belt that carried the cut plants to a rotary beater that loosened the grain kernels or beans from the stem. The thresher also had an arrangement of sieves and a fan for separating the loosened grain from the emptied stems, weed seeds, and other foreign matter.

The combination harvester (combine) unifies the operations of the cutting machines and the thresher. The combine cuts the crop, elevates it to a beating cylinder that loosens the grain, and then by means of sieves and fans produces a stream of clean grain. The emptied plant parts are deposited in the field behind the machine.

The cornpicker has functions similar to those of the combine but is adapted to handle the larger corn plant. A set of rollers pulls the corn ear from the stalk, which may or may not be cut off. The ear is then husked by a second set of tighter rollers. Some machines then shell the ears by rotary beating action.

HAY AND SILAGE MACHINES

Hay and silage machines harvest crops used for animal feed, such as alfalfa, clover, grasses, and green corn. The machines used are the mower, hay crusher, side-delivery rake, baler, and forage harvester. As in the harvesting of small grains, the first operation in haymaking is cutting. A mower cuts the alfalfa

and grasses in essentially the same manner as does the reaper described under grain machines. The crop is then dried. A hay crusher, which breaks the stems open with rollers, may be used to speed up the drying. The side-delivery rake picks up a wide swath of the cut, dried plants and lays them in rows. The hay baler moves down these rows, picks up the plants with a pronged cylinder, and elevates them to a compressing chamber. Here the loose plants are rammed into rectangular bundles and then tied. The baler then drops the hay bales to the ground or ejects them onto a trailer.

The forage harvester is a combination machine that cuts the green corn or other animal-feed plants and chops them into small pieces in preparation for ensilage.

ROOT-CROP MACHINES

Root crops harvested by machine include potatoes, sugar beets, peanuts, carrots, radishes, and turnips. The machines that harvest most of these crops (except sugar beets) are of the same general type. The initial operation is lifting; in this operation the plants are cut underneath with any of several types of blades or shovels. The plants are then elevated, and the dirt is cleaned from the roots by agitating or shaking them.

Sugar beets, the only root crop completely harvested by mechanization, are lifted by a large spiked wheel or by converging wheels that press the beet upward. The beet tops are cut off by revolving disks, and the dirt is knocked off by kicker wheels or by shaking. Because of their tendency to bruise, carrots

The modern combine cuts and separates grain in one operation. The entire grain stalk is cut with a sliding cutter and swept under the threshing cylinder, where the stalk is broken up. Beaters, 1 and 3, loosen the grain from the head of the stalk. Actual separation occurs at the raddle 2, where the grain is shaken through moving bars. Waste material, 4, is conveyed to the rear of the machine and dumped. Rotary fans, 5, blow chaff from the grain as it falls into the shoe, 6, and is conveyed to the hopper for removal.

Courtesy of Allis-Chalmers

1156

Harvesting machines developed for special purposes (below) have eliminated much labor.

Courtesy of Ford Motor Company

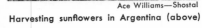

Ace Williams—Shostal

Harvesting sunflowers in Argentina (above)

This tobacco harvester eliminates walking.

Cucumber picker travels at 1½ miles per hr.

Celery harvester cuts and trims celery.

Tomatoes are picked by soft rubber fingers.

Asparagus picker cuts and boxes asparagus.

Peanuts are threshed, cleaned, and sacked.

Small motorboat carries wild-rice harvester.

Lima bean picker reduces labor by one-half.

and turnips are harvested by machine only if they are to be canned.

ROW-CROP MACHINES

The major row crops harvested by machine are cotton, green beans, spinach, and green peas. The cotton picker and the cotton stripper are the two major cotton harvesters. On the picker several hundred barbed, rotating spindles enter and leave the cotton plant as the machine moves down the row. The cotton is removed from the barbed spindles by rollers. Vacuum apparatus then pulls the cotton into a trash-separation chamber and then into the storage basket. Stripping machines with rollers remove both husk and cotton. Green beans are harvested by rollers that pull them from the plant. Spinach and peas are harvested by cutting only.

TREE-CROP MACHINES

Plums, cherries, walnuts, pecans, and almonds are among the tree crops harvested by machine. The machines are either shakers or pickup machines. Shakers use tractor power to vibrate the tree limbs. Fruit that is harvested in this way falls on canvas conveyers. It is sorted by hand as it is carried on the conveyers to loading boxes. Walnuts, prunes, and almonds are allowed to fall to the ground, where they are collected by vacuum apparatus, brushes, or rollers.

This modern pea harvester can operate easily and efficiently on a large and hilly Montana farm.

Courtesy of the Green Giant Co.

Bob Taylor—FPG

Machines have replaced manual cottonpickers in some areas. This machine harvests a cottonfield in eastern Texas.

Courtesy of Ford Motor Company

Joe Barnell—Shostal

Large rice crops are grown in southern Brazil. The harvesting work is made easier by use of threshing machines.

The small farmer can now afford a variety of machinery. This combination cornpicker and sheller is very economical for small fields.

Old-fashioned methods are still used to harvest wheat in Chile; however, modern machinery is being introduced.

This potato harvester scoops potatoes from the ground mechanically. The workers are freed from digging and need only clean and sort the potatoes.

Rosene—Shostal

Courtesy of North Dakota Soil Conservation Committee

HARVEY, WILLIAM (1578-1657), an English physician, was born in Folkestone, Kent. He took his degree in arts at Caius College, Cambridge, in 1597, and after five years' study at Padua, in Italy, he obtained his diploma as doctor of medicine in 1602.

He returned to England in the same year, and after receiving his doctor's degree from Cambridge, he settled in London as a physician. In 1609 he was appointed physician to St. Bartholomew's Hospital and in 1615 Lumleian lecturer at the College of Physicians, which was a life appointment.

It is generally supposed that in his first course of lectures (in the spring of 1616) he expounded those original and complete views on the circulation of the blood with which his name is indelibly associated. It was not until 1628 that he gave his views to the world at large in his celebrated treatise entitled *Essay on the Motion of the Heart and the Blood.* It was accurate, save for one detail. Harvey had no idea of a system of capillaries uniting arteries and veins. Marcello Malpighi, 30 years later, supplied this information. Harvey was appointed, successively, physician to James I and Charles I. In July, 1656, he resigned his Lumleian lectureship, which he had held for more than 40 years.

HASTINGS, WARREN (1732-1818), first governor general of all English possessions in India, born in Oxfordshire. He greatly strengthened British power in India by his able rule. He was honest and was sympathetic to the people he governed but unscrupulous when British power was threatened.

At the age of 18 Hastings went to India as an employee of the British East India Company. Seven years later he became the company's resident at the court of the Indian ruler of Bengal. His attempts, in this position, to rid the company of corruption aroused so much resentment that after he returned to England in 1764 he was given no work for four years. However, in 1772 he was appointed governor of Bengal. Here he put into effect the greatest of his reforms. He improved and reorganized the financial and tax-collecting systems and sought to administer justice according to the Islamic and Hindu traditions of the people.

From 1774 to 1784 Hastings served as governor general of India. Here he was less successful than before, largely because of the opposition of Philip Francis, one of the members of his governing council. Francis' opposition was based on prejudice and personal ambition. During his term as governor general

Hastings was involved in various wars. One was a four-year, inconclusive fight with the Maratha Confederacy, which was finally settled by a treaty that brought 20 years of peace. Hastings also took territory from the French in India.

Hastings returned to England in 1785. Philip Francis had stirred up many English politicians against Hastings, and they had mistakenly come to regard him as a symbol of all that was corrupt in the East India Company. The result was that Parliament impeached Hastings. His long trial, prosecuted before Parliament by Edmund Burke, Richard Brinsley Sheridan, and Charles James Fox, ended in 1795 with Hastings' acquittal.

HASTINGS, BATTLE OF. In this, perhaps the most decisive battle fought on English soil, the army of William, duke of Normandy, defeated the forces of Harold II, Saxon earl of Wessex and king of England, on Oct. 14, 1066.

William invaded England with an army numbering between perhaps 7,000 and 8,000 men. When he landed at Pevensey in September, Harold was at Stamford Bridge, where he had shortly before defeated an invading army of the Norwegian king. As soon as Harold received the news of William's landing, he hastened his weary and depleted troops to London. He remained there a few days while collecting a fresh army. Meanwhile, William encamped his men near Hastings and raided the countryside for provisions.

Harold planned a surprise night attack on the Normans and sent out ships to blockade William's navy. But Harold was too impatient to wait until his whole army assembled. On October 11 he sent out from London for Hastings. The English army was slightly inferior to the Norman in numbers. It was composed of the fyrd (the national militia) and the housecarls (the mounted cavalry), both of which fought mostly on foot. The Norman army was made up of a skilled, armored cavalry of knights and an infantry armed with crossbows.

Harold's march to Hastings exhausted the English, and the surprise attack was given up. Harold took up a position along a ridge and prepared for a defensive battle. William's first attack, which occurred in the morning, failed to break the English center, and the Norman left wing was pressed back. Then William feigned a retreat to

William Harvey explains blood circulation in one of his lectures at the College of Physicians.
Courtesy of and © 1959, Parke, Davis & Co.

Norman invaders won the Battle of Hastings.

lure the English from the hill. Part of Harold's army fell into the trap. As evening approached the English wall disintegrated. Harold was hit in the eye by an arrow and fell shortly after. Two months later William was named king of England by the Witan.

HAT, a head covering, distinguished from the cap or bonnet by having a brim around it. The hat, as a roomy, brimmed head covering, is the direct descendant of the petasos of the ancient Greeks. The petasos was distinguished from the other Greek headgear, the pilos, by the brim, which was useful for protecting its wearer from the rays of the sun. These Greek hats were made of felt, a material widely used for headgear in early times.

Hats were first made in Paris by a Swiss in 1404. When Charles VII made his triumphal entry into Rouen in 1453, he wore a hat lined with red velvet and trimmed with a rich plume of feathers, and hats were thenceforth the fashion of France.

The use of felt hats became known in England about the period of the Norman conquest. The merchant in Chaucer's "Prologue" to the *Canterbury Tales* is described as having "on his hed a flaundrish bever hat."

About the time of Queen Elizabeth I beaver felts, in many shapes, became common, and for three centuries thereafter fine beaver hats, mostly dyed black, formed the head covering of the higher classes in Great Britain. But now, though felt hats are the everyday wear of the community, there is no longer such a thing as a genuine beaver felt hat.

Hats of the present day are fashioned of an endless variety of materials and, especially in the case of those worn by women, are so diversified in form that they defy all definition. With all these variations, three principal classes of hat manufacture may be distinguished. They are the felt hat, the cloth hat, and the straw hat.

The opera hat, or crush hat, consists of a covering of merino wool stretched over a spiral steel frame, which flattens down on pressure so that it can be easily carried. The manufacture of Panama and straw hats forms entirely distinct branches of the hat trade.

HATCHET. See Ax.

HATE is an acquired emotion closely related to anger and fear. The person experiencing hate wants to destroy that which he hates. (See EMOTION.) Hate may be directed against an individual or against a group and may be rational or irrational. Rational hate develops as a reaction to a threat to freedom and security. It protects life and mobilizes a person for action. It tends to disappear when the threat is removed. Irrational hate arises out of the linkage of anger and fear to definite people, objects, and situations in a way that deprives an individual of sound judgment. For example, an individual may have an unpleasant experience with a member of a particular social or racial group. By a process of association the feeling becomes connected with

all members of the group. The same applies to experiences with individuals. A feeling toward an individual, justified by a single experience, becomes fixed in relation to all the activities of that individual and gives rise to irrational hate. Psychotherapy has proved useful in eliminating irrational hate.

HATFIELDS AND McCOYS, two families involved in a bloody feud from the time of the Civil War until about 1890. The Hatfields lived near Williamson, W. Va., and the McCoys lived just across the border in Kentucky. Although the family arguments were passed down from one generation to another and some of the stories were woven into mountain ballads, accounts of the beginning of the fight differ. Some say that the quarrel began when a Hatfield was accused of stealing a McCoy hog. Others attribute the trouble to a disagreement over the ownership of some timber. Part of the story is that Harmon McCoy, a Union private at the time of the Civil War, was killed by "Devil Anse" Hatfield, a rebel, on a lonely mountain pass. Jonse Hatfield, son of "Devil Anse" and the only a baby, grew up in the midst of the trouble. As a young man he fell in love with Rosanna McCoy. These two became the Romeo and Juliet of the mountains, their love thwarted by family hatred. The Hatfields and the McCoys killed each other singly when they met and made forays across the state line to do more damage to each other. Finally legal measures brought their feud to an end.

HAUPTMANN, GERHART (1862-1946), German dramatist and winner of the Nobel prize for literature in 1912, was born in Obersalzbrunn, Silesia. A failure in school and in his attempts to make a career as a sculptor and as a farmer, Hauptmann turned to literature. His *Before Dawn*, with its emphasis on the natural in both speech and environment, was to some extent the beginning of naturalism in drama. In *The Weavers*, a play on the 1844 revolt of Silesian weavers, a new concept of theater was introduced: The hero was the collective group of miners in revolt instead of an individual. In 1893 appeared Hauptmann's ironic satire on bureaucracy, *The Beaver Coat*, and in 1894 *The Assumption of Hannele*. Additional works by Hauptmann include *The Sunken Bell, Rose Bernd, The White Saviour,* and *Till Eulenspiegel.*

Shown below are a number of hat styles that have been worn in the past 2,000 years. Men's hats are: **1,** 9th-to-11th-century Anglo-Saxon cap; **4,** 14th-century Italian hood; **6,** 16th-century French hat; **9,** British top hat, 1840's. Women's hats are: **2,** ancient Roman; **3 and 5,** medieval European; **7,** French, 1770's; **8,** British, 1820's; **10,** French, about 1910.

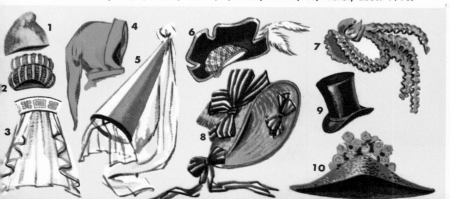

HAVANA is the capital of Cuba, lying on Havana Bay on the northwestern coast of the island. An important seaport, it is the largest city in the West Indies and one of the busiest commercial centers in Latin America. Sheltered Havana Bay, entered through a deep and narrow channel, provides an excellent and large harbor. All phases of Cuban life focus on Havana. The city has three distinct sections—the old part of town, the new, and the suburbs. It lies on level ground, although the suburbs of Vedado and Marianao stretch westward into the hills. The old section, with its narrow, crooked streets and surviving landmarks of Spanish colonial days, lies along the waterfront. Wide, landscaped boulevards and imposing buildings are found in the newer section. Havana has a population of about 1,000,000.

Cigar manufacturing is perhaps the city's most famous industry, but with the increased use of cigarettes this industry has declined considerably. Other industries include sugar refining, rum distilling, brewing, meatpacking, and textile milling. Havana's extremely profitable tourist trade, especially during the winter, was reduced by the anti-United States feeling of the government of Fidel Castro.

The city's oldest building, La Fuerza (The Fortress), stands just off the Plaza de Armas, around which Havana grew. Here also is the City Hall, a good example of colonial architecture. The nearby cathedral, dating from the 17th century, contains many art treasures. For many years it contained the supposed remains of Christopher Columbus. However, these remains, taken to Seville, Spain, in 1898, were most likely those of the discoverer's brother or son.

On either side of the narrow entrance to Havana Harbor stand two massive forts, built about 1590. Morro Castle, the larger, is perhaps the most famous landmark of Havana. La Punta stands on the other side. During the 17th and 18th centuries heavy chains were stretched between the two to keep enemy ships out of the harbor. La Cabaña, Havana's largest fortress, stands up the hill from Morro Castle.

The Parque Central, in the new section of Havana, is today the heart of the city. Near the park stands the magnificent white limestone Capitol, erected in 1929. The Prado, a beautiful broad promenade lined with palm trees, shrubs, and flowerbeds, leads to the Capitol from the Malecón, an attractive wide boulevard around Havana Bay. The University of Havana is the chief center of learning. There are also museums, libraries, and other cultural institutions.

Havana, originally founded on Cuba's southern coast, was probably established on its present site in 1519. Its safe and spacious harbor resulted in rapid growth; in less than 40 years it replaced Santiago as Cuba's capital. Havana was the early base for Spanish exploration in the New World. Hernando de Soto set out from here in his attempt to conquer Florida, which resulted in the discovery of the Mississippi River. Ships from Portobelo and Veracruz, loaded with riches, gathered periodically at Havana to be convoyed to Spain. For several centuries the city's great wealth invited repeated pirate attacks. To withstand these attacks Havana's fortresses were built. In 1898 the U.S. battleship *Maine* mysteriously blew up in Havana Harbor. This event brought on the Spanish-American War, which resulted in the end of Spanish rule in Cuba.

HAWAII, called the Aloha State, is the 50th state of the Union. Hawaii is composed of 20 islands in the North Pacific. It is about 2,400 miles from San Francisco.

The state's land area is slightly over 6,400 square miles. It ranks 47th in area. The inhabited islands are (from northwest to southeast) Niihau, Kauai, Oahu, Molokai, Lanai, Maui, and Hawaii. Honolulu, the capital, is situated on Oahu. The islands had a 1960 population of 632,772. An additional 50,000 persons are military personnel. The main group of islands is mountainous and of volcanic origin, rising from sea level to 13,825 feet (Mauna Kea, on the island of Hawaii).

The statue of King Kamehameha, known as Kamehameha the Great, stands in Honolulu.

The Hawaiian people are of a mixed racial stock. The fullblooded Hawaiians are Polynesians, who were the original inhabitants. Most of the people are from Asia, the Japanese being the most numerous. There is great racial harmony and almost no discrimination.

The Hawaiian Islands, inhabited for many centuries by Polynesians, were discovered by the British explorer James Cook in 1778. He named them the Sandwich Islands. Some historians contend that Spanish ships visited the archipelago as early as 1555. At the time of Cook's discovery the various islands were governed by local rulers. They were united in the late 18th century by Kamehameha I. Because of the islands' strategic location, whalers and traders began using Hawaii as a port of call. In 1820 the first group of New England missionaries arrived and began to play an important role in the development of the islands.

The Hawaiian Islands were annexed to the United States in 1898.

Havana, the chief city and port of Cuba, was once a lively tourist center.

Photo, Delta Air Lines

Ewing Galloway

Two years later they became known as the Territory of Hawaii, with Sanford B. Dole as governor. William F. Quinn became the first governor of the state of Hawaii.

HAWAII

Nickname: Aloha State

Seal: Coat of arms of monarchy in center—Goddess of Liberty on right holding state flag, King Kamehameha I on left—below shield, a phoenix

Flag: The British Union Flag at upper left—eight alternating red, white, and blue stripes on field

Motto: *Ua Mau Ke Ea O Ka Aina I Ka Pono* (The Life of the Land Is Perpetuated in Righteousness)

Flower: Red hibiscus

Bird: Néné (Hawaiian goose)

Capital: Honolulu

Largest city: Honolulu

Area: 6,435 sq. mi.

Rank in area: 47th

Population: 632,772 (plus 50,000 military personnel)

Chief university: University of Hawaii

Highest mountain peak: Mauna Kea (13,825 ft.)

Average temperature: Honolulu, 72° F. (Jan.), 78° F. (July)

Average annual rainfall: Less than 20 inches to over 450 inches

Chief economic activities: Agriculture, food processing, tourism

Chief crops: Sugarcane, pineapples

Chief manufactures: Processed sugar and pineapple

Notable attractions: Hawaii National Park, Mauna Loa, Waikiki Beach, Pearl Harbor

Important historical dates:

1778 Islands inhabited by Polynesians discovered by British explorer James Cook

1795 Various islands united by King Kamehameha I

1894 Republic of Hawaii declared

1898 U.S. annexation

1941 Attack on Pearl Harbor

1959 Became 50th state on August 21

An islander throws his fish net into the sea. Fishing is a sport and a serious business.

Above, the islanders prepare for a race in their outrigger canoes. Water sports, as boat racing, surfboard riding, water skiing, and swimming, are especially popular at Hawaii's most visited beach, Waikiki Beach in Honolulu.

Pineapple is harvested with mechanical aid at this vast plantation. Sugar and pineapple are the major agricultural products of Hawaii. Most of the world's canned pineapple is packed here.

Hawaii Visitors Bur.

Richard S. Yeo

Hawaii is one of the most popular vacation lands in America. Striking mountain scenery (left), luxuriant vegetation, rare plants, and many fine beaches (below) attract thousands of tourists annually.

Ray Atkeson

Location map

The official flag of Hawaii

The popular red hibiscus, Hawaii's state flower

The Néné, or Hawaiian goose, the state bird of Hawaii

Hawaii's colorful state seal

KAUAI

LEHUA

NOHILI PT.
Mana

Puuwai 1,281 FT.
NIIHAU
PUEO PT.
KAWAIHOA PT. KAUAI COUNTY

Haena Kilauea
Hanalei Bay
Hanalei Anahola
4,409 FT.
KAWAIKINI PK. Kealia
5,170 FT. Kapaa
Wailua
Kekaha Kalaheo Lihue Hanamaulu
Waimea Hanapepe Puhi
Kaumakani Koloa
Makaweli Eleele
Wahiawa MAKAHUENA PT.

KAUAI

P a c i

Kaulakahi Channel

Kauai Channel

Kawela KAHU
Ka
L
Waialua Haleiwa
Mokuleia Schofield
KAENA PT. Barracks
HONOLULU Wahia
Waianae Waipahu Kan
Nanakuli Ewa Pear
COUNTY
BARBERS PT. Pearl Harbor
Honolu

Kauai Channel

KAHUKU PT.
Waialee
Paumalu Kawela
KOOLAULOA Kahuku
Maunawai Laie
Kamananui
Kawailoa Beach Waimea Hauula
Camp
Haleiwa Kawailoa
Anahulu
KAENA PT. Mokuleia Opaeula Kahana
Waialua Camp
Helemano Kaaawa
Camp 2 KOOLAU
Makua Poamoho
KAALA PK. Whitmore Village
4,025 FT. Poamoho Camp
Schofield Wahiawa Waikane Kaneohe
Barracks WAHIAWA Bay KAPAPA
WAIANAE MOUNTAINS Kahaluu MOKU MAN
Kunia Waipio Camp Heeia MOKA
Waianae OAHU Waiawa Kaneohe
Lualualei E W A Coral Kailu
MAILI PT. PALIKEA Gardens La
3,098 FT. Waipahu Halawa NUUANU
Nanakuli Aiea PALI FUU
Middle PASS KONAHUANUI
Village Pearl City Salt L. 3,150 FT.
Waimanalo Fernandez
Village Village Ewa Pearl Harbor W
Gilbert SAND Kaimuki
Ewa Beach EWA BEACH Honolulu
BARBERS PT. Waikiki Maunalua Bay
Mamala Bay DIAMOND
HEAD

1″ = 8 Statute Miles

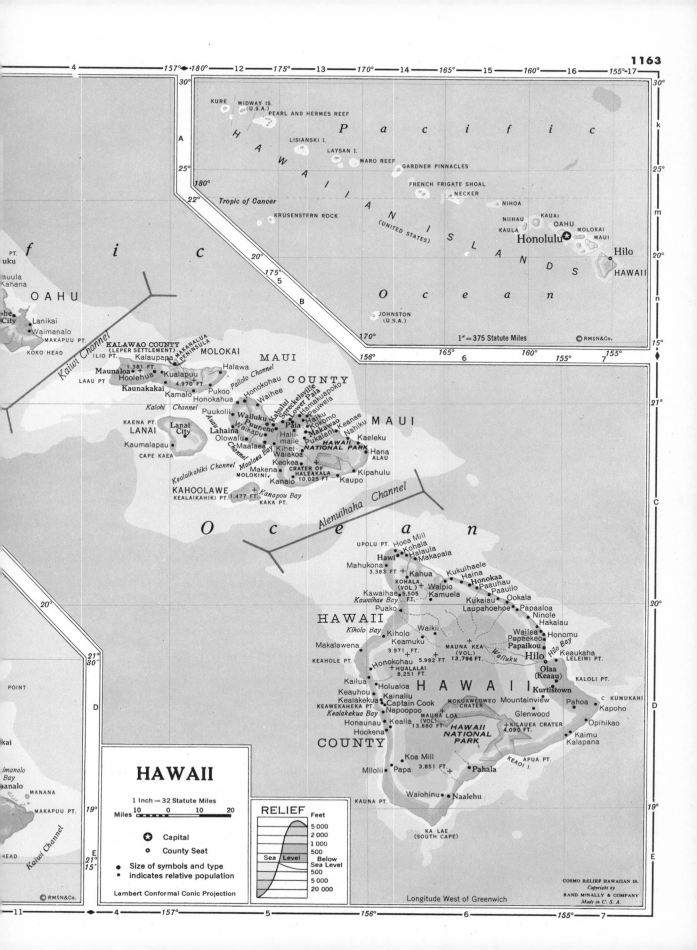

HAWAII NATIONAL PARK is one of the most spectacular volcanic areas in the world. The park includes two separate areas, the Kilauea-Mauna Loa section, on the island of Hawaii, and the Haleakala section, on the island of Maui. The park was established in 1916 and contains about 247,000 acres.

The chief attractions in the park are Mauna Loa, with its volcano Mokuaweoweo, and Kilauea, with the molten lava pit of Halemaumau. Kilauea erupted in 1959. Hawaii National Park also has a luxuriant tropical forest, native birds, spectacular cliffs, and a rugged coastline.

HAWKINS, SIR JOHN (1532-1595), an English admiral during the reign of Queen Elizabeth I, was born in Plymouth into a family of sailors and shipbuilders and learned the sea at an early age. He first earned fame by stealing slaves from Portuguese ships off the coast of Africa and smuggling the captured slaves into Spanish possessions in America. His first voyage of this kind began in 1562 and was followed by similar expeditions in 1564 and 1567. On the third voyage he was trapped by a Spanish fleet in the harbor of Veracruz, in Mexico, and escaped with only two ships. For several years after his return to England he did not return to the sea.

In 1573 Hawkins became treasurer of the navy and shortly thereafter was appointed its comptroller as well. These positions made him the navy's principal administrative officer. He kept Queen Elizabeth's ships in good order, although some suspected him of fraud in office. He returned to the sea in 1588, serving as a rear admiral in the English defeat of the Spanish Armada, for which he was knighted. In 1590 and

Sir John Hawkins

HAWAII NATIONAL PARK

The golden eagle, left, is a bird of the mountains; the bald eagle prefers shores and rivers.

again 1595 he participated in treasure-hunting voyages, neither of which was successful. On the second of these voyages, which was led by his cousin Sir Francis Drake, he died and was buried at sea off the coast of Puerto Rico.

HAWKS, KITES, EAGLES, related large birds of prey. Over 200 species are found worldwide, and 25 of them are in North America. Some are majestic birds of enormous size; some are as small as doves. All have hooked talons for grasping their prey and hooked bills for tearing it apart. They have powerful wings and keen vision. They feed mostly on fish, reptiles, amphibians, birds, and small mammals. Some small species also feed on large insects.

The female hawk is always larger than the male and is sometimes very differently colored. The pairs seem to mate for life, and both share in nest building, egg incubation, and the care of the young. The nest, a platform of sticks, is often seen high in a tree but is sometimes on a ledge or on the ground. The down-covered young are helpless; sometimes they cannot even stand until they are several weeks old.

This bird family, called the hawk family, includes groups known as kites, accipiters, buteos, eagles, and harriers. Falcons are also hawks, but they belong to a different family.

Kites live in warm regions. They are graceful birds with a long tail. Their long wings are often held on a dihedral as the birds expertly soar and glide. North America has four species: white-tailed, swallow-tailed, Mississippi, and everglade. The everglade kite is a fast-disappearing species because it feeds only on a particular kind of very scarce snail.

Accipiters, the true hawks, are recognized by their short, rounded wings and long tail. Worldwide there are 46 species. Best known in North America are the goshawk, the sharp-shinned hawk, and the Cooper's

hawk. These are the hawks that dart swiftly at their prey and sometimes take birds and poultry. In the Old World some accipiters have been trained for falconry.

The large hawks known as buteos (called buzzards in England) have broad wings and short tails. They often soar in circles high in the sky. North American buteos are the red-tailed, Swainson's, zone-tailed, white-tailed, short-tailed, rough-legged, ferruginous, gray, Harris', and black hawks.

The eagles and sea eagles of this large hawk family are represented in North America by the golden eagle and the bald eagle. See EAGLE.

The harrier, or marsh hawk, glides low over meadows and marshes in search of prey. It is found from the Gulf of St. Lawrence to the Gulf of Mexico. Its wings and tail are long. The male is gray with dark wingtips; the female is brown. Both are identified by a conspicuous white rump patch.

Falcons have long pointed wings, a long tail, and a rapid wingbeat. In North America they include the gyrfalcon, sparrow hawk, pigeon hawk, peregrine falcon, prairie falcon, and Aplomado falcon. See FALCON.

Hawks are among the best wild friends of the farmer. While it is true that some hawks do kill chickens and wild birds, most kinds of hawks are beneficial, for they eat large numbers of rats, mice, and other rodents harmful to agriculture.

Although some hawks can stand cold weather, the majority migrate to warm regions. They go down the broad river valleys, along the mountain ridges, and down the coast. Like gliders they take advantage of air currents to speed them on their way. Certain spots, such as the tip of Cape May Peninsula in New Jersey and Hawk Mountain near Hamburg, Pa., have become famous for the large numbers of hawks seen migrating there.

HAWKS, KITES, EAGLES

Marsh Hawk

Goshawk

Swallow-Tailed Kite

Sparrow Hawk

Everglade Kite

These birds of prey include four from North America and one (Brahminy kite) from Asia and Australia. The goshawk feeds largely on mammals. The marsh hawk searches meadows for small prey. The swallow-tailed kite and the sparrow hawk feed on small animals and large insects. The everglade kite eats a rare species of large snail; the Brahminy kite feeds on small animals and carrion.

Brahminy Kite

HAWTHORN, a thorny shrub or small tree belonging to the rose family. Hawthorns have numerous spreading branches and simple leaves, which have saw-toothed margins. The lovely five-petaled flowers look somewhat like crab-apple blossoms. Usually ranging in color from white to rose, they are sometimes deep crimson. They are borne in flat-topped clusters and often are very fragrant. The small, roundish fruits, called haws, are usually red, although in some species they are orange or yellow, and in a few they are purple. They are $\frac{1}{4}$ to 1 inch in diameter and resemble crab apples or tiny red apples. They sometimes hang on all winter and are always very decorative. In some regions these fruits are gathered after frost and eaten raw or made into jelly.

More than 1,000 different kinds of hawthorns are native to the United States. They are found in almost all parts of the country and are known also as haw, red haw, or thorn tree. The English hawthorn is much used for hedges in England and is planted to some extent in gardens in the United States. For many centuries its flowers were strung into garlands for the English May Day celebrations. For that reason the tree is often called the May tree.

The scarlet haw, whose leaves, flowers, and fruits are shown below, grows wild in woods and meadows of the eastern and midwestern United States. The small fruits are green at first but turn red during autumn. Thorns grow from the smaller branches. Hawthorns belong to the same family as apple trees.

HAWTHORNE, NATHANIEL (1804-1864), an American author. Two of his novels, *The Scarlet Letter* and *The House of the Seven Gables*, are among the most famous books of American literature.

Hawthorne was born in Salem, Mass. His father, a ship's captain, died when Hawthorne was four years old. The shock of her husband's death caused his mother to retire into solitude. This way of life probably contributed to Hawthorne's later solitary habits.

NATHANIEL HAWTHORNE

In Salem, Mass., Nathaniel Hawthorne's birthplace, stands the "House of the Seven Gables," according to tradition the setting of the author's novel of the same name.

When he was 14 years old, Hawthorne spent a summer at a remote Maine lake. This experience gave him a love of life in the wilderness and an ability to be contented when he was alone. He later attended Bowdoin College and was graduated in 1825.

For the next 11 years Hawthorne lived a generally solitary life in Salem. He began his writing career during this time. His first novel, *Fanshawe*, was a failure. Hawthorne then turned to short stories and wrote such tales as "The Maypole of Merry Mount," "Endicott and the Red Cross," and "The Ambitious Guest." Most of his stories dealt with moral and religious conflicts in New England, and this theme became Hawthorne's favorite. Many of the stories were collected and published in 1837 as *Twice-Told Tales*.

Beginning in 1836 Hawthorne worked for two years as a magazine editor in Boston. From 1839 to 1841 he served as an official in the Boston Custom House. He spent several months in 1841 and 1842 living at Brook Farm, the idealistic community in West Roxbury in which such leading authors as Ralph Waldo Emerson and Henry David Thoreau were interested. Hawthorne was

married to Sophia Peabody in 1842. The couple moved to Concord, Mass., and lived in a house called the Old Manse. He continued his career as an author and wrote such short stories as "Young Goodman Brown" and "Rappaccini's Daughter." These and other stories were collected and published as *Mosses from an Old Manse*.

Hawthorne worked as surveyor of the port of Salem from 1846 to 1849 and wrote little during this period, but after leaving this post he wrote two of his masterpieces, the novels *The Scarlet Letter* and *The House of the Seven Gables*. These books, dealing with spiritual conflict in New England, brought him worldwide fame. He followed them with *The Blithedale Romance* and two books for children, *A Wonder Book* and *Tanglewood Tales*. He also wrote the short stories "Ethan Brand" and "The Great Stone Face."

As a reward for writing President Franklin Pierce's campaign biography, Hawthorne was appointed United States consul to Liverpool, England. He served from 1853 to 1858 and then traveled in England and Italy. He wrote *The Marble Faun* and *Our Old Home* about his European experiences. He returned to Concord in 1860. During his last years Hawthorne began several books but completed none of them.

HAY, JOHN MILTON (1838-1905), U.S. secretary of state under Presidents William McKinley and Theodore Roosevelt, is best known as the sponsor of the open-door policy toward China and as the negotiator of the Hay-Pauncefote Treaty, an Anglo-American agreement that made possible the building of the Panama Canal.

John Milton Hay

Hay was born in Salem, Ind., and grew up on the Illinois frontier. After being graduated from Brown University in Rhode Island he returned to Illinois and took up the study of law in his uncle's office in Springfield. There he met Abraham Lincoln, whose assistant private secretary Hay became in 1861. This position he obtained through the recommendation of Lincoln's private secretary, Hay's old friend John G. Nicolay. After Lincoln's death Hay served as a diplomatic official in several European countries. In 1870 he returned to the United States, where he worked as an editor for the New York *Herald Tribune*, wrote poetry and a travel book, and began a ten-year collaboration with Nicolay on their biography of Lincoln. Hay was assistant secretary of state from 1879 to 1881 and in 1897-1898 was ambassador to Great Britain.

From 1898 until his death he served as secretary of state. In this position he worked for the cession of the Philippine Islands to the United States and supported the suppression of the Philippine rebellion for independence, led by Emilio Aguinaldo. During 1899 Hay worked for the acceptance of the open-door policy, a policy by which the various powers having commercial interests in China agreed not to discriminate economically against one another. Not so well known but perhaps more important was Hay's determination that the Boxer Rebellion should not be used as an excuse to further impair Chinese sovereignty. Hay's clever handling of the Alaskan Boundary Dispute, postponing the decision from 1899 until 1903 when all sides were calmer, resulted in a decision favorable to the United States. Finally, Hay is known for his negotiations on the subject of the Panama Canal. The first of these

resulted in the Hay-Pauncefote Treaty with Great Britain; the second, in the Hay-Herrán Treaty and the Hay-Bunau-Varilla Treaty. The Hay-Herrán Treaty provided for the lease from Colombia of the land through which the canal was to be built. Columbia rejected the convention because the price was too low. Shortly thereafter Panama revolted from Colombia, and Hay negotiated the Hay-Bunau-Varilla Treaty with the Panamanian representative. This treaty provided for the lease of the land from Panama. It gave the United States sovereignty over the land leased as well as the right to fortify it, though the canal zone was to be neutral, as provided by the Hay-Pauncefote Treaty. See HAY-PAUNCEFOTE TREATY; OPEN-DOOR POLICY.

HAY, dried grasses or legumes that are fed to livestock. The grasses that are dried to make hay include timothy, orchard grass, brome grass, fescue, and Bermuda grass. The legumes that are dried to make hay include clovers, alfalfa, lespedeza, birdsfoot trefoil, vetches, field peas, and cowpeas. Hay is made from the stems, blossoms, and leaves of grasses and legumes.

Most hay crops should be cut after the plants are fully grown but before their seeds have formed. After being mowed, the crop must be cured, or dried, before it is stored, so it will not rot. Another reason for drying hay is that undried hay piled in a stack either inside or outside a barn may generate enough

heat to set itself on fire. It is often dried by being raked into long, low, narrow heaps, called windrows, and left in the sun and wind for a period of from one-half day to several days, depending upon how hot and dry the weather is. The old adage "Make hay while the sun shines" arose from the fact that persistent rain or damp weather spoils drying hay. Some farmers dry their hay artificially in the haymow or on a wagon. While drying, the grass or alfalfa loses some of its green color. After it is dried, the hay may be stacked and left in the field or stored in the haymow. Many farmers press and tie it into rectangular or cylindrical bales and store it in the barn.

Hay is a nutritious food for cattle, horses, and sheep and is fed to them during winter or at other times when green pasture grass is not available. Hay will last for several years if kept dry.

HAYDN, FRANZ JOSEPH (1732-1809), a famous Austrian composer and the first great master of the symphony and of the string quartet, was born at Rohrau, Austria. His father was a wheelwright; his mother, a cook in a nobleman's family. But both were musical, and the evenings of Haydn's early childhood were spent listening to his father play the harp while his mother sang the folksongs of Hungary. A family cousin named Frank, who was a music teacher, noticed the boy's talent and undertook to teach him all that he knew. It was at his house that Haydn saw Reuter, the chapel-

After the ripened grass in the photograph has been mowed, it will be left in the sun to dry further. The drawings are of grasses and legumes that are commonly made into hay. Brome grass has large clusters of spikelets that contain many seeds. Meadow fescue is grown for hay in many parts of North America. Timothy grass is tall and has long, slender leaves.

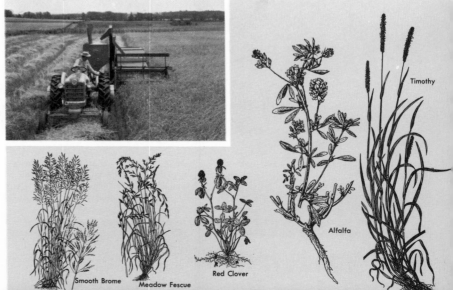

Timothy

Alfalfa

Smooth Brome

Meadow Fescue

Red Clover

master of the cathedral in Vienna. He was looking for choirboys and gave the lad a chant to sing at sight. Reuter was surprised at the beauty of Haydn's voice and made him a chorister in the church at St. Stephen. Haydn studied and sang there for nine years, but at the age of 17 his voice broke. For some childish prank he was expelled from the school and was thrown upon the world penniless. Ten years of poverty, starvation, and struggle followed, but during it all he devoted himself to music. At last he was made director of Prince Esterházy's orchestra, at that time the finest in Austria, and he held this position for 30 years. In 50 years Haydn wrote over 500 pieces of music. During an 18-month visit to England he wrote an opera, *Orfeo*, nine symphonies, and accompaniments to more than 100 songs. A later composition was the Austrian national anthem.

Rutherford B. Hayes

HAYES, RUTHERFORD BIRCHARD (1822-1893), 19th president of the United States, was born in Delaware, Ohio, Oct. 4, 1822. He was graduated from Kenyon College in 1842. He studied law at Harvard and was admitted to the Ohio bar in 1845. He was established in Cincinnati, Ohio, in 1850 and was affiliated with the Whig party until the Republican party arose, after which he was consistently a Republican. During the Civil War he served the Union first as a major, then as a major general. He was elected to Congress in 1864 and was reelected in 1866. In 1867 he was elected governor of Ohio and was reelected in 1869. His administration was noted for its sound and progressive measures. The Republican party nominated him for the presidency

in 1876, and he ran against Samuel Jones Tilden. The election was disputed because both parties claimed the electoral votes of Louisiana, Florida, Oregon, and South Carolina. A special commission was to decide which votes were valid. As part of an agreement to have the Southern electoral votes counted in his favor, Hayes ended the military occupation of the South, and the Reconstruction Period came to an end. He also pursued conciliatory policies toward the South and encouraged civil service reforms. He opposed cheap-money policies and resumed specie payments on the public debt. His party did not agree with him on many policies. Hayes did not choose to run for another term and retired at the end of four years. He devoted the rest of his life to humanitarian reforms. He died in Fremont, Ohio.

HAY FEVER is one of the forms of allergy seen in persons who are allergic to pollens, to other airborne substances, and to some foods. The principal symptoms are the result of severe irritation of the membranes of the upper respiratory tract and the eyes.

Seasonal hay fever may be caused by any pollen to which a person is sensitive. Fall hay fever in the United States begins in August and lasts until frost and is usually caused by the pollen of ragweed. Most persons having hay fever are sensitive to the pollen of more than one plant; the symptoms parallel the seasons of pollination of the plants to which the person is sensitive. Attacks begin and end at the same times each year.

The symptoms of hay fever are very similar to those of a severe head cold. Common complications of hay fever are sinusitis and asthma, the latter being present in up to 20 percent of the cases.

In determining the specific substances that cause the symptoms of hay fever, skin tests with a number of test substances may be necessary. The treatment of hay fever may include the use of such drugs as ephedrine to shrink the mucous membrane of the nose, control the discharge, and relieve itching. Taking such drugs by mouth is also effective. In many cases the antihistaminic drugs will effectively control symptoms. For the prevention of the occurrence of symptoms, desensitizing injections may be given well in advance of the hay fever season. These injections consist of very dilute solutions of the substances to

which the person is sensitive. The strength of the solution is gradually increased with the object of building up the person's tolerance to exposure to the offending allergens. Symptoms may also be prevented by avoiding exposure to the exciting allergens. This entails eliminating the allergenic substances from the environment, by such measures as air-conditioning, or avoiding contact with the substances by moving to a region where plants producing the offending pollens, for example, do not grow. See ALLERGY.

HAYMARKET MASSACRE was a violent incident in U.S. labor history. It occurred on May 4, 1886, during a labor demonstration in Haymarket Square, Chicago, protesting the shooting by police of various men who had been striking unsuccessfully for an eight-hour day. As police tried to break up the demonstration, someone threw a bomb into their midst, killing 7 policemen and injuring about 70. Eight anarchists were arrested, for anarchists had been active in organizing the demonstration. Although the prosecution could not prove that any of the arrested men had thrown the bomb or had had anything to do with the plan to throw it, all were convicted of conspiracy because of their beliefs. Four were hanged, one committed suicide, and three remained in prison until Illinois Governor John Peter Altgeld pardoned them in 1893 on the ground that the trial had been highly biased. The thrower of the bomb was never found.

HAY-PAUNCEFOTE TREATY, a treaty with Great Britain, signed Nov. 18, 1901, which made possible the building of the Panama Canal by the United States. Under the provisions of an earlier treaty Britain and the United States had agreed that any canal across Central America should be protected jointly by the two countries. (See CLAYTON-BULWER TREATY.) The new treaty gave the United States the right to build and regulate a canal. It also provided that the canal be open to ships of all nations at equal and reasonable toll rates. The right of the United States to fortify the canal was not mentioned in the treaty but was taken for granted by the governments of both countries.

The treaty was a revision of an earlier Hay-Pauncefote Treaty (Feb. 5, 1900), which had been rejected by Great Britain after amendments unacceptable to it had been made by the United States Senate.

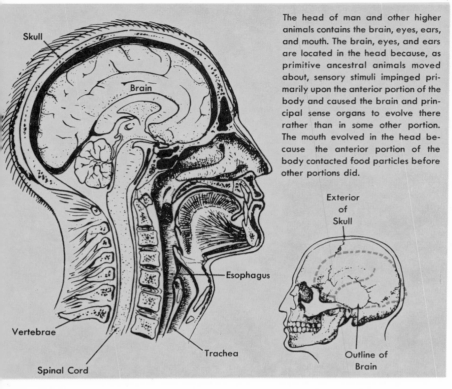

Skull

Brain

Esophagus

Vertebrae

Trachea

Spinal Cord

Exterior of Skull

Outline of Brain

The head of man and other higher animals contains the brain, eyes, ears, and mouth. The brain, eyes, and ears are located in the head because, as primitive ancestral animals moved about, sensory stimuli impinged primarily upon the anterior portion of the body and caused the brain and principal sense organs to evolve there rather than in some other portion. The mouth evolved in the head because the anterior portion of the body contacted food particles before other portions did.

HAZE, fine dust or salt particles scattered through the atmosphere. These particles are so tiny that they cannot be seen without a microscope, but they cut down visibility and give the atmosphere a hazy appearance. Haze casts a bluish or yellowish veil over the landscape and subdues its colors. These colorations make haze different from mist, which is grayish. See Fog; Smog.

HAZEL, one of several species of trees and shrubs that belong to a single genus of the birch family. All species are native only to the North Temperate Zone. Some bear edible hazelnuts or filberts and are cultivated for these nuts.

The native European species of hazel is a shrub that grows from 10 to 15 feet high. The nut produced by this species is about ¾ inch long. Although this hazel is cultivated in Europe for its nuts, it is cultivated in North America chiefly for ornamental purposes.

The Turkish hazel, which is native to western Asia and southeastern Europe, is a tree that may attain a height of 60 feet. Although this species bears edible nuts, it is grown in Europe and North America chiefly for ornament.

The species that bears the oblong nuts known as filberts is a shrub that grows from 10 to 30 feet high. Native to western Asia and southeastern Europe, this hazel is cultivated in Europe and North America both for its nuts and for ornament.

HEAD, the part of the body of an animal—such as a mammal, a bird, or an insect—that contains the brain, certain special sense organs, and the mouth. The head is located at the anterior end of the body or, as in man, at the highest level. Even in a worm there is a tendency for the development of a head, that is, for concentration of sense organs and food-gathering structures at the anterior end of the body. See Ear; Eye; Mouth; Nose.

In man the bony framework of the head is the skull. It is set on the summit of the vertebral column and is composed of the cranium and the bones of the face. The cranium is a strong bony case enclosing the brain. The bones of the face surround the mouth and nose and, with the cranium, make up the orbital cavities, which enclose the eyes. All the bones of the skull except the jawbone are firmly united. In babies there are temporary gaps, or fontanels, in the skull; these gaps form soft spots on the baby's head. The skull has many holes in it, some large and some small, through which arteries, veins, and nerves enter and pass out. Cavities in the bones of the head are known as sinuses. There are sinuses over the eyes, under the eyes, and behind the nose.

HEADACHE, a pain in the head. It is a common symptom of disease of both the body and the emotions. Many headaches are trivial and last such a short time that only the mildest of remedies, such as aspirin, is needed. However, headache can also be a symptom of serious disease. Determining the cause of persistent headache is difficult. Often the physician must perform a complete physical examination.

Migraine is a distinct type of headache with dramatic symptoms. On waking in the morning the victim may feel confused. He has zigzag bright spots before his eyes, followed by blackness in one half of his field of vision; a dull, boring, throbbing headache is present on the opposite side of the head. He also experiences nausea and vomiting. The underlying cause of migraine is unknown. Emotional disturbances are believed to be important in bringing on an attack of migraine. Some authorities believe that allergy is of major significance.

HEADHUNTER. A headhunter is one who decapitates enemies and preserves their heads. Heads have been almost universally taken as trophies in war. The practice has persisted even in recent times among primitive tribes of South America, the

These macabre trophies are facsimiles of the shrunken heads of foes slain in battle by the Jivaro Indians of Ecuador.

Roy Pinney—Monkmeyer

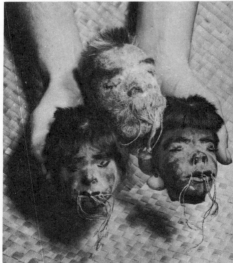

eastern frontier of India, the Malay Peninsula, New Guinea, and small islands of the South Pacific.

Headhunting was practiced by precursors of Western culture. The ancient Babylonians and Assyrians cut off the heads of slain enemies. The Hebrew David cut off Goliath's head and brought it before King Saul. The Celts also took heads as trophies of battle.

Among primitive tribes heads were often preserved as skulls or as mummified or shrunken heads. The Jivaro of Ecuador became expert head shrinkers. Initial contact with Westerners actually encouraged headhunting through a new industry—the collecting and shrinking of heads for sale as curios.

Among most headhunting tribes heads were more than mere trophies; taking heads was a means of gaining prestige. Among the Dyaks of Borneo, for example, heads were required for all great events. No Dyak man could marry without first taking a head. Headhunting was the basis of this people's religion. No man's house or fields were blessed unless he had a large collection of heads.

Recent attempts of governments to stamp out headhunting have greatly disrupted tribal cultures. In spite of such attempts headhunting is presumed to continue among isolated tribes in some areas.

HEALTH. A healthy person is free from disease or other ailment. However, in one sense, health is relative. An aged person, a handicapped person, or a person with disease under control may be healthy. This may be true even though his body does not function as efficiently as a body without such a disability.

Health is preserved only through the combined efforts of the government, the family, and the individual. The government takes an interest in our health at birth and throughout life. It recognizes that the health of the individual and of the community may depend on measures that have to be enforced by law. Such laws are designed to eliminate disease-producing conditions in the community, to prevent the occurrence of disease, and to control the spread of disease once it does occur. See PUBLIC HEALTH.

In a person's infancy, the family lays the groundwork for that person's continued health. This is done when parents provide proper food, proper physical and mental activity, proper rest, and proper conditions for emotional development. In addi-

FUEL FOR THE HUMAN MACHINE

PROTEIN

CARBOHYDRATE

FAT

The body compared to an automobile:
1. *rotary joints = wheels*
2. *muscles = cylinders*
3. *nerve endings = spark plugs*
4. *nerve system = distributor*
5. *arteries = fuel line*
6. *lungs = carburetor*
7. *heart = fuel pump*
8. *digestive organs = fuel system*
9. *nerve impulses = ignition*
10. *waste = exhaust*
11. *oxygen = air intake*

To maintain good health, a person must eat proper amounts of the foods necessary to movement and growth. Some of these foods are stored; others are used immediately. Several processes in the body are analogous to processes in an automobile, as shown above.

Good personal habits in everyday living improve a person's chances for having good health.

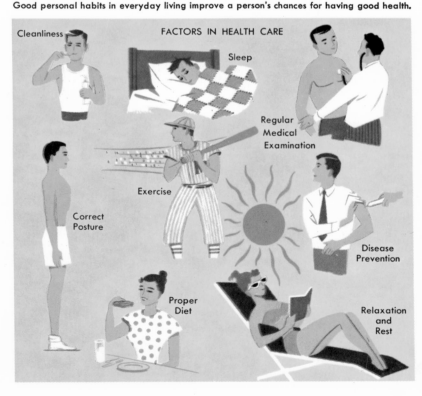

FACTORS IN HEALTH CARE

Cleanliness

Sleep

Regular Medical Examination

Exercise

Correct Posture

Disease Prevention

Proper Diet

Relaxation and Rest

tion, specific diseases are prevented by inoculations, for example, by vaccination for smallpox.

The individual's responsibility for health begins with a proper regard for the needs of his body. For the body to function properly and to fight off disease and the effects of unavoidable injury, it needs foods that supply the essentials for energy, growth, tissue repair, and function. (See NUTRITION.) It needs an adequate supply of oxygen in the air ("fresh" air) for the oxidation (burning) of food. It needs rest and sleep to permit it to recover from physical and mental exertion. Emotional health is also important to physical health; in fact, ill health can be an excuse for failure to resolve an emotional conflict. Personal cleanliness promotes health by eliminating conditions that encourage the multiplication and spread of disease-producing organisms. Finally, periodic physical examinations, particularly as a person grows older, may reveal conditions that may be corrected before they undermine the health.

HEALTH, EDUCATION, AND WELFARE, UNITED STATES DEPARTMENT OF, an executive branch of the U.S. government, created in 1953. It was established for the purpose of improving the administration of those agencies of the government whose major responsibilities are to promote the general welfare in the fields of health, education, and economic security. The affairs of the department are supervised and directed by the secretary, who

is a member of the president's cabinet. The major operating agencies of the department are: the Social Security Administration, which is responsible for the administration of the system of old age, survivors, and disability insurance and of public-assistance and child-welfare programs and for chartering and supervising federal credit unions; the Office of Education, which collects information on school systems and administrative procedures and conducts studies to guide educational practices; the Public Health Service, which conducts and supports medical research, provides medical care to eligible beneficiaries, and assists the states and other governments in the prevention and control of disease; the Food and Drug Administration, which enforces laws protecting consumers against impure foods, drugs, and cosmetics; and the Office of Vocational Rehabilitation, which cooperates with the states in providing services to handicapped persons to prepare them for employment and to place them in jobs.

HEARING is the ability to perceive sound. (See SOUND.) Both arthropods and vertebrates have true organs for hearing, that is, organs sensitive to stimulation by sound waves. In vertebrates this organ is called the ear. (See EAR.) In all mammals, including man, the organ of hearing has a sound-collecting

attachment surrounding an opening, or canal, leading into the head. Lower vertebrates have no sound-collecting attachment. For example, the frog has eardrums on both sides of the head to receive sound waves by air and water.

In the arthropods the simplest auditory organ consists of a nerve ending with accessory cells connected with the body wall. The organ is presumably stimulated by vibrations from the body wall. Such insects as the grasshopper and the mosquito have a more complicated organ for hearing. In a grasshopper the organs for hearing are located on the sides of the abdomen. In a mosquito these organs are located at the base of antennae.

Animals other than man are able to perceive sounds of higher and lower frequencies than those heard by man. Partial or total loss of hearing is known as deafness. See DEAFNESS.

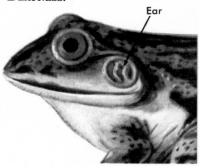

Ear

The frog lacks external ears, such as are found in man. It hears by means of the exposed eardrums lying just behind each eye.

The frequency range of human hearing is compared below with the ranges of various musical instruments and the human voice.

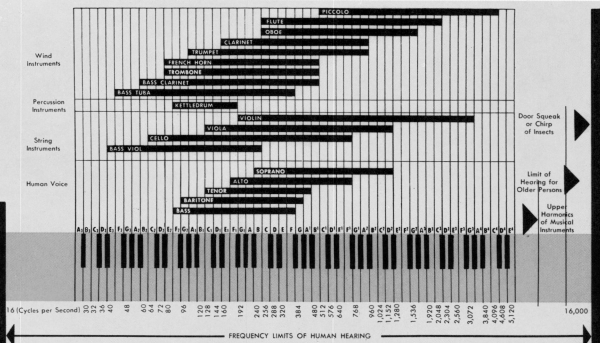

FREQUENCY LIMITS OF HUMAN HEARING

HEARST, WILLIAM RANDOLPH

(1863-1951), an American publisher of newspapers and magazines. He established and owned one of the largest chains of newspapers in the United States.

Hearst was born in San Francisco, the son of George and Phoebe Hearst. His father was a wealthy mine owner, and his mother became noted for her financial gifts to the University of California. George Hearst bought a daily newspaper, the San Francisco *Daily Examiner*, in 1880. When he entered the United States Senate in 1886, he turned over the operation of the newspaper to his son William.

For the next 50 years William Randolph Hearst concentrated on establishing a large chain of newspapers throughout the United States. At one time he was the owner and publisher of 31 daily and Sunday papers. Among them were the New York *Mirror*, New York *Journal-American*, Chicago *Herald-American*, Boston *American*, and Los Angeles *Examiner*. He also published such magazines as *Good Housekeeping*, *Harper's Bazaar*, *Town and Country*, and *House Beautiful*.

Hearst served in the United States House of Representatives from 1903 to 1907 as a Democrat from New York. He ran for governor of New York as a Democrat in 1906 but was unsuccessful. In 1919 Hearst began building San Simeon, a huge mansion on the California seacoast between Los Angeles and San Francisco. The structure, surrounded by 245,000 acres of land, was completed 18 years later at a cost of about 30 million dollars. The state of California now owns San Simeon and has made it into a memorial to Hearst.

HEART, a hollow muscular organ located in the chest cavity between the lungs. It weighs less than 1 pound and is only a little larger than the fist. Its job is to pump blood to all the body tissues. It has a tough, muscular wall that rests in a fiber-like bag and is lined by a thin, strong membrane. A wall divides the heart cavity down the middle into a right heart and a left heart. Each side of the heart is divided into an upper chamber (auricle) and a lower chamber (ventricle). Valves regulate the flow of blood through the heart and to the arteries. The heart receives a blood supply to its own muscles from two arteries that branch from the aorta, the main artery carrying blood from the heart

to the whole body. The heart is really a double pump. One pump (the right heart) receives blood from the body and pumps it through the lungs, where it gets rid of a gas (carbon dioxide) and picks up a fresh supply of oxygen. The second pump (the left heart) receives this reconditioned blood from the lungs and pumps it out through the main artery, the aorta, to be distributed by smaller arteries to all parts of the body. Its pumping rate is controlled by two sets of nerves. One set slows or stops the heartbeat; the other set speeds up the heartbeat. See CIRCULATION.

In heart operations it is sometimes necessary to maintain circulation artificially. This is done by a

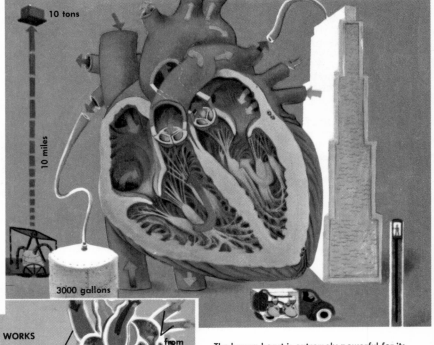

10 tons

10 miles

3000 gallons

The human heart is extremely powerful for its size (above). It pumps about 3,000 gallons of blood daily. In a 70-year lifetime it could pump 77,000,000 gallons of blood—enough to fill a skyscraper—or raise 10 tons 10 miles. A heart supplies enough power to raise a man five floors per hour in an elevator. The power of two hearts could drive a truck around the world in two years.

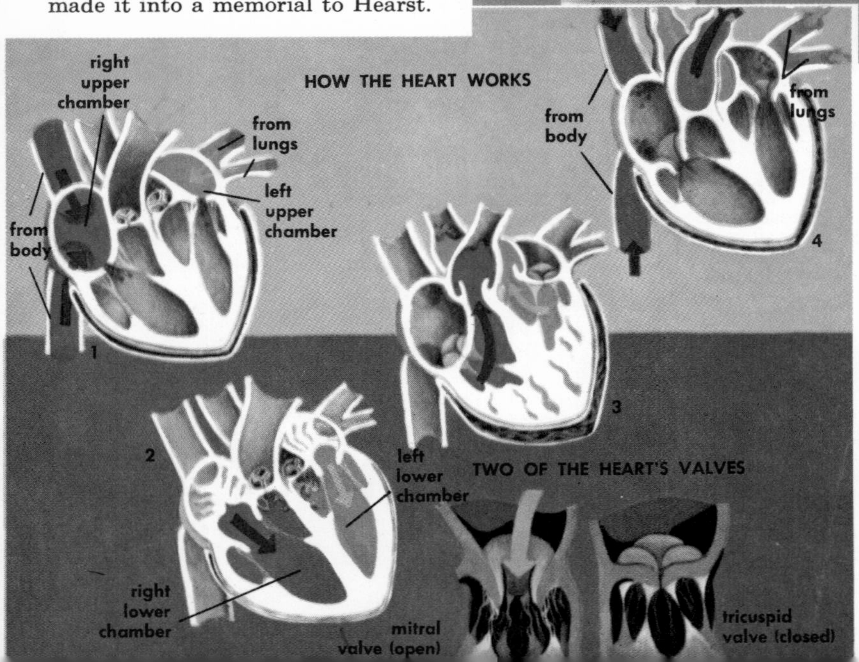

Stages in the heart's cycle are shown at left. **1.** Blood from the veins enters the auricles. **2.** The auricles contract and force blood into the ventricles. **3.** The ventricles contract, closing valves from the auricles and opening valves to the arteries. Blood from the right ventricle goes to the lungs; blood from the left ventricle goes to the body. **4.** The cycle begins again.

HOW THE HEART WORKS

right upper chamber

from lungs

left upper chamber

from body

from body

from lungs

left lower chamber

right lower chamber

mitral valve (open)

TWO OF THE HEART'S VALVES

tricuspid valve (closed)

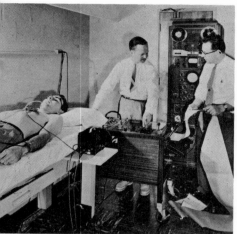

Wide World Photo

Heart sounds that are inaudible through a physician's stethoscope can be recorded by using this special electrical machine.

device known as the artificial heart. This device is really a mechanical pump that also provides oxygen for the blood. Plastic tubes connect it both to the veins to the heart and to the arteries from the heart. When the artificial heart operates, it takes over the functions of both the lungs and the heart. In order to keep blood free of air the tubes are filled with blood before they are inserted in the blood vessels. The heart tissues are supplied with blood through arteries branching off from the main artery into which the artificial heart feeds. This keeps the heart beating feebly without having the job of pumping.

HEART DISEASE. Any disease of the heart interferes with the heart's function of pumping blood through the body to nourish the tissues. There are many symptoms of heart disease. One is shortness of breath at rest or on slight exertion. This symptom is an indication that the heart is not pumping blood at a sufficient rate to meet the demands of the tissues for oxygen or to remove waste products such as carbon dioxide. Heart disease may be classified as congenital or acquired.

Congenital heart disease results from anomalies (defects) of the heart or circulatory system. Such defects are caused by maldevelopment of the embryo during the first three months, the time when the heart and great vessels are formed. The aorta may narrow over part of its length a few inches beyond its beginning (coarctation of the aorta). The persistence after birth of a large vessel joining the aorta and pulmonary artery (ductus arteriosus), which plays an important part in the fetal circulation, is a common congenital defect. Some defects re-

sult in poor physical development. Others cause cyanosis, or blueness of the skin, the outstanding symptom of so-called blue babies. The cause of congenital heart disease is unknown. However, German measles in the first three months of pregnancy may result in congenital deformities in the offspring.

Acquired heart disease may be classified as rheumatic heart disease, arteriosclerotic heart disease, and heart disease secondary to disease elsewhere in the body.

Rheumatic heart disease is a consequence of acute rheumatic fever. This disease usually occurs in childhood or adolescence and results in inflammation of the whole heart. The heart valves tend to become scarred as they heal. They are further damaged by repeated acute attacks of rheumatic fever. The deformed valves interfere with the pumping action of the heart. By the use of antibiotics, repeated attacks of acute rheumatic fever can be prevented. By surgery many valvular deformities of rheumatic heart disease can be corrected.

Arteriosclerotic heart disease results from a degenerative process in the walls of the blood vessels supplying the heart. It is commonest among men of middle age and older. Narrowing of the blood vessels interferes with the function of the heart muscle supplied by them. If a blood vessel to the heart is suddenly blocked by a clot, a heart attack results. If enough of the blood vessels are narrowed, heart failure results. If the supply of blood to the heart muscle is insufficient for heart action during exertion, the pain of angina pectoris occurs. The cause of arteriosclerosis is unknown. However, possible contributing factors are diet, way of life, and the presence of diabetes. Operations have been designed to increase the blood flow to the heart.

In heart disease secondary to other diseases the treatment depends on controlling the underlying disease and improving circulatory function.

An instrument used in the diagnosis of heart disease is the electrocardiograph. This instrument records the changes in electric potential displayed by muscular activity of the heart. The art of interpreting this record and diagnosing heart conditions therefrom is called electrocardiography.

About the middle of the 19th century it was established that the contraction and relaxation of the heart gave rise to a change of elec-

trical potential within the human body. Thirty years later it was demonstrated that this change could be recorded on a galvanometer, an instrument for detecting an electric current. In 1903 Willem Einthoven, a Dutch physiologist, devised the first electrocardiograph, which used a camera to make a photographic record of the changes shown by a galvanometer.

Development of the vacuum-tube amplifier and of more rugged and accurate galvanometers of the oscillographic type made possible the construction of the amplifier type of electrocardiograph now most commonly used. The galvanometers employed are 10,000 times more sensitive than the galvanometer Einthoven used. A mirror is attached to the moving element of the galvanometer, and records of the movement are made on a film.

HEARTS is a card game. It is called hearts because one of the basic objectives is to avoid taking heart cards in tricks.

From three to six persons may play the common varieties of hearts. An ordinary deck of 52 cards is used, with the cards in each suit ranking from the ace down to the 2. The dealer gives the first card to the person on his left and then continues, dealing one at a time clockwise, until the entire pack is dealt. (If necessary, remove some of the deuces from the pack before dealing so that all players will receive the same number of cards.)

Heart diseases impair the functioning of the heart by interfering with the operation of heart valves, **A**, the flow of blood, **B**, and the circulation to the heart muscle, **C**.

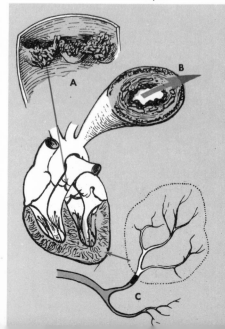

To begin play, the player to the left of the dealer takes out of his hand any card he wishes and places it face up in the middle of the table. Each player, in turn, must then follow by placing a card of the same suit on the table. The highest card of the suit led takes all the others and is said to have won the trick. That player leads to the next trick. When a player does not have a card of the suit led, he may discard from any other suit.

The object of the game is for each player to avoid taking heart cards in his tricks. For each heart card that he must take, the player is penalized either one or more points or one or more chips.

Many variations of hearts exist. In one game the players also try to avoid taking the queen of spades because it counts 13 points against the player who takes it. In another version a player may try to take the queen of spades and every heart card in the deck. If he succeeds, every other player has 26 points scored against him, and the successful player scores none. Another variety of hearts requires each player to pass three cards from his hand to the player on his left, immediately after the deal.

Most of the features of present-day hearts are found in a game called reverse. This game supposedly was originated in Spain. During the late 1800's reverse gradually gave way to hearts.

HEAT is a form of energy. It is the energy that a body possesses because its molecules are in motion.

The molecules of all substances possess kinetic energy, the energy of motion. The molecules of a gas, for example, move with great speed. Any one molecule is free to move in any direction. It moves on some path until it collides with another gas molecule or a surface that it cannot penetrate. If one gas molecule collides with another gas molecule, the course of both molecules is changed, and they speed off in new directions. If a molecule collides with a surface, the course of the molecule is changed, and force is exerted on the surface. The molecules of liquids are much closer together than the molecules of gases. A molecule of a solid is not free to move in some direction until it collides. A molecule in a solid vibrates back and forth about some definite position.

When a body has the energies and velocities of its molecules increased, its temperature rises. The energies of molecules can be increased in two different ways: Mechanical work can be done on a body, or a body can be put in contact with a second body at a higher temperature. We know that when air is compressed, its temperature increases. Air in a bicycle pump becomes warmer when the piston is pushed down. When air is compressed, work is done to it. We also know that a kettle or pot put on an electric burner soon becomes hot. Energy is transferred from the burner to the pot, and the atoms or molecules of the pot vibrate more violently.

The increased movement of molecules in bodies whose temperatures have been raised is indicated by the expansion of the bodies or the increased pressure exerted by the bodies.

Heat is conveyed from one substance to another or from one place to another by conduction, convection, or radiation. (See CONDUCTION, CONVECTION, RADIATION.) Heat always moves from objects of higher temperatures to objects of lower temperatures.

Heat is usually measured in units related to temperature changes. (See BRITISH THERMAL UNIT; CALORIE.) But one should always remember that when heat is added to a body, the temperature rise depends upon the mass of the body and on the material of which the body is made. For example, suppose you place two pans of water, one large and one small, over identical gas burners.

If you measure the temperature of the water in each pan after a few minutes, you will find that the water in the small pan has the higher temperature. Both pans of water have received the same amount of heat. The heat affecting the large pan had to be distributed over a large mass and could affect each part of that mass only moderately. The heat affecting the small pan was concentrated on a small mass.

Suppose you place a lump of lead and a lump of aluminum, both of the same mass, over two identical heat sources. If you measure the temperature of each lump after a few minutes, you will find that the temperature of the lead is higher than the temperature of the aluminum. Both lumps received the same amount of heat. The amount of heat that is necessary to raise one unit of mass of a substance one degree of temperature is called its specific heat capacity. The specific heat capacity of aluminum is 0.217 calories per gram-degree; it takes 0.217 calories to raise the temperature of 1 gram of aluminum 1° C. The specific heat capacity of lead is 0.031 calories per gram-degree. Since it takes less heat to raise 1 gram of lead 1° C. than it takes to raise 1 gram of aluminum 1° C., and since both lumps received the same amount of heat, it is easy to see why lead acquired a higher temperature than aluminum. Each substance has its own specific heat capacity.

HEATHER, a very handsome shrub, growing from 6 inches to 3 feet in height. Its stems are thickly covered with scalelike leaves, and its small pink, purple, or white flowers are borne in long, erect, rather dense clusters. The plant is native to western and northern Europe and to Asia Minor, where it often covers large areas of dry, rocky, hilly land. In parts of Scotland it is such a striking and common feature of the landscape that it is the theme of much Scottish poetry and song.

Heather is planted in gardens in the eastern part of the United States. It is especially attractive when planted as a border around beds of flowers or around evergreen shrubs. In Scotland heather is used for many purposes. The stems are made into brooms and brushes. They are also used for weaving baskets and wattled fences or for thatching roofs of cottages. The heath, a plant closely related to heather, has little bell-shaped flowers. These are the heather bells of Scottish song.

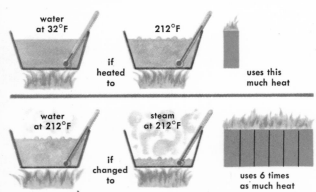

water at 32°F   if heated to   212°F   uses this much heat

water at 212°F   if changed to   steam at 212°F   uses 6 times as much heat

A pound of water absorbs 180 Btu's to change its temperature from 32° to 212° F. It absorbs 1 Btu of heat for every degree of temperature rise because of its specific heat capacity. A pound of water needs 970 Btu's to change to steam at 212° F. This quantity of heat is called the heat of vaporization of water.

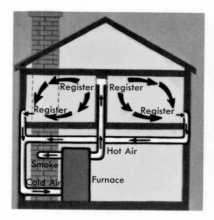

In a warm-air system heated air rises in a duct to wall registers. Cooled air enters floor registers and returns to the furnace.

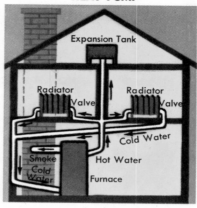

An expansion tank is necessary in a hot-water heating system because water expands and contracts as it heats and cools.

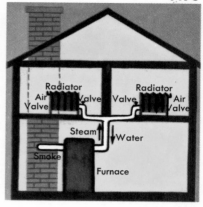

In this system steam goes to radiators. As steam loses heat, it condenses to water and flows back to the furnace to be reheated.

HEATING SYSTEM. This term is generally used to define the combination of components used to provide and distribute heat in a building or home. In the oldest type of heating system each room was heated by a fireplace or open stove. Since that time heating systems have been changing rapidly in accordance with new ideas of health, convenience, and comfort.

Heating systems are most popularly classified by the medium (steam, hot water, or warm air) used to convey the heat from the central heat source to the space to be heated. The systems are further classified by the method in which the medium is conveyed from the central heat source to the rooms. The term "gravity circulation" is used if transportation of the medium is accomplished solely by the changes in the density of the medium as it is heated and cooled; the term "forced circulation" is used if transportation of the medium is aided by some mechanical means.

Early steam and hot-water heating systems used gravity circulation for transportation of the heating medium. These systems required large boilers, radiators, and piping. Today a hot-water system using a pump to accomplish forced circulation is the more popular of the two systems. The use of a pump, along with improved design of boilers and radiators, has greatly improved the heating performance of the original systems. Also, large, conspicuous radiators have been replaced by small baseboard units, and boilers and piping are only a fraction of their original size.

Warm-air furnaces are of two types—the pipeless and the ducted. The older type, the pipeless, is installed in the center of the basement with a large register directly above it on the first floor. The air warmed in the furnace rises from the center of the register, while cool room air passes down around the furnace from the sides of the register. Rooms off the central hall or living room are heated through open doors. This system employs gravity circulation to convey the air to and from the furnace.

The ducted warm-air system has pipes or ducts that carry the warmed air to each room. The room outlets of the ducts are equipped with registers or grills for directing the airflow in the room. The first ducted systems were of the gravity circulation type; however, today almost all the systems installed are equipped with blowers for forcing the air through the duct system. The use of a blower, along with improved furnace design, has greatly improved heating performance and reduced the size of the components.

Panel heating—heating through walls, floors, or ceilings—is accomplished by using either hot water or warm air. In hot-water systems copper or iron pipe coils are embedded in concrete floors or plaster walls and ceilings. In warm-air systems the joist or stud spaces are used as warm-air ducts and in turn heat the floors, walls, or ceilings. Ceiling and wall panels are not seriously affected by placement of furnishings; however, the performance of floor panels is decreased by use of heavy floor coverings. In addition to hot-water and warm-air panels, newly developed electric radiant panels may be used for panel heating.

Solar-energy heating systems are also in use. These systems are predominantly hot-water systems and are most popular in mild climates.

HEAT PUMP, a device for extracting heat from low-temperature bodies and transferring the heat to a place where it is wanted. A heat pump has the same main parts as a compression refrigerator. (See REFRIGERATOR.) A heat pump can be run as a cooling device, as in a refrigerator, or it can be run as a heating device.

A typical heat pump has a heat absorber, or evaporator, a compressor, a condenser, an expansion valve, and a fluid to carry heat through the machine. If the heat pump is used as a heating device, the evaporator coils are exposed to the heat source. The heat source may be a lake, a river, well water, the ground, or air. The fluid in the machine, as it passes through the evaporator coils, absorbs heat from the heat source. The fluid absorbs heat as it evaporates to a vapor. The fluid then goes to a mechanical compressor. When the fluid is compressed, its temperature is raised. The compressed fluid flows through the condenser coils. The fluid gives off heat to the cooler material surrounding the coils as the fluid is condensed from a vapor to a liquid. If the material around the condenser coils is air, the heated air is blown where it is wanted. Water may be used to transfer to radiators the heat given off by the condenser coils. After the fluid leaves the condenser, it goes to an expansion valve. When the fluid expands, its temperature is lowered, and it is ready to go back to the evaporator coils to absorb more heat. If the heat pump is run as a cooling device, the direction of flow of the fluid is reversed in the machine.

Heat pumps require a large low-temperature body so that there will be sufficient heat available to extract. The power to run the mechanical parts of the machine must be cheap, or the heat pump will be too expensive to operate. Most heat pumps are used in the heating and air-conditioning systems of large buildings.

HEATSTROKE. See SUNSTROKE.

HEAVY WATER is deuterium oxide, or the combination of heavy hydrogen with oxygen. The element hydrogen is composed of two stable isotopes, one with a mass approximately twice that of the other. (See HYDROGEN.) For many years scientists tried to separate these two isotopes, but it was not until 1933 that G. N. Lewis, while working at the University of California, actually achieved a separation by means of electrolysis. (See ELECTROLYSIS.) Since ordinary hydrogen consists almost entirely of the lighter isotope, the heavier isotope, heavy hydrogen, called deuterium, could only be isolated in very small quantities.

During World War II methods for obtaining heavy water were greatly improved, and large quantities were obtained for use in experimental research. One of the uses to which heavy hydrogen has been put is that of an isotopic tracer. By tracing the course of heavy-water molecules through living matter much information has been obtained about biological processes. Heavy water has also been used as a moderator in atomic reactors. It is considered to be superior to graphite for this purpose. See ATOMIC ENERGY.

HEBREW, a Semitic language spoken by early tribes of Israel before and during the time they lived in Canaan. Hebrew is the language of the Old Testament and of most later Jewish sacred writings. The Israelites left Canaan about 600 B.C. and settled in Babylonia. During their stay there and in other lands to which they later migrated, they adopted the languages of their neighbors. In Babylon the Israelites spoke Aramaic. Hebrew was still spoken in Judea until the beginning of the Christian Era, when Aramaic replaced it in most of the country. Hebrew always remained a learned language studied by the Jews, who read their sacred books and prayers in the language of the Old Testament.

The chief characteristic of Hebrew, as of the other Semitic languages, is the three-consonant root.

בראשית Genesis	מלכים ב 2 Kings	נחום Nahum	רות Ruth
שמות Exodus	ישעיה Isaiah	חבקוק Habakkuk	איכה Lamentations
ויקרא Leviticus	ירמיה Jeremiah	צפניה Zephaniah	קהלת Ecclesiastes
במדבר Numbers	יחזקאל Ezekiel	חגי Haggai	אסתר Esther
דברים Deuteronomy	הושע Hosea	זכריה Zechariah	דניאל Daniel
יהושע Joshua	יואל Joel	מלאכי Malachi	עזרא Ezra
שפטים Judges	עמוס Amos	תהלים Psalms	נחמיה Nehemiah
שמואל א 1 Samuel	עבדיה Obadiah	משלי Proverbs	דברי הימים א 1 Chronicles
שמואל ב 2 Samuel	יונה Jonah	איוב Job	דברי הימים ב 2 Chronicles
מלכים א 1 Kings	מיכה Micah	שיר השירים The Song of Songs	

Superimposed on the Star of David is the Jewish Bible index, in Hebrew and English.

For instance, the root *L-M-D* means "learning." From it are derived the words *lamad*, meaning "he learned"; *limmed*, meaning "he taught"; and *talmud*, meaning "study." Adjectives always follow nouns and are defined by the nouns they modify.

The Hebrew alphabet is derived from a Canaanite alphabet that was in use after 1600 B.C. In the following alphabet list, one sound for each letter is given: Alef (glottal stop: silent in English), Beth (English *b*), Gimel (English hard *g*), Daleth (English *d*), He (English *h* voiced), Vaw (*w*, later *v*), Zayin (*z*), Heth (English *h* unvoiced), Teth (emphatic *t*), Yod (*y*), Kaf (*k*), Lamed (*l*), Mem (*m*), Nun (*n*), Samekh (*s*), Ayin (guttural, silent in English), Pe (*p*), Sade (emphatic *s*, later *ts*), Qof (back-throated *k*), Resh (*r*), Sin (*s*), Shin (*sh*), and Tav (*t*). Hebrew, like the other Semitic languages, has three basic vowels (*a*, *i*, and *u*); but with diphthongs and variations there are 14 vowel signs used.

Hebrew is written from right to left. Originally, the signs were of three basic shapes: square, circular, and triangular. Gradually the Hebrew scribal tradition squared them, so that modern Hebrew has letters that are all nearly square in form.

European and English-speaking people have taken over many of the words, phrases, and expressions of the Hebrew language. Such words and phrases are called Hebraisms. Such words as *Sabbath*, *cherub*, *amen*, and *hallelujah*. Expressions such as "after one's own heart," and "a drop in the bucket" are other examples.

Within the past 150 years Jews have revived Hebrew as a spoken language. The greatest impetus for the revival was the sentiment developing for a national Jewish homeland in Palestine. The rapid colonization of Palestine following World War I brought acceptance of Hebrew as a spoken language, and it became one of three official languages of Palestine. It is now the official language of the state of Israel. Modern Hebrew has been modernized along the lines of the European languages.

HEBREWS were a Semitic people and spoke a language akin to Arabic and Syrian. Some of the Hebrew tribes settled in Palestine or Canaan as early as 1400 B.C., while others roamed the desert as nomads. The Hebrews called themselves Israelites because of their descent from the patriarch Israel (known also as Jacob), grandson of Abraham. Jacob's 12 sons were the ancestors of the 12 tribes of the Hebrew people.

Those belonging to the tribe of Joseph lived in northern Egypt. After the Egyptian Pharaoh compelled them to become slaves, these Hebrews, under the leadership of Moses and Aaron, fled Egypt about 1200. This is called the Exodus. According to the Bible, the Egyptian army in pursuit of the fleeing Israelites was swallowed by the Red Sea. The tribe of Joseph joined their brethren in Palestine. There the 12 tribes were at first ruled by the judges. Being threatened by the neighboring peoples, the tribes united and elected Saul as their king about 1028. David became king of all Israel shortly after he killed the Philistine Goliath in personal combat. David made Jerusalem his capital, and his successor, Solomon, built the Temple where the Israelites worshiped their god, Yahweh.

After Solomon's death in 933, Israel was divided. In the north was the kingdom of Israel, which was occupied by the Assyrians in 722. The southern kingdom of Judah, with its capital in Jerusalem, did

This map shows how, according to the Bible, the land of the Canaanites was divided among the 12 Hebrew tribes after the Hebrew conquest. Each of the tribes bore the name of the son of Jacob from whom, by tradition, the tribe was descended. It has been suggested that the number of tribes was not fixed, and that King Solomon's dividing of Israel into 12 parts for administrative purposes aided in setting the traditional number of tribes at 12. Today, this area is divided between the states of Israel and Jordan.

Asher
Naphtali
Benjamin
Zebulun
Issachar
Manasseh
Ephraim
Gad
Dan
Judah
Reuben
Simeon

not succumb to foreign invasion until 586. Then Jerusalem was captured by king Nebuchadnezzar of Babylonia, and the people of Judah were deported. For centuries afterward the Israelites lived under foreign rule. Under Persian domination they built a second Temple in Jerusalem. Despite foreign domination they managed to keep their religious unity and the purity of their faith.

Palestine was eventually conquered by the Romans. Angered by the rebellious Hebrews, they destroyed the Temple in Jerusalem A.D. 70. Thereafter most of the Hebrews, by now called Jews, left Palestine and dispersed into all parts of the world. During the Middle Ages the Jews numbered about 1,500,000. They were an important element in Spain and later in the Ottoman Empire. Today there are about 12,000,000 Jews throughout the world. About half of them live in the United States and about 15 percent in the newly founded state of Israel. See JUDAISM.

This ancient Jewish lamp was probably in use in early biblical times.

HECTOR. See TROJAN WAR.

HEDGE, a row of bushes whose branches, twigs, and leaves have become so interlaced that they appear to be a dense, continuous mass of foliage. Many hedges are trimmed so that their top and side surfaces are flat and unbroken or smoothly rounded.

Low hedges are used to divide areas in flower gardens. Higher hedges may serve as windbreaks, barriers, screens, backgrounds, or enclosures for privacy. They can also be used to mark the boundaries of properties and to keep out trespassers. Well-trimmed hedges give an air of formality to a garden. Untrimmed hedges are less formal. Perfectly shaped hedges were a dominant feature of the English formal gardens of the 18th and 19th centuries.

Many plants whose natural growth is dense and compact are suitable for hedges. Privet, box, laurel, yew, barberry, holly, and hawthorn are examples.

Careful pruning is necessary for the cultivation of a well-shaped hedge. During the first two or three years after the young bushes are planted, the new branches growing from their tops and sides must be pruned frequently so that other branches will grow profusely at their bases and will result in a dense, unbroken mass of foliage extending along the ground. The top of a hedge should be narrower than the base.

HEGEL, GEORG (1770-1831), German philosopher. Hegel's is one of the most difficult of philosophical systems. He himself was supposed to have said: "Only one man understands me, and even he does not." Many British and American academic philosophers of the 19th and 20th centuries were Hegelians. John Dewey, for example, was influenced for a time by Hegelianism. Hegel's thought has influenced Protestant theologians, and his *Philosophy of History* influenced political thinkers. In his youth Karl Marx was profoundly influenced by Hegel, although the Marxist system contains a greatly modified Hegelianism.

Hegel was a fine teacher who inspired his pupils with confidence. His lectures at Berlin were popular, although he was not a brilliant speaker. Hegel was born in Stuttgart, in southern Germany. His early school career was unremarkable. He received a Ph.D. in theology at Tübingen, in Germany, in 1793. He was adjudged an able student but rather weak in philosophy. Hegel became a private tutor at Bern, Switzerland, where he read

An evenly trimmed hedge may serve as an attractive barrier between two yards.

Eugene Z. Dodd

Hedge shrubs (below) should be pruned to a height of 6 inches when planted. They should be cut to a height of 12 inches after the first summer and 18 inches during the second summer. The growing shrubs should also be pruned regularly to make the bases wider than the tops so that sunlight can reach the lower leaves and stimulate growth.

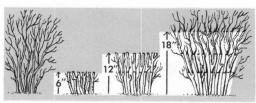

GOOD GOOD GOOD

POOR

The Bettmann Archive

Georg Hegel

extensively on Christianity and wrote a life of Jesus. He also read Hume, Montesquieu, and Gibbon. Hölderlin, a school friend, helped Hegel obtain a post at the German city of Frankfurt am Main, where Hegel wrote several essays on economics and government and began to sketch his philosophical system. At Jena, in Germany, in 1801, Hegel helped Schelling, another old school friend, edit the *Critical Journal of Philosophy*. He also taught classes in logic and metaphysics and read Homer, Aristotle, and Plato. He left Jena to accept a rectorship in Nuremberg. In 1816 he accepted a teaching post at Heidelberg. Two years later he became a professor of philosophy at Berlin. He died of cholera after only one day of illness.

It is not possible to summarize well a philosophy that ambitiously tried to reorganize modern thought. Hegel's *Encyclopedia of Philosophical Sciences* was meant to expound his system as a whole to students attending his lectures. Hegel did not believe in the separateness of things. Nothing was real except as it related to the whole. Hegel called the whole the Absolute, which was spiritual. The Absolute was similar to Aristotle's idea of God: thought thinking about itself. The basis of Hegel's metaphysics is his logic, and his *Science of Logic* is one of his important books. Logical speculation was called dialectic. Dialectic moves from thesis ("The Absolute is Pure Being") through its opposite, or antithesis ("The Absolute is Nothing"), to the resolution of these contradictory statements in the synthesis ("The Absolute is Becoming"). But the synthesis is not really the whole truth, and the philosopher tries to correct the errors of these too abstract statements. By so doing, he develops a view of Reality.

Hegel's grasp of history was somewhat limited, but he developed a philosophy of history in *The Philosophy of Law* and *The Philosophy of History*. History, Hegel tried to show, also developed according to the dialectic, approaching Reality in the organization of the Prussian state. The significant vehicles of historical truth were the nation and the military hero (Marx emphasized the social class). Hegel also glorified war and considered Immanuel Kant's idea of the League for Peace a mistake. Hegel was, of course, undemocratic. He contended that the individual, whom men like John Locke emphasized, existed only through the state.

HEIFETZ, JASCHA (1901-   ), one of the outstanding violinists of the 20th century. He was born in Vilna, Russia (now in Lithuania). At the age of three he began taking violin lessons, and he first played in public when he was five years old. Four years later he went to St. Petersburg (now Leningrad) and studied under Leopold Auer. Heifetz appeared as soloist with both the Kiev and Odessa symphony orchestras when he was ten years old. For the next six years he traveled throughout Europe and played with orchestras in Berlin and Leipzig, Germany, and in Vienna, Austria.

When the Russian Revolution broke out in 1917, Heifetz left his native land and moved to the United States. He made his American debut in New York in 1917. He continued to live in the United States but traveled to all parts of the world to appear with orchestras and in recital.

Jascha Heifetz

Allied Arts Corp.

HEIGHT, BODY. Heredity plays an important part in the height of the human body. However, environment (including climate, diet, and living standards) determines whether inherited possibilities are realized. In many parts of the world with a rising standard of living there is a tendency for children to be taller than their parents. This tendency is in large part the result of better nourishment. Other influences are the control of communicable childhood diseases and improved sanitation. All children have their individual rates of growth, even in cases in which they have the same hereditary tendency to tallness or shortness. For this reason hasty conclusions should not be drawn from a study of charts listing averages of height for age groups. Occasionally, there are glandular disturbances that lead to excessive tallness. Regular consultation with a doctor makes possible the discovery of such conditions.

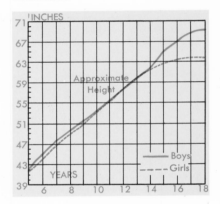

This chart shows the height of girls and boys in the United States. Notice that after age 13, boys begin to grow much taller than girls. The chart is based on measurements taken from 1937 to 1939. However, average heights may differ from decade to decade and from country to country.

HEINE, HEINRICH (1797-1856), German lyric poet and journalist, was born in Düsseldorf. He studied law and was admitted to the bar, but he never seriously practiced. His first book of poetry was published in 1821. But he did not become famous until the appearance of his *Book of Songs* (1826), one of the most enduring books of lyrics in world literature. This fame gained Heine the post of associate editor of the *General Political Annals*, but because of his extremely liberal writings he was fiercely attacked and had to flee to Paris in 1831. In France Heine wrote for various German newspapers, and his articles are collected in three volumes: *French Affairs*, *The Salon*, and *Lutetia*. His *New Poems* appeared in 1844 and his *Last Poems* in 1853-1855. Among Heine's most popular lyrics are his "Thou Fair Fisher-Maiden," "On the Wings of Song," and "In the Lovely Month of May," while his ballads include "The Lorelei" and "Belshazzar." His travel books are entitled *Pictures of Travel*.

HEISENBERG, WERNER (1901-), a German physicist, born at Würzburg. Educated at the University of Munich and under Max Born at Göttingen and Niels Bohr at Copenhagen, he later taught at the University of Leipzig. In 1942 he was appointed director of the Max Planck Institute at Berlin. Three years later he was given a professorship at Göttingen. He is primarily noted for his formulation of the uncertainty principle and for his theory of quantum mechanics, generally known as matrix mechanics. The uncertainty principle states that all measurements concerning atomic particles have a limited accuracy because any method of measurement affects the behavior of the particles. He was awarded the Nobel prize for physics in 1932. During World War II Heisenberg headed atomic-weapons research for the German government, but after the war he joined with many other physicists throughout the world in calling for the cessation of atomic-weapons testing. In 1958 he outlined a new theoretical equation to explain the basic nature of all matter, a further development of his theory of quantum mechanics.

HELENA, the capital of Montana, seat of Lewis and Clark County, in the west-central part of the state, near the Missouri River, 50 miles north-northeast of Butte. It is the trade center of a rich mining and farming region. The 1960 population was 20,227, which makes Helena one of the smallest of all the state capitals. Among the points of interest in the city are Carroll College, Roman Catholic and Episcopalian cathedrals, and the Algeria Shrine Temple. The city was settled in 1864 when gold was discovered in Last Chance Gulch, now occupied by Main Street. Helena became the capital of the Montana Territory in 1875 and capital of the state in 1894. A severe earthquake in 1935 caused widespread damage.

HELEN OF TROY. See TROJAN WAR.

Helicopters are sometimes called rotary-wing aircraft. The rotors serve as wings.

HELICOPTER, a type of aircraft with lifting rotors that rotate horizontally. The concept of the helicopter first appeared in the Chinese top, with two airscrews made of feathers that turn in opposite directions. The origin of this top is unknown, but it does antedate the sketches made by Leonardo da Vinci in the 16th century. However, the first truly successful helicopter appeared in 1936 with the Focke-Wulf FW-61 in Germany. In 1937 Igor Sikorsky built and flew his VS-300.

In the helicopter the power of the engine is used to drive the blades of the rotor, which provide both suspension and propulsion. It is because of this dual function of the rotor that the helicopter is superior to the autogiro.

Helicopters have special value in wartime for carrying troops and supplies to inaccessible places and as a means for rescue operations. During peacetime they are used for mail-carrying service and for various other operations, such as the passenger shuttle service between a city and an outlying airport. Regularly scheduled passenger service has been set up in various cities in Europe. In the United States several cities have helicopter service to their airports. One-man helicopters were developed in the 1950's.

Helicopters are becoming increasingly useful in construction work. They are used in building bridges, erecting buildings, pouring concrete, and laying electric-power lines. Also they are used to plant trees and to dust crops. Approximately 100,000 lives have been saved since World War II by the use of helicopters, including the rescue of ship crews and passengers and of the populations of flood-stricken areas.

HELIOGRAPH, an apparatus devised by Henry Christopher Mance for telegraphing by means of the sun's rays. It is composed of a circular mirror, revolving on a horizontal axis, adjusted to the required angle of incidence with the sun by a telescopic rod. The light from the sun is reflected by the mirror in whatever direction the operator desires. A person receiving the message is able to do so by watching the flashes of light. The operator of the heliograph moves the mirror so that it emits the reflected light as short flashes. The message can be sent by Morse code or some semaphore system.

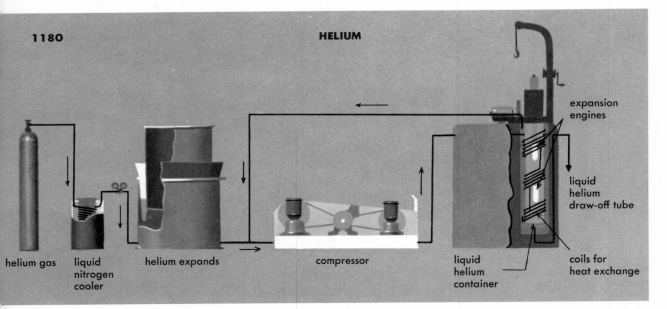

helium gas   liquid nitrogen cooler   helium expands   compressor   liquid helium container   expansion engines   liquid helium draw-off tube   coils for heat exchange

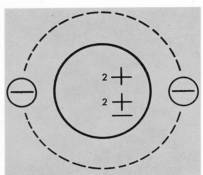

Helium (at. no. 2, at. wt. of most abundant isotope 4) has 2 electrons (−) around a nucleus containing 2 protons (+) and 2 neutrons. It is a rare gas.

HELIUM, a rare gas belonging to the argon, neon, and krypton group. It is one of the elements and has the symbol He. It dissolves less in water than any other gas; it is not combustible, nor will it support combustion; and its buoyancy, or lifting power, is over nine-tenths that of hydrogen. For these reasons it makes an excellent gas for filling balloons, dirigibles, and so forth, as there is no chance of its catching fire, as hydrogen does.

Strangely enough, helium was discovered in the sun before it was found on earth. In 1868 Sir Norman Lockyer, an English astronomer, was making a spectroscopic examination of the sun's corona during an eclipse and discovered a bright-yellow line, which up to that time had been thought to be one of the sodium lines. From its position he believed it to belong to a hitherto unknown element, which he named helium. (See SPECTROSCOPE.) About 30 years later Sir William Ramsay

identified it as being both associated with uranium ore and present in very small quantities (five parts per million) in the atmosphere.

Eventually it was discovered that the natural gas produced in some districts—especially in Texas—was rich in helium, the content sometimes running as high as 2 percent.

The very low boiling point of helium enabled it to be easily separated from the other gases that came from the natural-gas wells. The gas was pumped into a pressure chamber and chilled to a very low temperature. One by one the other gases liquefied and could be removed. Finally only the helium was left.

Helium plants are at Fort Worth and Amarillo, Tex. From them come the huge quantities of helium needed for inflating giant airships. The United States has a practical monopoly on helium production, as very little natural gas is obtained in other countries, and such as there is does not contain any helium.

HELLENISTIC AGE, the period of the spread and decline of ancient Greek culture that began with the conquests of Alexander the Great and continued into the period of the Roman Empire. The Hellenistic Age was marked by a decay of Greek political power and by the loss of the youthful creativity of Greek culture, which had become rather superficial. Nevertheless, although Greek cultural roots decayed, the fruits of that remarkable culture were spread far and wide. Hellenism was the basis for Islamic science and philosophy after the conquests in the 7th century A.D. The Renaissance witnessed a new flowering of Hellenism that continues to influence the modern world.

Even before Alexander's conquests (334-323 B.C.), Hellenistic culture had influenced much of the ancient world. With Alexander's aid it spread as far as the Indus River Valley. Rome felt the influence of Hellenism after it incorporated the Greek cities of southern Italy and Sicily, especially the city of Syra-

This coin depicts Alexander the Great, whose conquests spread Greek culture.

cuse, in the 3d century B.C. When Rome gained control of Asia Minor about 133 B.C., it continued the process of Hellenization.

Literary and artistic achievement was largely critical and learned rather than vigorously creative. Men traveled much and read more. Many libraries were founded. Ptolemy I and Polybius wrote historical works. The poetry of Callimachus became overripe with learning. The poems of Theocritus of Syracuse were almost alone in their freshness. Art flourished at Pergamum, which vied with Alexandria as an intellectual center. Alexandria, however, under librarian-scholars like Aristophanes of Byzantium and

Artha Hornbostel

The Temple of Jupiter at Baalbek is a monument of Syrian Hellenistic architecture.

Aristarchus, outshone other cities. Science showed great progress. The medical schools were vigorous. Euclid (geometry), Eratosthenes (astronomy and geography), and Archimedes (physics) were among the foremost scientists.

Generally, the Hellenistic Age was economically prosperous, but the political devices of the Greeks declined. The Greek city-states joined in leagues that might have become federations but did not. Athens became a revered intellectual center of no political import. Only Sparta, until about 146 B.C., retained a political and military significance.

The unique religion of the Greeks decayed. Under the Roman Empire the Jews made converts in the Hellenistic world, and the worship of Persian or Egyptian gods enjoyed a fad. The Academy of Plato survived, but its thinkers became skeptical about attaining truth. The Aristotelians devoted themselves to history and science. Two new cosmopolitan philosophies, Stoicism and Epicureanism, were founded and became very influential in the Roman Empire. Also, the interplay between Hellenism and Christianity was profound, for the early Christians used Greek philosophical terminology and adapted some of the Stoic ethics to Christianity.

HELMHOLTZ, HERMANN VON (1821-1894), a German scientist and philosopher, born near Berlin. For a while he was an army physician. He became a professor of physiology and anatomy at Königsberg in 1849 and later taught in Bonn and Heidelberg. He became professor of physics at Berlin in 1870 and held this position until his death.

Helmholtz's writings, especially his *Manual of Physiological Optics* and *The Doctrine of Sensations of Tone*, laid the foundations for modern studies of the eye and the ear. Helmholtz satisfactorily explained the mechanisms and processes of binocular vision, the sensation of color, color blindness, and the ability of the eye to focus by alteration of its curvature. The ophthalmoscope, which he invented in 1851, is an instrument of great value and is still used by doctors in determining eye diseases. He studied the ear and was the first to give an accurate description of the inner ear, the function of the cochlea in distinguishing pitch, and the effects of harmonics in giving sounds their distinctive timbre. Helmholtz also studied new ways to conserve energy and wrote on philosophical problems.

HELMONT, JAN BAPTISTA VAN (1577-1644), a Flemish chemist and physician, born at Brussels. After attending the University of Louvain and a visit to London, he determined to devote himself to the medical care of the poor.

As a result of studying medical chemistry Van Helmont became the first to show that gases had a material character. The term *gas* was, in fact, coined by Van Helmont. He also recognized the existence of many different gases. A gas he called "gas silvester"—although he did not actually isolate it—is now known as carbon dioxide.

HELOISE. See ABELARD, PETER.

HEMINGWAY, ERNEST (1899-1961), American novelist and short-story writer, born in Oak Park, Ill. He became a newspaper reporter and then an ambulance driver for the Italian army during World War I. During the Spanish Civil War as well as during World War II he was a war correspondent. His work was influenced by writers Ezra Pound and Gertrude Stein. In short stories he exhibited a hard-fisted attitude of mind and a technique for which he became famous.

As a leading spokesman for the "lost generation" of the 1920's

Hemingway expressed the feelings of a war-weary people in such novels as *A Farewell to Arms* and *The Sun Also Rises*. *For Whom the Bell Tolls* is a novel of the Spanish Civil War. His other works include *To Have and Have Not*, *Green Hills of Africa*, *Across the River and into the Trees*, and *The Old Man and the Sea*. In 1954 he received the Nobel prize in literature. He died from a gunshot wound in 1961.

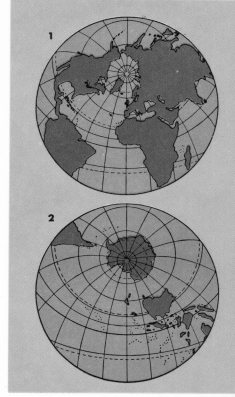

A hemisphere is half of a sphere. The earth is divided into the Northern Hemisphere and the Southern Hemisphere by the Equator.

HEMISPHERE, a half of a sphere. The term is usually applied to the halves of the earth, which is somewhat spherical in shape. The earth may be divided into an infinite number of hemispheres. In each case, however, the boundary line between the two halves must be the circumference with the maximum diameter obtainable. The Equator is, for example, a circumference of maximum diameter, and so it makes a logical line for dividing the two hemispheres into the Northern Hemisphere and the Southern Hemisphere. The earth can be similarly divided into the Eastern Hemisphere and the Western Hemisphere or any other pair of half-spheres.

Hemlock needles are short, flat, and green.

HEMLOCK, one of several species of cone-bearing evergreen trees native to North America, China and Japan. Hemlocks belong to the same family as the pines, firs, and spruces.

The species known as eastern hemlock, which is native to eastern North America, may attain a height of 100 feet and a trunk diameter of 4 feet. Its crown of branches is pyramidal. Its flattened needles, which grow thickly on the twigs, are about $\frac{2}{3}$ inch long and $\frac{1}{16}$ inch wide. The eastern hemlock is found most frequently on shaded northern slopes and in cool ravines. The tannin extracted from its inner bark is used to tan leather. Its lumber is used for beams, rafters, and joists in houses and other buildings.

The western hemlock is native to the mountains of western North America. Its lumber is used for flooring and is made into boxes and crates. Both eastern and western hemlocks are cultivated for ornament in yards and parks.

Hemming is done to prevent raveling.

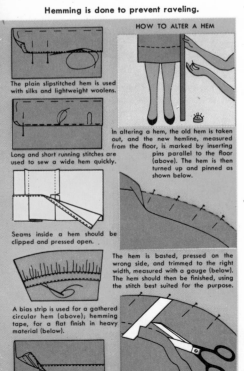

The plain slipstitched hem is used with silks and lightweight woolens.

Long and short running stitches are used to sew a wide hem quickly.

Seams inside a hem should be clipped and pressed open.

A bias strip is used for a gathered circular hem (above); hemming tape, for a flat finish in heavy material (below).

HOW TO ALTER A HEM

In altering a hem, the old hem is taken out, and the new hemline, measured from the floor, is marked by inserting pins parallel to the floor (above). The hem is then turned up and pinned as shown below.

The hem is basted, pressed on the wrong side, and trimmed to the right width, measured with a gauge (below). The hem should then be finished, using the stitch best suited for the purpose.

HEMMING, finishing the border of a garment or a household article by folding the edge and sewing it down to prevent raveling. It may be done by hand or on the sewing machine. The hand stitch most commonly used in hemming is the slipstitch. To do this, first make a tiny stitch in the garment; then push the needle into the fold at the top of the hem and slip it along inside the fold for about $\frac{1}{4}$ inch. Now pull the needle through and make another tiny stitch in the garment. Working from right to left, continue sewing this way all around the edge, with the open side of the hem toward you. Stitches on the right side of the garment should be almost invisible.

Edges to be hemmed may be curved or straight, sewed directly to the material, or faced with a bias strip. The bias strip is needed for circular or flared edges and for heavy materials, such as tweed, that are difficult to fold. On skirts, one edge of the bias strip is stitched to the hem, and the other edge is stitched to the garment. If the skirt is circular, the hem must be gathered at the upper edge before it is sewed to the bias strip. Before sewing a hem on a circular skirt, let it hang for some time, so that the bias seams will sag before you take measurements, not afterward. Ordinary skirt hems and dress hems are about 2 inches wide.

Whether you are working on a table napkin, finishing a dress, or making alterations on a skirt, you should press the material you are hemming after the edge has been turned under and basted. This will keep a straight, firm line in the hem and thus make sewing easier. Pressing is especially important where a seam crosses a hem, for the flaps of the seam inside should lie flat and open. Otherwise the surface of the garment will look bumpy. Press hems from the wrong side of the garment and use a damp cloth under the iron.

For decorative effects, hems on household articles may be trimmed with simple embroidery stitches.

HEMORRHAGE. See BLEEDING.

HEMP, an annual herb native to Asia but now grown in many parts of the world for the fiber, seeds, oil, and drugs that it yields. Hemp grows 3 to 18 feet tall and has a straight, slender stem and compound leaves, each made up of five to seven rough, coarsely toothed leaflets arranged like the fingers of a hand. The inner bark of the rough,

angular stem is made up of tough fibers from 3 to 9 feet long.

When the plant is grown for its fiber, it is cut while the staminate flowers are in full bloom, soaked in water, and dried. Then the fiber is removed, either by hand or by machinery. Hemp fiber is coarser than flax but longer and stronger. It is used in the manufacture of strong twine, canvas, sailcloth, and rope. Tarred ravelings of hemp rope (called oakum) are used for calking joints of pipes and seams of boats.

HENDERSON, RICHARD (1735-1785), American land promoter, was born in Virginia and grew up on the North Carolina frontier. He was a lawyer, sheriff, and judge until, at the age of 38, he retired to devote himself to land promotion in what is now Kentucky and Tennessee.

Several years before retiring he had formed a land company, hired Daniel Boone as his agent, and sent Boone to investigate the land west of the Appalachians. In 1774 he formed the Transylvania Company and the following year purchased from the Cherokee Indians a large tract of land extending from the Kentucky River to the Cumberland River. With Boone again blazing the trail, Henderson established the town of Boonesborough in a colony to be known as Transylvania. He depended upon the British government to uphold the legality of his colony; when the Revolutionary War removed this support, Virginia and North Carolina, which held charters for the land, asserted their control, and the colony collapsed.

In the winter of 1779-1780 Henderson was a member of the commission that surveyed the Virginia-North Carolina (now Kentucky-Tennessee) border. That same winter he helped promote the settlement of what is now Nashville, Tenn.

Although Henderson's major project, the Transylvania colony, failed, his efforts were an important part of the beginning of American westward expansion.

Tall, thick stalks of Manila hemp are being cut by workers in North Borneo.

B.I.S.

HENIE, SONJA (1912-   ), world-famous ice skater, was born in Norway. Her father gave her her first pair of skates when she was only six years old. Her older brother, Lief, gave Sonja her first lessons. She also took ballet lessons and learned to ski. Both of these added to her natural poise and balance.

From the very first, Sonja Henie showed unusual talent on the ice. When she was only eight years old, she won the children's figure-skating championship of Oslo. Her formal education at this time was placed in the hands of tutors, and she received coaching from a prominent skating instructor. She also took courses in ballet from Karsavina, who was a famous Russian ballerina. When Sonja was ten years old, she won the national figure-skating championship of Norway.

For ten years Sonja Henie was the world's amateur champion ice skater. In three successive Olympic Games contests she won the women's figure-skating title. In 1936 she ended her amateur career and made a series of professional appearances in the United States. Later she starred in ice revues and motion pictures, toured army hospitals as an entertainer during World War II, and wrote a book about her career and her technique, *Wings on My Feet.*

She became a citizen of the United States in 1941.

HENNEPIN, LOUIS (1640?-1701?), the Flemish missionary, friar, and explorer who discovered and named the Falls of St. Anthony, the site of the future city of Minneapolis. He was born in the province of Hainaut in the Spanish Netherlands.

In 1673 Louis Hennepin went to Canada, and in 1678 he became chaplain to a group of shipbuilders set up by the Sieur de La Salle on the Niagara River. In 1679 he accompanied the great French explorer La Salle on a trip through the Great Lakes, and in 1680, under Michel Aco, he helped explore the upper Mississippi River. On this latter trip the party of explorers, including Hennepin, were captured by Sioux but were finally released.

In 1682 Hennepin returned to France and there published his *Description de la Louisiane*, a work that has been called the most interesting of the early American narratives of exploration. Hennepin published two other works, *Nouveau Voyage* and *Nouvelle Découverte*, both of which tell of his voyages in North America.

HENRY VIII (1491-1547), second Tudor monarch of England, born at Greenwich. The second and only surviving son of Henry VII, he was well educated in the New Learning, a true man of the Renaissance—proficient in three languages, able in theology, and accomplished as a musician, poet, horseman, swordsman, runner, and wrestler. Upon the death of his elder brother, Arthur, in 1502 Henry became Prince of Wales. In 1509 he succeeded to the throne and married his dead brother's widow, Catherine of Aragon, the daughter of Ferdinand and Isabella of Spain.

For approximately the first 18 years of his reign Henry VIII did little toward effecting much-needed social and religious reforms within England. He was a loyal son of the church, having written in 1521 the *Assertion of the Seven Sacraments* in answer to the criticisms of Martin Luther. For this work Pope Leo X conferred upon him the title "Defender of the Faith." Two years before Luther nailed his 95 theses upon the door of the Cathedral of Wittenberg, Henry, in submitting to the pope a dispute (between the Lords, Commons, and judges on the one side and the church on the other) over the power of church courts, had told his chancellor, Thomas Wolsey, that "kings of England have never had any superior but God alone." Also during this period Henry and Wolsey, who yearned to be pope, began to meddle in the politics and wars of the Continent. In 1511 Pope Julius II, the state of Venice, and Ferdinand V of Castile formed the Holy League (later joined by Holy Roman Emperor Maximilian I) against France. Henry joined the league, since he was jealous of French military successes in Italy, was anxious to show off his navy, was loyal to the church, and was influenced by his father-in-law.

Around 1520 Henry, after a succession of royal mistresses, began to tire of his wife, and by 1526 he decided on divorce. He convinced his own conscience that his marriage was null because of the death of all of his children except Mary Tudor. This he considered a sign that Heaven had viewed with disfavor the marriage to his brother's wife and that the papal dispensation permitting the marriage had been given on false grounds. Henry appealed to Pope Clement VII, but the pope was unable to reverse the decision of former Pope Julius II, on doctrinal grounds and on the practical

Few portraits have so well captured the personality of a man as does this painting of Henry VIII by Hans Holbein the Younger.

grounds that Rome was at the mercy of Charles V, Holy Roman emperor, king of Spain, and nephew of Catherine of Aragon. Henry, determined to obtain the divorce and marry Anne Boleyn, submitted the question to the universities of England and Europe, many of which decided in his favor. As a result he married Anne (Jan. 25, 1533), broke with the church of Rome, and confiscated the annates. The pope, in turn, excommunicated Henry (who now and until his death continued to regard himself as a good Catholic) and annulled Henry's divorce from Catherine.

In 1534 Parliament passed the Act of Supremacy, appointing the king and his successors "Protector and only Supreme Head of the Church and Clergy of England," an act that may be considered as the undisputed beginning of the English Reformation. In 1536 the smaller monasteries were suppressed. Three years later the larger ones were suppressed and their property was confiscated.

In 1536 Henry had Anne Boleyn beheaded on a charge of adultery and Elizabeth, the child of that marriage, proclaimed illegitimate. His other marriages were to Jane Seymour (1536), who died a year later after the birth of her son, the future Edward VI; Anne of Cleves

Arms of Francis I of France

Arms of Henry VIII of England

Chief   Pale   Bend

Fess   Bar   Chevron

Cross   Saltier   Pile

Vair   Countervair

Rampant Gardant   Combattant

The fields (left) are said to represent the fur of squirrels. Above are honorable ordinaries; at right, common charges.

Names are given to each part of the shield (the right side is the dexter; the left, the sinister): **1,** dexter chief canton; **2,** chief point; **3,** sinister chief canton; **4,** dexter flank; **5,** center point; **6,** sinister flank; **7,** dexter canton of base; **8,** base point; **9,** sinister canton of base; **10,** honor point; and **11,** nombril point.

added by such men as governors of provinces to their own arms in order to show superiority or prior right of jurisdiction; (5) arms of alliances, arms borne by the children of heiresses in order to show their maternal descent; (6) arms of assumption, arms assumed by a person with the approval of the sovereign, for example, the arms of a prisoner of war may be borne by his captor and transferred to the captor's heirs; (7) arms of succession, arms borne quartered by the family arms of those inheriting fiefs or manors by will, entail, or donation; (8) arms of concession, those in which a part of the sovereign's arms have been granted to the bearer as a mark of distinction; (9) arms of adoption, arms borne by an adopted heir; and (10) paternal, or hereditary, arms, arms transferred by the first possessor to his descendants.

All of these classes of arms are displayed on an escutcheon (shield) and by charges (anything depicted on a shield). Most escutcheons have been represented as approaching a triangular form, with the top horizontal and point down. To facilitate description, the field of the escutcheon is divided into points.

The charges are divided by heralds into three classes: the honorable ordinaries, the subordinaries, and the common charges. The honorable ordinaries, which include old and frequent bearings representative of the wood or metal strengthenings of the old shields, are generally considered to be nine. However, some heralds consider the quarter, the upper right-hand fourth of the shield cut off from the rest of the shield by a vertical and a horizontal line, to be one of the honorable ordinaries. But most heralds class it with the subordinaries. The common charges are more or less conventional representations of familiar objects, which have no necessary relation to the shield but are emblematic in their concern with individual or family history and character. Among the commonest animals used in coats of arms is the lion.

Coats of arms are distinguished from one another not only by their charges but also by the color of the charges and of the field on which they are placed. These colors, known technically as tinctures, are seven. They consist of two metals—or (gold) and argent (silver, represented on the shields as white)—and five other colors—gules (red), azure (blue), sable (black), vert (green), and purpure (purple). These tinctures were sometimes varied by the use of two more representing furs, ermine and vair (a species of squirrel). The former is represented by black spots or tails on a white field; the latter, by a series of adjoining conventional shapes of blue and white in alternation. No example has been found in English heraldry of a shield of plain color or metal, although the French can show a few.

HERB, a plant whose stem develops little or no tough, woody tissue and remains relatively slender, soft, and green. Herbs comprise many thousands of different species of plants, including the violet, primrose, petunia, daisy, carrot, tomato plant, spinach, marjoram, and hyssop. Many other cultivated flowers and vegetables are classified as herbs. Most herbs are of small size, but some, such as prairie cord grass and the banana plant, are relatively larger. Although the majority of herbs are annuals, many are biennials or perennials.

Some herbs have been utilized by man for hundreds or even thousands of years. Their roots, leaves, flowers, or seeds were eaten as vegetables or condiments, or healing medicines or agreeable scents were extracted from them. Manuscripts, stone carvings, and drawings on the walls of tombs indicate that the ancient Egyptians, Greeks, and Romans were familiar with many herbs and with their medicinal and culinary uses. These ancient peoples learned which herbs were beneficial and which were harmful by the laborious and sometimes dangerous method of trial and error. At first, useful herbs were gathered from where they grew wild in meadow or forest. Later, they were cultivated in gardens. During the Middle Ages descriptions and drawings of various herbs and of their uses were compiled in books called herbals. During the 16th and 17th centuries some physicians and apothecaries kept gardens wherein they cultivated those herbs from which they extracted their medicines. The

science of pharmacy developed from the old apothecaries' lore concerning the medicinal uses of herbs.

Marjoram, which was known to the ancient Greeks, is an herb whose leaves are still used to season roast beef, fish, and salads. When variously diluted and compounded, marjoram leaves were also prescribed for head colds, stomach ache, and rheumatism. Basil, whose fragrance is like that of cloves, is an herb whose leaves were used as a spice by the ancient Hindus. In Europe salads and turtle soup were seasoned with basil leaves, whose oil was distilled into a perfume. Hyssop is a flowering herb that is mentioned in the Bible as a purgative, or cathartic. In medieval Europe the flowers of hyssop were made into a tea or a sirup that was believed to be a good remedy for coughs. Other herbs with a long history of culinary and medicinal usage are fennel, tarragon, and chives.

HERBARIUM, a systematic collection of dried plant specimens, including samples of trees, shrubs, algae, fungi, bryophytes, lichens, and so forth. A small plant is taken whole; if the herb, shrub, or tree is large, only a part or fragment is used. Upon being placed in a herbarium, a plant sample is pressed, dried, and mounted on a sheet of paper. The sheet is then labeled so that observers will know the scientific name of the plant, the name of the collector, where and when it was collected, and its normal habitat. Photographs showing the plant growing in its normal habitat may also be included so the observers can see its natural manner of growth. The plants are sometimes arranged systematically according to their botanical class, subclass, order, family, and genus. Sometimes the collection is arranged alphabetically by family.

Herbariums range in size from the smaller private ones of botanists

and amateur naturalists to the larger public ones of botanical gardens and universities. The herbarium of the Royal Botanic Gardens, in Kew, England, contains approximately five million specimens. Before World War II the herbarium of the national botanical garden of Berlin contained approximately four million specimens. The herbarium of the New York Botanic Garden contains a few more than two million specimens.

HERBERT, VICTOR (1859-1924), Irish-American composer, was born in Dublin, Ireland. He studied at Stuttgart, Germany, and came to the United States in 1886 as first cellist of the Metropolitan Orchestra in New York. He conducted the Pittsburgh Symphony Orchestra from 1898 to 1904, after which he devoted all his time to composing. His works include the operas *Natoma* and *Madeleine*. Among his 35 operettas are *Sweethearts*, *Babes in Toyland*, *Naughty Marietta*, and *The Red Mill*.

HERBIVOROUS ANIMAL. See ANIMAL.

HERCULES was a hero in Greek and Roman mythology. His name in Greek mythology was Heracles. One of the most widely worshiped of the heroes, he was a huge man, whose great strength and courage became the subject of many myths and legends.

Hercules was not a god, but a man. He was the son of Jupiter, the king of the gods, and Alcmene. Juno, the queen of gods, hated Hercules and sent two snakes to kill him in his cradle. But Hercules was already strong, and he strangled the snakes. He grew to be a powerful and brave man and performed such heroic deeds as killing the dangerous Thespian lion. However, Juno continued to hate him. She caused him to become insane and kill his children. As punishment Hercules was forced to perform the "Twelve Labors" for his cousin Eurystheus.

Each of the labors was difficult and required great skill and courage. In the first labor Hercules killed the lion of the Valley of Nemea. His second labor required him to kill the Hydra, a nine-headed water serpent. He next had to capture a wild boar and then a huge stag with golden antlers. Hercules' fifth labor was to destroy the Stymphalian birds, which had sharp claws and beaks. He next cleaned the

These herbs and many others have a long and varied history of medicinal and culinary use.

Basil

Hyssop

Fennel

Tarragon

Bay Leaf

Thyme

Camomile

The mighty strength of Hercules at rest is shown in the Farnese Hercules of Naples done by Glycon of Athens in the 1st century B.C.

Augean stables, which had not been cleaned for 30 years, by sending two rivers through them.

For his eighth labor Hercules captured the horses of Diomedes, which ate human beings. He next brought back the girdle of Hippolyta, the queen of giant, warlike women called Amazons. In his tenth labor Hercules had to kill a giant and his two-headed dog. He gained the apples of the Hesperides for his eleventh labor and finally completed his tasks by conquering Cerberus, the three-headed dog of the underworld.

Hercules died when he was accidentally poisoned by the blood of the centaur Nessus, whom he had killed for carrying away his wife. After his death Hercules was made a god by his father Jupiter.

HERCULES, or the Kneeler, a northern constellation between Draco and Ophiuchus. It is visible in the evening sky from midnorthern latitudes between April and October. The great globular cluster Messier 13 is located in this constellation. It is barely visible to the naked eye as a faint, hazy star between the two stars marking Hercules' waist and

hip along the rear side of the figure. It is actually a cluster of some 500,000 stars, measuring 160 light-years across, at a distance from us of 30,000 light-years. See STAR CLUSTER.

HERDSMAN, THE (constellation). See BOOTES.

HEREDITY, the inheritance of qualities or tendencies from ancestors. The science of heredity is known as genetics. The resemblance between parents and offspring is commonly recognized as being a matter of heredity. However, the features of resemblance should not be regarded as being inherited in themselves. What is inherited is a gene for each of the literally thousands of characters in man that are transmitted from parent to offspring. These genes are discrete unit particles carried in the reproductive cells of the mother (the egg) and the father (the sperm). An important fact about genes is that they maintain their individuality. When a new individual is formed by the union of egg and sperm, that individual carries every gene in duplicate, one from the mother and one from the father. These genes do not fuse but are carried individually, and when the offspring forms his own reproductive cells (egg or sperm), the paired genes separate and are incorporated

Hercules, famed in myth for his 12 great labors, unknowingly donned a tunic containing a deadly poison. At the highest point of the Oeta Mountains in Greece he died in the flames of a funeral pyre, but Jupiter raised the hero to a place in the stars.

in different reproductive cells. Consequently, each child in a family is likely to receive different sets of genes from the parents.

The laws of heredity were discovered by Gregor Mendel, an Austrian monk (1865). In his experiments he crossed pea plants that had easily recognizable opposite characters, such as tallness and shortness, smooth seeds and wrinkled seeds, yellow pods and green pods. He dis-

Animals with two unlike traits are mated. Black, **B**, and rough coat, **R**, are dominant. If resulting black-rough animals are mated, their offspring are black-rough, black-smooth, white-rough, and white-smooth in a 9:3:3:1 ratio.

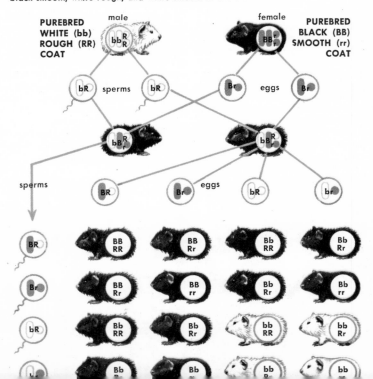

covered that in breeding plants with opposite characters and following them through two, three, or more generations, opposite characters would not appear in a haphazard fashion in the offspring but would be transmitted according to a regular plan. In some instances one of the opposite characters is dominant and the other is recessive. For example, tallness is said to be dominant in a plant when the character of tallness predominates in plants carrying genes for both tallness and shortness. Some characters are said to be sex linked, that is, the sex chromosomes, in carrying genes other than those concerned directly with sex, are responsible for the transmission of certain characteristics such as color blindness and hemophilia.

Throughout most of the 19th century, biologists generally accepted the Lamarckian theory of heredity. This theory, expressed by Jean Baptiste Lamarck.in 1809, states that characteristics acquired by an individual may be inherited by its offspring. August Weismann, conducting the first experimental tests of the theory in 1880, cut off the tails of mice for 20 generations and found no shortening of tails in the last generation. His conclusion, accepted by most Western geneticists today, was that acquired characteristics are not inherited.

Michurinism, a Lamarckian theory extended by Trofim Lysenko, is the accepted theory of heredity in the U.S.S.R. This theory considers heredity a function, like metabolism, of every particle of the living body. Michurinism emphasizes the "shattering" of heredity by changing environmental conditions or by grafting of plants. Thus in the process of vernalization, discovered by Lysenko, winter wheat treated with moisture at low temperatures is made to behave like spring wheat. Lysenko claims that by a variation of this process the change may be made hereditary.

HERMES. See MERCURY.

HERMIT, a person who lives alone or who has as little contact with others as possible. Stories of hermits who have secluded themselves with their hoards of wealth are quite common. More interesting, however, are those who became hermits for religious reasons, shunning the distractions of this world. They are called anchorites or eremites (inhabitants of the desert).

Only one hermit appears in the Old Testament. This is Elijah, who prophesied before Ahab, a king of Israel, a terrible drought that lasted three years. Both John the Baptist and Jesus dwelt in the desert for periods of time as contemplative hermits before they began to teach. Christian eremites became more numerous during the Roman persecutions of Christians. Thus, St. Paulus became a hermit A.D. 250 during the cruel reign of Emperor Decius. His biographer, St. Jerome, also spent periods of time as a hermit in the desert near Antioch (now in Turkey) and Bethlehem. Egypt seemed to lend itself to the hermitic life. It was in the Egyptian desert in the 4th century that St. Anthony dwelt for 20 years in a ruined fort atop a mountain. Although St. Anthony lived alone in contemplation, people sought him out for religious counsel. He received these occasional visitors with courtesy and sympathy.

During the Middle Ages monasteries sometimes grew up around a hermit's cell. The church was interested, too, in bringing hermits together into religious orders, and strict monastic orders, such as the Carthusians and the Camaldolites, were founded for that purpose. However, many hermits remained independent of any religious order, and they were common even into the 17th century throughout Europe.

HERMITAGE, Andrew Jackson's mansion near Nashville, Tenn. The log cabin he had lived in since 1804 was replaced in 1819 by a brick building, which was expanded in 1831. After this burned in 1834, the present structure was built. Jackson and his wife, Rachel, are buried in the plantation graveyard. The Hermitage, furnished with pieces the family actually used or with furniture typical of Jackson's time, is now maintained as a memorial, open to visitors.

The Hermitage is also the name of a world-famous art museum in Leningrad, the U.S.S.R.

The Hermitage is a splendid example of antebellum architecture. It is typical Southern-plantation-owner's home.

HERODOTUS (484?-425? B.C.), a great Greek historian, was born at Halicarnassus, of a noted family. When a young man, Herodotus went into exile because of local troubles. He traveled in Egypt and in other parts of the classical world. In later years Herodotus was a citizen of the Magna Graecia city of Thurii, but he visited Athens and is reported to have given a public reading of *The Persian Wars* in 446 B.C. Besides *The Persian Wars* Herodotus is said to have written other works, which have not survived. The masterpiece that has survived is the first great creation of Greek prose.

HEROD THE GREAT (73-4 B.C.), king of the Jews, was the son of Antipater. After the Battle of Philippi he gained the favor of Antony, and in 37 B.C. he was appointed king of Judea by Antony and Octavius, the rulers of the Roman Empire. An explanation of Herod's later violence and ruthlessness is thought to be found in his Idumaean birth. The district of Idumaea, lying between the Dead Sea and the Gulf of Aqaba, was one of the few examples of forced conversion to Judaism. Placed in this light such an action as his Massacre of the Innocents, as recorded in the Gospel of St. Matthew, becomes more understandable.

A violent struggle for power marked the reign of Herod. He attempted to consolidate his kingship by marrying Mariamne, a princess from that prominent family of Jewish patriots, the Maccabees.

The tragedy of Herod and Mariamne has been the plot of over 40 dramas. The story tells that Herod, before going on a trip to Rome to defend himself for his murder of Mariamne's brother Aristobulus, instructed his brother-in-law Joseph to kill Mariamne if he failed to return. He returned unharmed and was convinced by Joseph's wife that Mariamne and Joseph had conspired in his absence. Joseph was executed, but Mariamne was spared. On a later trip Herod left the same orders, and on his return his sister told him again of Mariamne's guilt. This time Herod had his wife executed.

Among the achievements of Herod's reign were the building of some cities, the rebuilding of the Temple at Jerusalem, and other architectural improvements. Herod also constructed pagan temples in Judea and was responsible for the inauguration of Greek games.

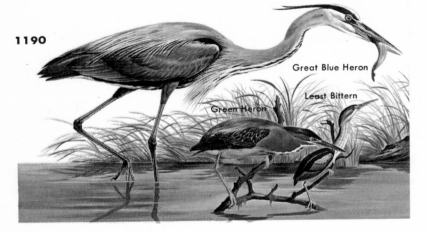

Great Blue Heron

Least Bittern

Green Heron

HERONS, EGRETS, BITTERNS, wading birds with long legs, long neck, and sharp, pointed bill that acts as a spear in securing food. These birds are found in most parts of the world. They feed largely on fish, aquatic animals, and insects. In sustained flight most members of this family fold the neck back in an S-shape (unlike the crane, which flies with extended neck). The wingbeats are slow, deliberate, and usually powerful.

Herons and egrets are usually found in open water or along the edges of swamps and streams. They often nest in large colonies, with several species in the same heronry. Bitterns, however, are shy birds that live among the reeds and grasses of swamps; they do not nest colonially.

Herons vary in size. The widely distributed green heron is about 18 inches long, with a wingspread of about 25 inches. The great blue heron is about 46 inches long, with a wingspread of about 70 inches. The great white heron (probably a color phase of the great blue heron) of the Florida Bay area is even larger—about 49 inches long with wings that extend about 75 inches. Other North American herons are the little blue heron, the Louisiana heron, the black-crowned night heron, and the yellow-crowned night heron.

Egrets have beautiful nuptial plumes, known in the millinery trade as aigrettes. In the early 20th century the great demand for these plumes resulted in the near extinction of the beautiful snowy egret and the American egret; they were saved only by the efforts of the Audubon Society. Now the birds are protected by law in the United States. Two other egrets are found in North America, chiefly in the southern parts—the reddish egret and the cattle egret. The cattle egret is one of the most recent bird arrivals in the United States. Apparently it crossed the South Atlantic to British Guiana and then came into Florida. Now it is found along the eastern

Here are a few of the 64 species that make up a family of unusual aquatic birds. Most of them feed while wading. The long neck enables the bird to use its sharp beak as a spear to impale its prey under water or to use its mandibles as pinchers. These birds are also characterized by powder downs, patches of small feathers that grow on the chest and rump and are easily crumbled into fine powder. With its bill the bird crumbles the feathers and distributes the powder over oily spots on its plumage. The powder absorbs the oil, and the bird then combs it out with a serrated device on its middle claw.

coast to Canada. It is a white egret with buffy breeding plumage on the head, chest, and back. It often walks among grazing cattle and feeds on the insects stirred up by their trampling feet.

Bitterns have a unique method of escaping danger. Instead of flying they freeze into position. By pointing the head and bill upward they closely resemble the reeds about them and are often unnoticed. North America has two species, the American bittern and the least bittern. The American is a brownish streaked bird about 28 inches long; its call is a most unlovely sound, often described as a stake-driving or bog-pumping noise. Its nest of bent-over grasses is hidden in the reeds. The least bittern, only about 13 inches long, has a bold pattern of buffy yellow, chestnut, and glossy black. Its notes are low cooing sounds and a harsh cackle. Often it too freezes into position with its bill pointing skyward. If flushed from its grassy home it flies briefly and then drops back into the marsh.

Black Heron

Reddish Egret

Snowy Egret

Cattle Egret

Black-Crowned Night Heron

Yellow-Crowned Night Heron

Purple Heron

Common Egret

Little Blue Heron

HERRING, any of many species of fish belonging to the herring family, including not only the famous Atlantic and Pacific herrings but a number that have been given other names—the alewife, the skipjack, the sprat, the sardine, and the menhaden. Tarpons are close relatives of the herrings but belong to a different family.

The members of the herring family generally are flat (from side to side), have forked tails, lack the lateral line, and have silvery scales that are easily knocked off. The underside of the belly usually has a sharp keel.

The Atlantic herring and the menhaden are two of the most valuable of all American fish—the herring as human food, the menhaden as a source of fish oil, fertilizer, and meal. The meal is used in poultry and livestock feeds. The Atlantic herring, which is caught on both sides of the Atlantic Ocean, has been called the world's most important food fish. The annual catch in the United States amounts to 170 million pounds. Although fresh Atlantic herring is excellent when broiled, the greater part of the catch is salted, dried, smoked, or pickled.

Herrings move about in great schools and feed on small organisms, often crustaceans. Most herrings are under a foot in length. Many of the young herrings fall prey to such fish as cod, haddock, and halibut.

HERSCHEL, SIR JOHN (1792-1871), English astronomer and only son of Sir William Herschel, was considered a mathematical genius by his professors at Cambridge University. His book *Outlines of Astronomy*, first published in 1849, was reprinted a dozen times in his lifetime and was even translated into Chinese.

Herschel completed his father's work of observing new nebulae and clusters of stars and of recording his observations in catalogues. This research greatly increased knowledge of double and triple stars, their distances, and their positions.

Between 1834 and 1838 he lived near Cape Town, Cape Colony (now in the Union of South Africa), to study the distribution of the stars in the Southern Hemisphere.

During the course of his studies Herschel also carried out valuable experiments with new photographic processes and studied the chemical action of the rays of the solar spectrum on sensitized paper. He was the first to measure direct solar radiation satisfactorily. In addition he described new graphical methods of investigating stellar orbits.

HERSCHEL, SIR WILLIAM (1738-1822), a German-born astronomer living in England, was the discoverer of the planet Uranus. In 1782 he became court astronomer to King George III, who granted him a lifelong pension. To Herschel, who devoted the rest of his life to the study of the heavenly bodies, may be traced the beginnings of solar physics.

He cut, ground, and polished lenses for his telescopes himself. He also perfected a lens-polishing machine. He constructed a telescope of 40 feet focal strength. With this and other telescopes he was able to view for the first time the revolving rings of Saturn. His many discoveries included over 2,000 nebulae and clusters of stars, about 800 double stars, two satellites of the planet Saturn, and two of Uranus. He is also credited with the discovery of infrared solar rays. His sister Caroline Lucretia assisted him in his observations and independently discovered seven comets.

HERTZ, HEINRICH (1857-1894), a German physicist, born at Hamburg. He discovered that electromagnetic radiation is emitted whenever the direction of current changes in an electric circuit of the proper inductance and capacitance. The type of electromagnetic radiation emitted is what we call radio waves. The radiations are also called hertzian waves. Hertz's discovery was the basis for the invention of radio communication, television, and radar. Hertz made his discovery in 1888 while experimenting to confirm Maxwell's theory of electromagnetic radiation.

The pieces of laboratory equipment Hertz used to make his discoveries were the first crude radio transmitting and receiving apparatus. Hertz in his experiments also showed that radio waves, like light waves, can be reflected from suitable objects. The reflection of radio waves is the principle of radar and loran.

HERZL, THEODOR (1860-1904), founder of Zionism, was born to a well-to-do family in Budapest, Hungary. After being graduated with a law degree from the University of Vienna, he served for a while as an official in the Austrian law courts, but in 1885 he decided to devote himself wholly to writing. He eventually obtained a permanent position with a prominent Vienna newspaper, which sent him to Paris in 1892 as a journalist.

This stay in Paris, highlighted by the Dreyfus case, was the turning point in Herzl's life. Herzl had always been much concerned by the anti-Semitic literature and political activity rife at the time, but prior to the Dreyfus case he had thought that anti-Semitism would eventually disappear with the disappearance of the Jews through intermarriage with non-Jews or that the growth of mutual understanding between the two groups would eliminate anti-Semitism. The cries of "Death to the Jews" that Herzl heard in Paris during the Dreyfus affair convinced him that anti-Semitism was so deeply rooted that neither of these solutions was possible. Consequently, in 1896 Herzl wrote *The Jewish State*, in which he analyzed anti-Semitism and explained why he thought the amalgamation of the Jews with the surrounding peoples was impossible. He presented his solution of the Jewish state where Jews, who according to Herzl were always subject to persecution, could go.

After the publication of *The Jewish State* Herzl devoted himself to the organization of the world Zionist movement and to negotiations for land for a Jewish state with the sultan of Turkey, Emperor William II of Germany (through whom he hoped to influence the sultan), and the British government. In the midst of this work Herzl died of a heart attack.

HESSE, HERMANN (1877-   ), German-Swiss novelist and winner of the 1946 Nobel prize in literature, was born in Calw in southern Germany. His outspoken criticism of the enthusiasm shown for World War I brought against the already famous novelist the charge of traitor. He subsequently moved to Switzerland and became a Swiss citizen. Hesse's prose is musical and unpretentious. He often deals with the problem of man's spiritual loneliness. *Knulp*, one of Hesse's best loved works, tells of a childlike vagabond who brings happiness and a longing for freedom to everyone he meets. *Demian* reflects Hesse's knowledge of psychoanalysis. His interest in Indian mysticism dominates *Siddhartha*. *Steppenwolf* is a severe indictment of modern civilization. *Death and the Lover* portrays the contrast between the worldly and ascetic life. His later work includes *Magister Ludi* and *Journey to the East*. His poetry is steeped in German romanticism.

HESTIA. See VESTA.

HIBERNATION, the state of torpor or sleep in which many animals spend the winter months. Hibernation is undergone during cold winters by many coldblooded animals such as frogs, toads, snakes, and lizards. The body temperature of such animals fluctuates with that of their external environment. During winter the temperature of these animals is the same as that of their surroundings. If they are not in a warm enough place, the animals may even freeze.

Some warmblooded animals, such as the chipmunk, ground squirrel, and bat, also hibernate. Their body temperature is greatly reduced. They hibernate in places that remain above freezing.

During hibernation the rate of breathing, of heartbeat, and of blood circulation is greatly reduced in all animals. They eat no food but live on surplus fat acquired during autumn. Upon awakening in spring they are emaciated. Usually a hibernating animal can be awakened during winter only by bringing it into a warm room and letting it remain there for several hours.

The decreased physiological activity during hibernation enables an animal to survive the food scarcity and cold of winter. Animals hibernate in holes, caves, and other sheltered places. Some fish and insects also hibernate. See COLDBLOODED ANIMAL.

HICCUP, the peculiar sound that occurs when the glottis closes suddenly and checks a quick, involuntary intake of the breath. Hiccup is a reflex reaction. It is caused by stimulation of the nerves of the diaphragm (the muscular partition between the chest and the abdominal cavity) or by stimulation of the respiratory center in the brain. Any number of conditions, from a full stomach to a serious disease, can cause hiccup. Severe hiccup, for example, may follow an abdominal operation. Everybody has a favored way of curing simple hiccup. The most sensible treatment is to breathe and rebreathe into a paper bag. By this means the carbon dioxide content of the inspired air is increased; this, in turn, has a corrective effect on respiration.

HICKOK, JAMES BUTLER (1837-1876), also known as "Wild Bill" Hickok, was a famous soldier, border scout, stagecoach driver, and U.S. marshal in the days of the Old West. He always loved guns and hunting and was known as an excep-

tional shot. When he was just 16 he went from Illinois to the troubled Kansas Territory, seeking adventure. An enemy of slavery, Hickok fought on the side of the Kansas free-state faction. In 1856 he was elected constable of Monticello Township in Kansas Territory. "Bill" Hickok, as he was known, then became a stagecoach driver on the Santa Fe Trail and later on the Oregon Trail.

During the Civil War "Wild Bill" Hickok served as a scout and a spy for the Union. In many dangerous situations his coolness, poise, and ability to think quickly and his expert marksmanship saved his life. His reputation as a fighter grew, and soon he was famous throughout the West.

In 1866 "Wild Bill" was appointed deputy U.S. marshal at Fort Riley, Kansas, and managed to keep order

James Butler Hickok, marshal of Hays City for a time, maintained order in some of the wildest towns of the West.

in this frontier territory. Afterward he served the Army as a special scout and as an Indian fighter.

By 1869 Hickok's reputation was so great that he was appointed marshal of Hays City, the roughest town on the border. After establishing law there, he repeated his success at Abilene.

In 1872 "Wild Bill" Hickok left his beloved plains and joined Buffalo Bill's entertainment troupe in New York. After this eastern tour Hickok married Mrs. Agnes Lake, who was to join him on the frontier as soon as she settled her business affairs.

In 1876 shortly after his marriage, however, "Wild Bill" Hickok's fabulous career was abruptly ended. The famous law enforcer was shot in the back and killed by Jack McCall at Deadwood, in Dakota Territory.

A twig, compound leaf, piece of bark, and nut of the shagbark hickory are shown above.

HICKORY, one of several species of nut-bearing deciduous trees that belong to the same family as the walnut trees. Hickory trees are native to eastern North America and eastern Asia.

The shagbark, or shellbark, hickory tree, which ranges from Quebec and Minnesota to Florida and Texas, attains a height of 120 feet and a trunk diameter of 4 feet. It is so named because its gray bark is shaggy. The bark can be pulled off in long strips. The smaller branches of the shagbark hickory are reddish brown. Its compound leaves, which consist of five leaflets, range in length from 8 to 14 inches. The egg-shaped nuts have a hard shell and a sweet-tasting kernel. This hickory is cultivated in North America for its nuts.

Another shellbark hickory tree, which ranges from New York to Iowa and south to Tennessee and Oklahoma, also has shaggy gray bark. This hickory is also cultivated for its nuts, which are globe-shaped and have a sweet-tasting kernel.

HIDALGO, MIGUEL (1753-1811), was a Roman Catholic priest and a hero in Mexico's fight against Spanish domination. He was brought up on his father's farm near Guanajuato and later chose to become a priest. When Napoleon occupied Spain, many Mexicans saw an opportunity to get rid of the Spaniards. Hidalgo was one of those who conspired for the independence of Mexico. On Sept. 16, 1810, he rallied his parishioners in Dolores and seized the prison, which was thought to hold some Mexican patriots. He and his followers were joined by pro-Mexican soldiers of the regular army.

This ill-armed and undisciplined mob led by Hidalgo was not capable of opposing the pro-Spanish regular army of General Félix Cajella. Hidalgo collected a large mob at Guadalajara, but the revolutionists were beaten on Jan. 17, 1811, and Mexico City remained in the hands of the pro-Spanish army. Hidalgo tried to escape but was betrayed and taken prisoner. He was degraded from the priesthood and was shot as a rebel in July or August, 1811.

HIEROGLYPH, the name given by the Greeks to a symbol in the picture writing of the ancient Egyptians. The term has been used to cover all ancient picture writing, such as that of the Mayas. Hieroglyphs are either monumental or written. The former are found on monuments of wood or stone; the latter, on tablets of papyrus, leather, or wood. Written hieroglyphs eventually developed into abbreviated forms called hieratic and demotic writing.

The hieroglyphic writing of the Egyptians consisted of small pictures, some being pictures of the thing represented; some, symbols of an idea; some signifying certain sounds or syllables.

There was a method of spelling with sounds. For example, nine pictures were used to spell *Cleopatra*. To show that Cleopatra was a woman, the picture of an egg was added. Signs for sound, or phonograms, were rarely used. They were mingled with the other types of signs in the inscription.

The first hieroglyphs were pictures of such objects as the sun, the moon, animals, and plants. Then some pictures served as idea signs. (See IDEOGRAM.) Some of the signs represented sounds, or syllables, as well as ideas and yet partly kept their original meaning. The picture for an eye stood for the sound in the word for eye and for the idea of seeing. Egyptologists still argue about the interpretation of some of the signs.

The earliest hieroglyphic inscriptions found go back to about 5,000 years ago. They contain the same mixtures of symbols for sounds and for things as the later inscriptions.

In 1799 the discovery of a stone tablet at Rosetta, Egypt, provided a clue to the deciphering of the hieroglyphs. It had the same inscription on it in three different letterings—hieroglyphs, demotic, and Greek. Since Greek was known, scholars were able to decipher the rest. See ROSETTA STONE.

HIGH FIDELITY. Sound reproduction by radio or phonograph can be measured in a number of different ways, but each describes only one aspect of the reproduction. For example, one measurement might be made of how well the electronic equipment reproduced all the high and low tones, while another measurement might be made of the amount of unwanted background noise reproduced. For this reason a more general term is used to distinguish good overall reproduction from average or poor reproduction. This term is "high fidelity," often abbreviated to *hi-fi*. The word *fidelity* may be defined as faithfulness of

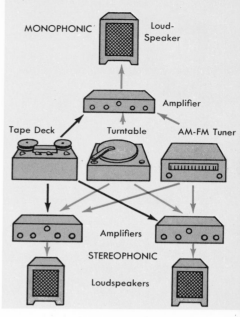

reproduction, and the term "high fidelity" indicates a high degree of that faithfulness.

Two things must be kept in mind when determining whether a sound-reproduction system is a high-fidelity system: high quality of technical reproduction and pleasantness to the ear. What may be technically exact reproduction usually includes all the little unwanted background noises that the listener is not conscious of when he hears a live performance. Such noises, however, can be very pronounced on a phonograph record and will distort the overall effect of the music. Various electronic techniques will overcome these defects and make the music pleasant to the ear, but they do this by modifying the original sound. Thus the pleasant-to-listen-to recording may not be technically accurate. High-fidelity recordings are the result of setting up a balance between the two objectives.

Above is a photograph of Egyptian hieroglyphic writing. The word *hieroglyph* comes from two Greek words: *hieros* meaning "sacred" and *glyphein* meaning "to carve." Greeks traveling in Egypt in ancient times saw the picture symbols and gave them a name in the Greek language. The Egyptian hieroglyphic mode of writing is very ancient: No one knows when it was first used.

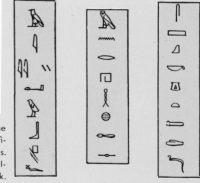

Hieroglyphs are used in picture writing. The Egyptian hieroglyphs at right represent definite sounds as well as objects and ideas. These hieroglyphs gave rise to phonetic alphabets, such as the Hebrew and the Greek.

Shown below are primitive ancient Mayan hieroglyphs that represent the date May 9, 751.

Another aspect of electronic reproduction that makes for a difference or distortion in the original sound is the limitation set by a loudspeaker. The reproduced sound is changed from electrical impulses into sound waves by the loudspeaker. (See LOUDSPEAKER.) But if there is only one loudspeaker, the sound will all come from that one alone; if there are two loudspeakers, the sound will come from two places only. In the original live performance, sound comes from every point in the room—from each musical instrument and from every wall where the sound waves are reflected back into the room. A high-fidelity system with two loudspeakers and specially designed phonograph records, called a stereophonic system, reproduces the sound with more high fidelity, or more realistically, than a system with only one loudspeaker. Yet the exact duplication of the original live performance is probably impossible. The best the high-fidelity system can do is to approximate it closely. The sound reproduced by a high-fidelity system, however, is far superior to that reproduced by the ordinary radio or record player.

HIGH JUMP. See TRACK AND FIELD SPORTS.

HIGHLAND FLING, a traditional dance of Scotland, originally performed as a solo dance by Highland warriors. It is a vigorous type of Scottish reel, characterized by high, kicking steps, which require great agility and precision. Music for the Highland fling is played on bagpipes in an even, flowing rhythm of four beats to the measure. Since this dance was taken over by the popu-

A kilted athlete throws the heavy stone in the Highland Games at Ballater, Scotland.
B.I.S.

A Highland Games hammer thrower winds up.
B.I.S.

lace, it has been performed with other country dances in Scottish balls. On these occasions it is danced by two or more couples.

The Highland fling is also performed in the annual Highland Games, which are held in the autumn at various spots in the north of Scotland. Skilled dancers in full Highland dress compete at these gatherings.

HIGHLAND GAMES are athletic and dance contests held every autumn at several places in the Highlands of Scotland. The chief events at the games are dance competitions and track-and-field contests. The dances are usually performed to the music of bagpipes and include the sword dance and the Highland fling.

The track-and-field contests almost always feature throwing the hammer and putting the shot. Races and jumping events are also usually included. The most famous event is one that was invented at the Highland Games. It is called tossing the caber and requires the contestant to lift the heavy trunk of a fir tree and hurl it as far as he can. The trunk sometimes must be cut down in size before any competitor can lift it. All contestants in the games must wear traditional Highland dress, including kilts and knee stockings.

The oldest and most famous of the Highland Games is held at Braemar, where they probably began during the 11th century. Other well-known Highland Games take place at Aboyne, Inverness, and Oban.

HIGH PRESSURE AREA. See ANTICYCLONE.

HIGHWAYMAN. See BRIGAND AND HIGHWAYMAN.

HIKING is the sport of walking through the countryside for pleasure. It is a popular activity in many parts of the world.

Any number of people may take part in a hiking trip. No special equipment is needed, but the hiker should wear strong and comfortable shoes if he plans a long or rugged walk. The shoes should be comfortably large because a person's feet often swell after he has hiked a long distance.

If the hiker plans an overnight trip, he generally carries the necessary camping equipment in a flat cloth bag, called a rucksack. Most hikers strap their rucksacks on their backs. See CAMPING.

HILLARY, SIR EDMUND (1919-), a New Zealand beekeeper and mountain climber, was the first person to reach the summit of Mt. Everest, the world's highest mountain. He and Tenzing Norkey, a Sherpa mountain guide, reached the summit on May 29, 1953. They were part of an expedition led by Sir John Hunt, a British army officer.

Hillary became interested in both mountain climbing and beekeeping while still in school. After service in World War II as a navigator in the Royal New Zealand Air Force, he resumed his mountain climbing, although he had been seriously wounded during the war. He participated in several major climbing expeditions before the Everest expeditions. In 1957-58 Hillary was responsible for stocking storage depots in Antarctica for the Trans-Antarctic Expedition of Sir Vivian Fuchs. On Jan. 4, 1958, he and four companions arrived, after a 16-day trip on three tractors, at the South Pole; there they met Fuchs, who had crossed Antarctica from the opposite direction.

Hillary lives in Auckland, New Zealand, where he devotes seven or eight months of each year to keeping bees. The remainder of the year he saves for climbing mountains.

Edmund Hillary and Tenzing Norkey had to wear oxygen masks to ascend Mt. Everest.

HIMALAYAS, the highest mountain system in the world. It lies in central Asia between the high plateau of Tibet and the plains of India. Between 100 and 150 miles wide, the range forms a wide curve about 1,500 miles long. The Indus, Ganges, and Brahmaputra rivers begin in these lofty mountains. There are three main ridges, the Great Himalayas, the Lesser Himalayas, and the Outer Himalayas. The northern ridge, or Great Himalayas, has a succession of snow-capped peaks reaching 20,000 feet. Here Mt. Everest, the world's highest peak, rises to 29,028 feet. Everest was first climbed to the top in 1953. The Lesser Himalayas are between 7,000 and 15,000 feet high. The Outer Himalayas, including the Siwalik Range, are between 2,000 and 5,000 feet in height. Beyond the Great Himalayas in the northwest, across the Indus River valley, lie the towering ranges of the Karakoram, which have the greatest number of high peaks, many exceeding 25,000 feet.

The Himalayan region from Nepal eastward has a heavy monsoon rainfall. This region rises sharply from the plains through belts of dense tropical forests, evergreen oak

Earth's highest mountains are the Himalayas.
Courtesy of TWA—Trans World Airlines

forests, conifers, and alpine vegetation to the snowline, which lies at about 16,000 feet. The western part of the Himalayan region is more complex and drier. It rises more gradually through scattered zones of bamboo and scrub, temperate forests, and alpine grasses to the snowline. Glaciers descend from the heights.

The Himalayas have long been a barrier to travel. No railroad crosses them, but there are a few trade routes through the mountain passes, which include Burzil Pass, Jelep La, and Natu La. The beautiful Vale of Kashmir is famous for its scenery. Of the many legends connected with the Himalayas perhaps the best known is that of the Abominable Snowman, which reputedly is a mysterious, manlike animal that wanders about the snow-covered peaks.

HINDEMITH, PAUL (1895-), contemporary German composer, was born in Hanau. He studied the violin as a child and later entered the Hoch Conservatorium at Frankfurt am Main. His unpublished String Quartet in C won the Mendelssohn prize. His Chamber Music No. 1 and his song cycle *Die junge Magd* were performed in 1922.

Hindemith was the founder of the Amar String Quartet and a viola soloist. From 1927 to 1937 he taught at the Berlin Hochschule. In 1938 he toured the United States as a violist. Later he taught at Yale University. In 1953 he went to the University of Zurich as professor of music theory.

In addition to his chamber music Hindemith has published the operas *Cardillac* and *Mathis der Maler*. In 1934 the latter work was made into a symphony. Theme with Four Variations and Symphony in E Flat are other notable works for orchestra by Hindemith. For voice he has written *Das Marienleben* from Rilke's poems and for ballet *Nobilissima Visione*.

HINDENBURG, PAUL VON (1847-1934), German military officer and statesman, was born at Posen (now Poznan, Poland). Hindenburg served in the Austro-Prussian War. In the Franco-Prussian War he was awarded the Iron Cross. Finally, he became a general in the infantry. Poor health forced him to retire in 1911, but in 1914 he was made a commander. After winning the Battle of Tannenberg in 1914, where he repulsed the Russian forces, he was made a field marshal and became the idol of the army. In 1916 Hindenburg became commander of the entire German army, a post he held until 1919. Until 1925, when he was elected president of the German Republic, Hindenburg kept remote from the politics that followed the German defeat in World War I. In 1932 he was reelected with the support of republicans who considered him a bulwark against the forces represented by Adolf Hitler, who ran second. Chancellor Heinrich Bruning, who had campaigned vigorously for Hindenburg, was forced to resign several weeks later and was replaced by Franz von Papen. Von Papen was replaced by General Kurt von Schleicher, who convinced Hindenburg that his plan to split the Nazi party by drawing the support of left-wing Nazis was the only way to avert civil war. The plan failed, and in January, 1933, Hindenburg, despite his dislike of Hitler, named him chancellor, on von Papen's advice that the Nazi leader could be managed. But Hitler amassed power, while Hindenburg, on whom the anti-Nazi conservatives based their last hopes, became a figurehead. Hindenburg was lost amid these political difficulties at a time when his own powers were weakened by age.

Paul von Hindenburg became commander of the German army in World War I.
UPI

The Hindu Temple of Jagannath (Sanscrit, Lord of the Universe) is located in Puri, India.

HINDUISM, the religion of more than 300 million people of India and millions more in Pakistan, Ceylon, and Burma. Hinduism is the oldest of the world's religions, stretching 4,000 years into the past. It served as the basis for Buddhism and has also inspired Western thinkers like Ralph Waldo Emerson and Schopenhauer. Hinduism is still very vigorous. It experienced a rebirth in the 19th century because of the teaching of Ramakrishna, whose followers founded missions in Europe and the United States.

Hinduism is an extremely complicated religion, for it means different things to each Hindu. The Westerner is struck by the many gods in the Hindu roster, but the kernel of the worship of those gods lies in the belief that they are facets of the supreme God. The Hindu religion has no central authority. Its devotees may or may not worship in the temples. Yet devout Hindus are among the most religious people in the world: Each act in the day has a sacred character for a Hindu. To the Hindu teacher Ramakrishna each Hindu sect and each variation in worship was a path toward the true knowledge of Brahma, or God.

The early Hindu sages were moved by the constant change in the universe. Not even mountains were permanent. Thus, man's desires within a universe of impermanence were doomed to failure. Man had to seek, through his karma (the deeds he did in the world), to attain the pure and unchanging reality behind the illusion of material things (or maya). The Hindu believes that by purity, detachment (of which one form is yoga), self-control, and compassion toward all things, he can attain closer and closer in each reincarnation to oneness with Brahma. Compassion is symbolized for Hindus by their feeling toward the cow, which they regard as sacred. The effect of a person's past deeds on his reincarnation is reflected by his caste. Originally, the caste system was introduced by ancient Aryan invaders. The system divided Hindu society into Brahmins (or priests), warriors, merchants, and workers. Untouchables were outside the caste system. Untouchability was abolished by the Indian government.

Hinduism may be highly intellectual, or the Hindu may direct his worship toward popular gods like Vishnu, the preserver, or Shiva, the destroyer. Rama, one of the reincarnations of Vishnu, is very popular and is regarded as the perfect example for men; his wife Sita, as the perfect example for women. As Gandhi, shot by an assassin, lay dying, he murmured "O Rama, O Rama." Another popular form of devotion is the pilgrimage to the holy city of Benares. The sick or the dying hope by this pilgrimage to obtain release from future reincarnations. In Benares, along the Ganges River, are innumerable cremation pyres.

Hinduism has affected all facets of Indian society. Just as Christianity has inspired great art, so has Hinduism stimulated Indian dance, drama, art, and social structure. To the Western mind the Hindu may appear otherworldly and too little interested in history and science. But the Hindu regards the Westerner as caught in the meshes of maya, the illusory material world, and doomed to disillusionment. See Yoga.

HIPPOCRATES (about 460 B.C.-about 377 B.C.), the greatest physician of ancient times, called the Father of Medicine, was born on the Island of Kos. He was a contemporary of Socrates and Plato. Almost nothing is known of his life. Writings attributed to Hippocrates included *Aphorisms*, *Epidemics*, and *Air, Earth, and Locality*. He was distinguished for his remarkable skill in diagnosis and his accurate and vivid analysis of morbid symptoms. Among the *Aphorisms* attributed to Hippocrates is the famous one, "Life is short, but the art is long, the opportunity fleeting, the experiment perilous, the judgment difficult." The Hippocratic oath, still taken by doctors, was probably not written by him.

Very little is known of the real Hippocrates, but he has come to symbolize the ideal doctor.